Endangered Species

Recent Titles in the
CONTEMPORARY WORLD ISSUES
Series

Student Debt: A Reference Handbook
William Elliott III and Melinda K. Lewis

Food Safety: A Reference Handbook, third edition
Nina E. Redman and Michele Morrone

Human Trafficking: A Reference Handbook
Alexis A. Aronowitz

Social Media: A Reference Handbook
Kelli S. Burns

Prisons in the United States: A Reference Handbook
Cyndi Banks

Substance Abuse: A Reference Handbook, second edition
David E. Newton

Campus Sexual Assault: A Reference Handbook
Alison E. Hatch

Sex and Gender: A Reference Handbook
David E. Newton

The Death Penalty: A Reference Handbook
Joseph A. Melusky and Keith A. Pesto

The American Political Party System: A Reference Handbook
Michael C. LeMay

Steroids and Doping in Sports: A Reference Handbook, second edition
David E. Newton

Religious Freedom in America: A Reference Handbook
Michael C. LeMay

Books in the **Contemporary World Issues** series address vital issues in today's society such as genetic engineering, pollution, and biodiversity. Written by professional writers, scholars, and nonacademic experts, these books are authoritative, clearly written, up-to-date, and objective. They provide a good starting point for research by high school and college students, scholars, and general readers as well as by legislators, businesspeople, activists, and others.

Each book, carefully organized and easy to use, contains an overview of the subject, a detailed chronology, biographical sketches, facts and data and/or documents and other primary source material, a forum of authoritative perspective essays, annotated lists of print and nonprint resources, and an index.

Readers of books in the Contemporary World Issues series will find the information they need in order to have a better understanding of the social, political, environmental, and economic issues facing the world today.

Endangered Species

A REFERENCE HANDBOOK

Jan A. Randall

ABC-CLIO™

An Imprint of ABC-CLIO, LLC
Santa Barbara, California • Denver, Colorado

Library of Congress Cataloging-in-Publication Data

Names: Randall, Jan A., author.
Title: Endangered species : a reference handbook / Jan A. Randall.
Description: Santa Barbara, California : ABC-CLIO, 2018. |
    Series: Contemporary world issues | Includes bibliographical
    references and index.
Identifiers: LCCN 2017035770 (print) | LCCN 2017054333
    (ebook) | ISBN 9781440849008 (ebook) |
    ISBN 9781440848995 (alk. paper)
Subjects: LCSH: Endangered species.
Classification: LCC QH75 (ebook) | LCC QH75 .R36 2018
    (print) | DDC 578.68—dc23
LC record available at https://lccn.loc.gov/2017035770

ISBN: 978-1-4408-4899-5 (print)
        978-1-4408-4900-8 (ebook)

22 21 20 19 18   1 2 3 4 5

This book is also available as an eBook.

ABC-CLIO
An Imprint of ABC-CLIO, LLC

ABC-CLIO, LLC
130 Cremona Drive, P.O. Box 1911
Santa Barbara, California 93116-1911
www.abc-clio.com

This book is printed on acid-free paper ∞

Manufactured in the United States of America

To by husband Bruce and all the species fighting for survival.

The decline in biodiversity, the amazing variety of plants, animals, and microorganisms bound together in a web of life, should be a major concern for anyone who inhabits planet Earth. In addition to the aesthetic value and enjoyment of nature's diversity and beauty, a healthy and diverse environment is also one of human survival. Biodiversity provides the natural services on which humans depend: pollination, medicine, wood products, food, clean water and air, nutrient storage and cycling, soil formation and protection, climate stability, and recovery from unpredictable events.

A manifestation of biodiversity loss is the continuous decline of species, and in some cases even species declared threatened and endangered are losing ground. Elephants and rhinoceros killed for their tusks and horns are only one example of how overexploitation continues to destroy species, despite efforts to protect them. Amphibian, bat, and marine starfish populations are in rapid decline from the spread of new diseases. Coral is bleaching and dying from warming oceans. Agricultural practices, livestock farming, urban development, invasive species, pollution, human disturbance, transportation, and fossil fuel production continue to destroy habitats as human populations grow. Global climate change is a threat that will only grow larger in the future.

The loss in biodiversity has become so acute that scientists propose we are in a new age of mass extinctions. The rapid decline of populations of many species of plants and animals is driven by the uncontrolled expansion of human populations, which have quadrupled in the past century. In 1950, 2.5 billion people inhabited the Earth; today there are about 7 billion people, and a conservative estimate predicts that the human population will grow to 9 billion by 2045.

Scientists, naturalists, and environmentalists believe extensive efforts are required to prevent further extinctions of plants and animals. They consider the Endangered Species Act (ESA), passed in 1973 and signed by Republican Richard Nixon, the best line of defense to prevent species extinctions and diversity loss in the United States. Under the ESA, there has been steady progress in species recovery as measured by prevention of extinctions and the large number of threatened and endangered species recovering on the schedule set by the U.S. Fish and Wildlife Service. Scientists know that recovery of endangered species is a complicated process because at-risk species often have very small populations and inhabit areas of limited habitat. Recovery, therefore, can be a long process that may take decades.

The ESA has critics who wish to weaken it. Some private property owners, conservative politicians, the fossil fuel industry, developers, and representatives of commercial interests claim the ESA is not working, and they resent the regulations imposed by the act and claim too much interference by the federal government in private property decisions. As measured by the number of species declared recovered and delisted, they deem the act ineffective. There is concern about effects on property rights and the cost to industry and jobs.

The debate over the ESA and its effectiveness has been brewing for a long time and may be reaching a climax. Environmental skepticism is high in the Trump administration as demonstrated by appointments to the cabinet of avowed climate change skeptics and a Congress consisting of the same politicians who introduced dozens of amendments, bills, and riders aimed at weakening and stripping away provisions of the

ESA in the last (114th) Congress. Efforts are being made to take powers away from the Environmental Protection Agency, and many of President Obama's executive orders affecting the environment are in the process of being reversed by new executive orders issued by Donald Trump. While environmentalists and their champions in Congress are committed to the prevention of a weakened ESA, those opposed to the law are equally determined.

Endangered Species is designed as a comprehensive resource guide for individuals who wish to learn about endangered species and the ESA. The majority of the book was written before the Trump administration entered office. Although I have updated the information in this book as much as possible before it was sent to press, there may be changes in endangered species, climate, and general environmental legislation and rules that are not covered in the book. The use of the resources in Chapter 6, however, especially the links in the section on the Internet, should be helpful in finding the latest actions and changes to the ESA and policy concerning the environment and endangered species.

I agreed to write this book as an opportunity to use my extensive background as a biologist and my concern about the increased losses of biodiversity. In the first chapter, I establish the seriousness of the rapid losses of biodiversity and the history and background of efforts to protect imperiled species and the habitats in which they reside. I include the biology responsible for species diversity, major points in the ESA, the history leading up to passage of the ESA, and the legal battles that followed. The second chapter discusses the issues, pro and con, that affect endangered species and the controversy surrounding the ESA. Two species are highlighted, the gray wolf and greater sage-grouse, as examples of two different approaches to dealing with species protection.

Chapter 3 is unique because it contains essays from individuals from different walks of life involved in various aspects of endangered species activities: a hunter, a fisherman, a major general in the Marines, an ecologist, an ecotourism guide and operator, a member of the IPPC on climate change, a marine biologist, an environmentalist, and a wolf biologist. Each person has a unique perspective to offer from their personal experience.

Chapter 4 offers descriptive bio sketches of individuals and organizations involved in endangered species actions and activities. Chapter 5 contains data and documents showing the effects of climate change, the loss of species, effects of ocean level increases on America's coasts, lists of species in various stages of listing, and excerpts from various documents on the topic. Chapter 6 references books, articles, Internet sites, and reports as resources to learn more about issues involving endangered species. Chapter 7 offers a chronology of the science of understanding biodiversity, laws protecting endangered species, and key events. The book concludes with a glossary of terms and a comprehensive index.

Endangered Species

The Sixth Mass Extinction

Human populations grow while other species decline. Scientists propose we are in a new age of mass extinctions called the "Anthropocene" (the "Epoch of Man"), more popularly known as the "sixth mass extinction." This designation describes the ongoing extinction of species from the last Ice Age at the end of the Pleistocene (approximately 11,700 years ago) to the present from five major factors: climate disruptions, loss of biodiversity, ecosystem loss, pollution, and overgrowth of human populations (Barnosky et al. 2014). Scientists estimate that humans have increased extinction rates as much as 1,000 to 10,000 times the historic background rates (Vignieri 2014).

The exact beginning of this mass extinction is debated by scientists. Some scientists propose it began 8,000 years ago with the beginning of agriculture. Some think it started at the beginning of the Industrial Revolution (1760), and others say it began after World War II (1945) with the beginning of the nuclear age. A new study suggests that humans engaged in activities that led to alterations of biodiversity as far back as the Late Pleistocene (around 20,000 years ago) (Boivin et al. 2016).

Bridal Veil Falls in Yosemite Valley, California. Established in 1890, Yosemite National Park is home to the endangered Sierra Nevada bighorn sheep and eight species of endangered or threatened plants. Over a thousand populations of federally listed and endangered species inhabit National Park Service units. (AP Photo)

Whatever the time period, the common thread is a widespread degradation of habitats based on human activities and the loss of biotic diversity leading to endangered and extinct species. A conservative estimate predicts that of the five to nine million animal species inhabiting the planet, the extinction rate is likely between 11,000 and 58,000 species annually. Vertebrates have experienced a mean decline of 28 percent, and of identified invertebrate species, about 40 percent are threatened (Dirzo et al. 2014, 401–402).

But species always have gone extinct. What about the dinosaurs? Fossil evidence shows that at least five mass extinctions have occurred in the last 540 million years or so when the Earth lost more than three-quarters of its species in a geologically short interval. The difference between these five extinctions and the Anthropocene is the rate of extinction. Not since the dinosaurs have so many species and populations died out so fast on both land and in the oceans (Barnosky et al. 2014). Species extinctions occurring now far outstrip "background" rates derived from historic extinction rates as calculated by extinctions per million species-years (Pimm et al. 1995). In a conservative estimate, the number of species that have gone extinct in the past 100 years would have taken, depending on the taxonomic group, between 800 and 10,000 years to disappear (Ceballos et al. 2015). Tom Lovejoy (2000), a prominent scientist who studies biodiversity, expressed deep concern about the biological trouble and extinctions unequalled since the dinosaurs. He warns: "The rate at which species disappear is about 1,000 to 10,000 times normal, and a quarter or more of all species could vanish within a couple of decades."

Not all scientists accept the idea of a "sixth mass extinction." They argue that current extinction rates have been overestimated and species extinctions during the past 500 years have occurred at a much slower pace (Briggs 2016). The methods used to determine extinction rates may not be robust enough for reliable estimates, and the lack of fossils for comparisons are a limitation. Estimates of extinctions depend on varying time scales, and different plant and animal groups are used by different scientists for comparisons. Gains in species diversity must be considered as well as losses.

As with most science, the rates of extinction and whether the planet is really entering into a sixth phase of a mass extinction will continue to be debated, but most scientists agree that extinctions are occurring at a high enough rate to generate serious concern. It seems clear we can attribute the current decline of populations of many species of plants and animals to expanding human populations and their per capita consumption as the likely drivers of the global changes in species numbers. Human populations have quadrupled in the past century. Conservative estimates predict that the human population will grow from its present number of 7 billion to 9 billion by 2045 with another half a billion added by 2050. Humans have converted about 43 percent of the Earth's land to agriculture or urban landscapes, with much of the remaining land in a network of roads and nonarable land (Barnosky et al. 2014). Clearly, if the planet is to support all of these humans and maintain its biodiversity at the same time, there is an urgent need for conservation measures.

Evolution and Biodiversity

Diversity is a beautiful thing. Diversity in living systems is called biodiversity and consists of an amazing variety of plants, animals, and microorganisms bound together into an interdependent assemblage of populations in a web of life. Every species (individuals in a population that reproduce together) is essential to keep the web in balance. The diversity among living organisms comes from genetic diversity, individual diversity (phenotypes) among members of the same species (blue eyes versus brown eyes), and the number and relative abundance of species. In an even broader perspective, biodiversity includes ecosystem diversity such as tropical rainforests, deserts, swamps, tundra, and coral reefs in mosaics of inter-connected ecosystems.

How many species are there on Planet Earth? For decades, scientists have been asking and trying to answer this question to find a reference to measure current and future loses of bio-diversity. A great deal is yet to be discovered about the diversity of living organisms that share the Earth with us. About 1.4 million species of microorganisms, plants, and animals have been identified on Earth with millions more that remain unidentified (Wilson 1992, 38, 133). A recent estimate places the number of species as high as 8.7 (plus or minus 1.3) million with 86 percent of species on Earth and 91 percent in the ocean still waiting description (Mora et al. 2011).

An interest in diversity in the natural world dates back to the ancient Greeks. Aristotle (384–322 BC) was a keen observer of nature and described in detail diverse kinds of organisms. His search to understand causes led him to be the first to make observations and to understand the value of comparisons. He developed his own classification system and placed species into different groups based on their shared traits. He thought that species were fixed and came into being by hybridization and direct adaptation. The concept of species fixed by divine design, as described in the first chapter of Genesis in the Bible, remained unchanged for the next 2,000 years (Mayr 1982, 149–154).

After Aristotle, little happened in the way of scientific inquiry until the Renaissance in Europe (1400–1700), when once again an interest in natural history developed. Herbalists and encylopedists revived the traditions of Aristotle and spent time discovering and describing in detail diverse kinds of organisms. Overseas travel and exploration of other continents were in full swing, and individual explorers brought exotic plants and animals back from other continents to add to vast collections of plant and animal specimens in Europe. These collections required organization, and it was the Swedish naturalist, Carolus Linnaeus (1707–1778), who developed the binomial classification system still used today (Mayr 1982, 340–341). The classification system consists of a hierarchy of biological classification ending with the most specific category, the species. Every individual species has its own scientific name and is a member of a group of species classified as a genus. For instance, domestic dogs are *Canis domesticus*. The species name *domesticus* is unique to domesticated dogs. The genus name, *Canis*, is shared by wolves, foxes, and other dog-like animals in the family Canidae. Dogs, cats, weasels, and other mainly predatory animals are grouped in the order Carnivora, and all are mammals.

It was Charles Darwin (1809–1882), however, who forever changed how diversity in the natural world is viewed. On his voyage around South America and to the Galapagos Islands as a young man on the HMS *Beagle*, Darwin observed the diversity of living organisms and their geographical distributions in different environments. He was fascinated by the unusual species he found there and how they differed but also shared characteristics. Island species did not look like other island species, but they shared traits with animals on the mainland. From his observations and the knowledge he gained from reading Charles Lyell's *Principles of Geology*, Darwin realized that the traditional belief of a static Earth only a few thousand years old with fixed species did not coincide with the diversity and adaptations he viewed in nature (Mayr 1982, 397–400). Darwin published *On the Origin of Species by Means of Natural Selection* in 1859 after the presentation of a joint paper with Alfred Russel Wallace (1823–1913), who had arrived at a similar interpretation of evolution from his travels in the Amazon and in Asia.

The Darwinian revolution had an unprecedented impact that demanded a rethinking of the concept of the world and humans' place in it (Mayr 1982, 501–509). Darwin made it clear that humans are merely part of the natural world. He replaced the static view of unchanging species with one that consisted of species changing and evolving. He explained that shared traits, which had been used as the basis of taxonomy, originate from common descent and similar species share a common ancestor (Mayr 1982, 209–213). His greatest contribution, however, was establishment of the theory of natural selection as the mechanism that drives the evolutionary process. Darwin observed that individuals produce more offspring than the environment can support because resources are limited. There is a struggle for existence and only a fraction of individuals survive to reproduce in the next generation. Those individuals have inherited traits that give them an advantage for survival and reproduction in the environmental conditions they inhabit. They pass on these favorable traits into the next generation. This unequal ability of individuals to survive and reproduce leads to gradual changes in populations with favorable traits accumulating over time to form a new species (Mayr 1982, 479–485).

In the 150 years since publication of *On the Origin of Species*, evolution has become a unifying theme for explanations of natural causes. Dobzhansky (1973), a prominent American geneticist, succinctly summarized: "Nothing makes sense in biology except in the light of evolution." The theory of evolution and its predictions have stood up through continual testing by experiment and observations. Genetics, biochemistry, ecology, animal behavior, developmental biology, neurobiology, and molecular biology (the molecular code of inheritance is the same in all species) have supplied powerful new evidence confirming evolution and the mechanism of natural selection. Evolution is an accepted scientific theory that explains many facts and provides a basis to predict further findings from additional observations and experiments (National Academy of Science Steering Committee on Science and Creationism 1999, 9–36).

Today, evolutionary biology is an integral part of conservation biology and an understanding of species interactions. Community ecology aligned with evolutionary ecology and island biogeography to foster a new line of research in which ecologists could investigate ways a shifting environment influences ecological stability (Steffes 2013, 391–396). Because endangered species are often found in areas of ecological instability, an understanding of their adaptations and life requirements is important for the formation of conservation policy. Scientists who study endangered species concentrate on how the species evolved and is adapted to its habitat and environment. They want to know if the species is a specialist or more of a generalist. Species that specialize and have very narrow requirements usually become endangered before generalists with more flexibility in their requirements. Scientists must understand how species compete and whether they are able to radiate into new locations and form new combinations with other species. This information seems especially important as the planet warms and climate change forces species into new environments.

Early Conservation Action in the United States and the Preservation of Public Lands

No single person has done more to preserve public lands than Theodore Roosevelt (1858–1919), the 26th president of the United States (1901–1909). Although Roosevelt was a passionate hunter who loved to kill big game in the United States and anywhere else in the world that offered hunting trophies, he also believed in preservation and was a dynamic force in the fledging conservation movement. As a boy, he learned to love nature and wanted to be a naturalist. He believed that if he did not protect public lands in an official system they would fall prey to special interests. As president, therefore, he created five national parks and provided federal protection to almost 230 million acres of land in 150 forest reserves and 51 federal bird reserves that became the National Forest System and the National Wildlife Refuge System respectively. In later years, many of the public lands preserved by Roosevelt became major refuges for endangered species (National Park Service 2017).

By the time Teddy Roosevelt became president, after the untimely assassination of President William McKinley in 1901, many populations of species once common and abundant in the United States were already disappearing and, in some cases, were either extinct or on the verge of extinction. American bison once roamed the Great Plains in huge numbers, but by the end of the 19th century, they had almost disappeared at the hands of hunters in a well-organized campaign to drive the native human populations of the plains onto reservations. Many bird populations were brought to near extinction during the 19th century from excess market hunting for meat and to decorate women's hats with spectacular plumage and stuffed birds (Souder 2013).

Legislation to protect species in the early part of the 20th century focused on birds. The passenger pigeon, a species of numbers so vast it was thought they could never be hunted to extinction, became a victim of overhunting; the last known specimen died in the Cincinnati Zoo in 1914. The plumage and market trades decimated bird populations, and by 1900, hunters had killed nearly 95 percent of Florida's shore birds for their plumage. Market hunters harvested game birds to near extinction to sell them to markets and restaurants. A national symbol, the bald eagle, was in decline. The demise of birds became so serious that Congress was finally compelled to take action and passed the Lacey Bird and Game Act of 1900. This act prohibited interstate transport of birds, thus making it a federal crime to transport birds in violation of any state law. The Lacey Act was poorly enforced, however, and it protected only those species valuable to commerce and recreation (Czech and Krausman 2001, 10–11). Furthermore, it had no provision to regulate the plumage trade. Although women organized a boycott of feathered hats with fancy bird plumage, it took the Weeks-McLean Act of 1913 to regulate the use of feathers in fashion and end the plume trade completely (Souder 2013).

The first protection of nongame birds was in 1918 when the United States and Canada entered into the Migratory Bird Treaty Act (MBTA). This important act, still in place today, protected all migratory birds, not just game species, and protected birds for their natural value, not just their economic value. Mexico was an important addition to the treaty in 1936. The act was challenged in the Supreme Court in 1920 on the grounds that the federal government had no jurisdiction over what should be a state matter (*Missouri v. Holland*). Justice Oliver Wendell Holmes, writing for the majority, declared that the protection of birds was in the "national interest" (Rozan 2014).

Perhaps, the greatest contribution to species' survival and biodiversity in the United States was the development of various laws and actions to preserve large areas of federal lands. Millions of acres of forest reserves became the National Forest System. Wildlife refuges were set aside with the express purpose to protect wild species in a variety of habitats. National parks and national monuments were established to protect unique natural scenery and cultural and archeological sites. Designated wilderness areas and wild and scenic rivers offered an opportunity for all species to seek solitude and escape the influences of human development.

National Forests

By the end of the 19th century, the federal government had given away or sold great swaths of public lands to railroads and private enterprises. Forests were logged at a rapid pace to meet a high demand for lumber. Erosion from logging clogged fresh waterways and western forest fires burned out of control. In response, Congress passed the Forest Reserve Act of 1891. It ended the giveaway of public lands and began the federal government's role in forest preservation. The act contained an important provision that gave the president authority to convert public lands into forest reserves. When Teddy Roosevelt came into office in 1901, he used this presidential prerogative to set aside large tracks of federal land into forest reserves. Western land developers, logging, railroad, and oil companies were openly hostile to these actions. In response, in February 1907, a senator sympathetic to development introduced an

amendment to an agriculture appropriations bill that prohibited the president from creating more forest reserves in Oregon, Washington, Idaho, Montana, Colorado, or Wyoming
without an act of Congress. On March 2, four days before the
amendment was scheduled for a vote, President Roosevelt released a document to Congress announcing that he had created by presidential action 32 new forest reserves consisting
of 16 million acres of timberland. Congress was furious.
Roosevelt was criticized and the executive branch sued for
using excessive executive power, but the U.S. Supreme Court
ruled in favor of the president. Many of the nation's forests
were preserved and saved from exploitation, and today they are
part of the National Forest System (Brinkley 2009, 676–681).

The Forest Reserve Act of 1891 provided no provisions to
manage or police the public forest lands. A miner or logger who
trespassed on a forest reserve would suffer no consequences. The
Forest Service Management Act of 1897 provided authority to
the General Land Office to manage forest reserves and provide protection. It clarified further that national forests could
be preserved to secure good water conditions and to furnish
timber for future generations. In 1905, President Roosevelt
transferred the forest reserves from the Department of Interior
to establish the U.S. Forest Service in the Department of Agriculture under the leadership of Gifford Pinchot (1865–1946),
America's first forester and an influential figure in the early
conservation movement (Brinkley 2009, 237–243).

The western national forests were formed from land already
owned by the federal government. In contrast, national forests
in the eastern United States were from land purchased from
private owners. Passage of the Weeks Law in 1911 gave the
federal government authority to acquire lands to protect watersheds of navigable streams. The necessity for these purchases
became apparent when water from logged and denuded lands
flooded valuable agricultural lands. Five million acre of forests
in the Appalachians and another million acres in the White
Mountains of New Hampshire comprised the first purchases.

President Herbert Hoover (1929–1933), an avid fisherman, proclaimed four new national forests; more were added during the New Deal of President Franklin Roosevelt (1933–1945). Most of the national forests in the east are small compared with those in the west, and only five are more than a million acres. When acquired, much of the land was logged or worn out farmland that required reforestation and reclamation (Shands 1992). Today, the National Forest System consists of 154 national forests and 20 grasslands in 44 states and Puerto Rico (USDA Forest Service 2014, 3).

Environmentalists began to question the forest management practices of clearcutting (removal of all the trees in an area) in the national forests in the 1960s. They objected to the erosion and soil damage, water pollution, and loss of habitat. On the other hand, professional foresters contended that clearcutting was the most desirable and economic method of tree harvesting, and local residents argued their economy depended on it. In response to public protests and a court case that ruled against the practice of clearcutting, Congress in 1976 passed the National Forest Management Act (NFMA) requiring smaller clearcuts and alternative management practices such as selective logging in national forests. Vast clearcuts still occur on private land, but restrictions and ecosystem practices have curtailed massive clearcutting in most national forests (Williams 2008). The exception is in Alaska's Tongass National Forest, where the Forest Service has approved logging on thousands of acres of old-growth rainforest and construction of more than 80 miles of road, a threat to the habitat of the rare Alexander Archipelago wolf (*Canis lupus ligoni*). In response to a law suit that argued the logging plan in the Tongass was inadequate, the court ruled that the Forest Service's plan was compatible with the NFMA (McCann 2017).

Another fight over logging in old-growth forests came to a head in the 1990s when environmentalist and loggers became locked in a bitter "war" over the cutting of mature trees in the Pacific Northwest (See Perspective by Brock Evans.). A species listed as threatened under the 1973 Endangered Species Act (ESA), the northern spotted owl (*Strix occidentalis*), was in the center of the controversy. After a series of court rulings that halted timber sales because they violated environmental laws, the Clinton administration adopted the Northwest Forest Plan (NFP) to safeguard what remained of the heavily logged old-growth forests. The plan, developed by a team of scientists, limited the timber industries' access to federal timber in Oregon, Washington, and northern California and provided a blueprint for restoring the badly overcut forests. Now, two decades later, the Forest Service is in the process of revising the NFP. Under the new plan, the timber industry expects to gain more access to timber (Koberstein 2015).

National Wildlife Refuges

In 1903, Theodore Roosevelt established Florida's Pelican Island Refuge by executive order as the first area to become part of the U.S. National Wildlife Refuge System (NWRS). This action was an important step for the future of endangered species, because national wildlife refuges are the only federal lands designated primarily for the benefit of wildlife. The refuges were founded on three concepts of "compatibility." First, wildlife and habitat protection are important primary uses of the refuges. Second, wildlife lands are to be sanctuaries and protected so natural processes can occur; third, there must be accountability in the use and management of individual refuges in the system (Curtin 1993).

Despite the "compatibility" directives, wildlife refuges have a history of being opened to recreational and economic uses that are incompatible with the wildlife that reside within them. For instance, the secretary of interior in the Eisenhower administration (1953–1961) opened refuges to oil and gas exploration. In 1958, an amendment to the Duck Stamp Act opened 40 percent of the refuges to hunting, and in 1966, the Refuge Administration Act authorized the use of any refuge within the system for any purpose to include hunting, fishing, and public recreations. The ESA increased the refuge system's responsibility to endangered species, but the ESA did little to clarify the meaning of compatibility within the system's mandate. Some clarity was achieved from a suit brought by an environmental organization, Defenders of Wildlife, in 1978. Defenders charged that waterskiing and motorboats in the Ruby Lake Wildlife Refuge in Nevada were incompatible with wildlife on the refuge. The court ruled for the environmentalists and specified that recreational use is permitted in wildlife refuges only when it will not interfere with the primary purpose for which the refuge was established. The U.S. Fish and Wildlife Service (FWS) continued to manage the NWRS under a variety of laws without comprehensive legislation spelling out how the refuges should be managed. Uses were not always compatible, and in 1989 a General Accounting Office Report indicated that activities harmful to wildlife were occurring on nearly 60 percent of all National Wildlife Refuges (Curtin 1993).

Incompatible economic and recreational uses of wildlife refuges, including grazing, farming, and motorized recreation, were addressed in the National Refuge System Improvement Act of 1997. Signed by President Bill Clinton (1993–2001), the act made a broad statutory commitment to ecosystem protection and spelled out how refuges are to be managed and used by the public to ensure the protection and conservation of the nation's wildlife resources. The act included a strong and singular wildlife conservation mission and directed the secretary of interior to maintain the biological integrity and diversity of the NWRS. It also recognized the recreational uses of hunting, fishing, wildlife observation, photography, and environmental education and interpretation. Refuges must develop and implement comprehensive conservation plans on cycles of 15 years or less (Meretsky et al. 2006). Today there are over 560 refuges on 91 million acres located in all 50 states. The refuges are home to more than 380 of the 1,311 endangered and threatened species. Fifty-nine national refuges were created specifically to help imperiled species (FWS 2015).

Alaska has the largest area in designated wildlife refuges. The Arctic National Wildlife Refuge (ANWR), created by legislation in 1980, is considered unique because it is the only area that protects a complete spectrum of the Arctic ecosystems in North America. The biologically rich, 19 million acres is home to 30 species of mammal, including the threatened polar bear (*Ursus maritimus*), 32 fish species, and more than 200 migratory bird species. Despite its importance as a wildlife refuge, ANWR has been the focus of several fights in Congress to open the coastal plain to oil exploration and development. The U.S. Geological Survey estimates there is recoverable oil there, but it would be expensive to produce and require construction of new infrastructure, such as pipelines and processing units, in a difficult environment. The amount of oil economically recoverable would depend on the price of oil, which is currently low. In January 2015, the Obama administration recommended that the Coastal Plain of ANWR be made a wilderness under the Wilderness Act of 1964 (Corn et al. 2015). However, because ANWR is yet to be protected by an act of Congress, its final status is uncertain, especially with the appointment of pro oil extraction members to powerful positions in the Trump administration. President Trump's budget proposal for fiscal year 2018 contains plans to open leases for oil and gas drilling in ANWR. Also in the budget is a plan to cut $90 million from wildlife refuges, which already experience low levels of funding for maintenance and operation (Akpan and Santhanam 2017).

Since 2010, drastic budget cuts and sequestration dropped the 2016 funding level of the NWRS by 15 percent, which has seriously curtailed some of the restoration work. Wetland restoration has fallen by 69 percent and restoration of forest habitat by 56 percent. Control of harmful invasive plants has dropped by 63 percent, despite the millions of acres overrun with invasive species. There has been delayed progress in recovering some of the more than 380 threatened and endangered species that depend on the NWRS (Green Investments 2016, 11).

National Monuments and the Antiquities Act

The Antiquities Act of 1906 became another important means to preserve habitat for endangered species. The act authorized President Theodore Roosevelt to designate areas on federal lands that contain "historic landmarks, historic and prehistoric structures, and other objects of historic or scientific interest." Its main purpose was to protect archaeological sites from theft and vandalism, but Roosevelt interpreted the act more broadly and established a system of national monuments in protected areas similar to national parks. Within two years after passage of the Antiquities Act, Roosevelt designated nine national monuments, and in January 1908, in the face of threats from development, he set aside 808,120 acres of the Grand Canyon as a national monument. All together Roosevelt created 18 monuments consisting of 1.5 million acres. Developers in Arizona sued the federal government over the Grand Canyon designation, but the U.S. Supreme Court upheld the president's authority to preserve unique landscapes as national monuments. Congress and President Woodrow Wilson (1913–1921) later created the Grand Canyon National Park in 1919 (McManamon 2014).

To this day, the Antiquities Act is available to provide presidents with flexibility in preserving natural areas already in the federal system. Because an act of Congress is not required, members of Congress and state and local officials often object to the president's action to protect areas. They object to the restrictions of no grazing or commercial fishing, and states sometimes lose revenue from taxes and grazing fees. However, the courts have supported the establishment of monuments of large sizes under the Antiquities Act and found that loss of income is not a legal basis to reject a monument's designation. Opponents have considered measures to restrict the president's authority to designate monuments. They think presidents have used the act too broadly and should not have the ability to declare unilaterally and arbitrarily national monuments and take away economic and environmental decisions from the states and local organizations. Supporters of the Antiquities Act counter that presidents of both parties have successfully used the act to protect valuable federal lands in areas that may be vulnerable to looting, development, and other changes. Monument designations that were once contentious, such as the Grand Canyon, are now areas widely supported; visitors provide an important source of revenue for nearby towns and other locales (Vincent 2016).

Nearly all presidents after Theodore Roosevelt have used the Antiquities Act to preserve federal lands. In 1978, when Congress failed to act, President Jimmy Carter (1977–1981) used the Antiquities Act to add millions of acres of pristine Alaskan wilderness to national monuments. President William Clinton (1993–2001) enlarged three areas and added 19 others. President George W. Bush (2001–2009) established a large marine monument (the Papahanaumokuakea National Marine Monument) in the Pacific Ocean off the coast of Hawaii before leaving office (Vincent 2016). President Barack Obama (2009–2017) protected millions of acres of land and water, including three monuments in the Californian desert at the request of Senator Dianne Feinstein, who was unable to gain passage in Congress of her California Desert Conservation and Recreation Act (Sahagun 2016). In August 2016, President Obama more than quadrupled the size of the Papahanaumokuakea National Marine Monument to 582,578 square miles.

In contrast to the legacy of other presidents, President Donald Trump called the designations of national monuments under the Antiquities Act a "land grab" and "egregious abuse of federal power." In April 2017, he signed an executive order directing a review of the 27 national monuments designated in the past 21 years "to give that power back to the states and to the people, where it belongs." Environmental and conservation groups worried that this action would open national monuments to oil and timber extraction, limit their size, and even repeal the designations (Fimrite 2017). These concerns were not unfounded. Interior Secretary Ryan Zinke submitted a report in August 2017, recommending large reductions in size of four national monuments: Bears Ears and Grand Staircase Escalante in Utah, Gold Butte in Nevada, and Cascade-Siskiyou in Oregon. Two marine monuments in the Pacific Ocean are slated for reduction, and a third monument on the Massachusetts coast would be modified to allow commercial fishing. The plan also allows logging in a newly designated monument in Maine and urges more grazing on sites in New Mexico. Other monuments, reserved for their natural beauty, historical significance, and species protection could be opened to mining, logging, and other development (Daly 2017).

National Parks

The National Park System (NPS) founded in 1916 may be the United States' greatest conservation accomplishment. Besides preserving large tracks of natural scenery in perpetuity in the United States, the NPS serves as a model for the preservation of unique parts of natural landscapes for other countries of the world. Ken Burns called his six-part series on national parks, "National Parks: America's Best Idea" (Duncan and Burns 2009). According to Burns, seeds for the NPS were sown in 1851 when Yosemite was discovered in California by the U.S. Army. Although preserving large tracks of land was a radical idea in the mid-19th century, and the United States was engaged in a bloody civil war, war-weary President Abraham Lincoln (1861–1865) took steps to preserve Yosemite in 1864 when he signed a law to transfer 60 square miles of federal land encompassing the Yosemite valley and Mariposa Grove of big trees to the state of California to be preserved for public use. Just six years later, in March 1872, President Ulysses S. Grant (1869–1877) signed the bill creating Yellowstone National

Park, the first in the history of the world. Yosemite became a national park in 1890 at the urging of John Muir, an early advocate for wilderness preservation. These unprecedented acts began a century of provisions to preserve the most beautiful landscapes of the United States. In doing so, parks and national monuments became the last refuge for many species of plants and animals.

The NPS celebrated its 100th birthday in 2016 with multiple celebrations all over the nation. On August 25, 1916, President Woodrow Wilson (1913–1921) signed the Organic Act creating the NPS. Until then, the nation's parks were supervised by different agencies creating a "bureaucratic mess." The Organic Act consolidated into the Department of Interior all the parks, monuments, memorials, and cemeteries with the mission to "preserve unimpaired the natural and cultural resources and values of the national park system for the enjoyment, education and inspiration of this and future generations." The NPS grew from managing a collection of scenic parks to administering hundreds of diverse sites and programs. Its legislative mandate now includes endangered species as well as clean air and water, protection of archeological resources, historic preservation, wild and scenic rivers, 40 national heritage areas, and large environmental and cooperative landscape projects (Keiter 2011).

The number of visitors to the national parks grows yearly, requiring more and more management of facilities for people and their automobiles. Over 305 million people visited national parks in 2015, an increase of more than 12 million visits over 2014, and even more were projected to celebrate the centennial year (Olson 2016). As much as the American people value their national parks, the NPS is chronically underfunded with decaying structures and roads. After an infusion of money in 1966, funding for the NPS failed to keep pace with the growing agency. Over 150 parks and preserves have been added to the system, including 13 huge parks and preserves in Alaska. The Alaska National Interest Lands Conservation Act signed by President Jimmy Carter in 1980 added a whopping 47 million acres to the struggling system. Each addition to the parks brings obligations for inventories, to create and organize collections, attend to wildlife and preservation, and develop educational programs and media. Congressional appropriations did increase slowly, but they often failed to keep up with inflation, and there was little new funding for park additions. A NPS study of approximately 100 parks found a budget shortfall to average 35 percent (Pitcaithley 2007). In 2014, the budget of the NPS was $2.6 billion (1/15 of 1% of the total federal budget) with a growing maintenance backlog of over $11.5 billion. Seven new parks were added and nine parks expanded in 2014 with no increase in funding. By 2015 the NPS consisted of 84.5 million acres in 407 units, compared with 25.7 million acres in 200 units in 1960 (Fretwell 2015).

Because congressional funding and user fees have not covered infrastructure and other expenses in national parks for many years, there has been more and more effort to support the parks via private donations, volunteer labor, and selling the rights to corporations to promote their brands in national parks. The national parks are so desperate for cash that Director Jonathan Jarvis proposed in March 2016 to expand the rules to allow corporate logos on prominent display in exchange for donations to the parks. In another concession to increase funding, the policy against taking money or advertising support from companies that make alcohol was lifted in a $2.5 million deal with beer maker Anheuser-Busch. Park advocates are very critical of these actions and the creeping commercialism they promote. They believe that corporate advertising has no place in the park system and are worried that corporations will demand privileges and try to influence park policy (Rein 2016).

National parks in the 21st century may face other problems besides lack of funds and decaying infrastructures. No park exists in isolation, and some parks are becoming natural islands in the middle of areas developed for agriculture, logging, mining, and urban development. A uranium mine is adjacent to the rim of the Grand Canyon National Park. Although not allowed in national parks, logging, mining, and petroleum prospecting can pollute the air and water in the parks. Species protected in the park do not recognize boundaries and may not survive when they travel out of the park area. Invasive species are a huge problem. More than 6,500 invasive species, mostly plants, have been found in the U.S. National Park System (National Geographic 2016).

The Environmental Movement Takes Off in the 1960s: Three Decades of Environmental Legislation

During much of the first 50 years of the 20th century, the United States was preoccupied with two world wars and the Great Depression. There was little action to protect the environment or endangered species until the 1960s, when an environmental movement was spurred by a surge of public interest after publication of Rachel Carson's 1962 book, *Silent Spring*. Carson, who had a scientific background, recognized the harm insecticides developed during World War II could do, especially the insecticide DDT that was sold and used on a large scale in agriculture and domestically after the war. She was particularly disturbed by the potential of the chemicals to travel through the food chain. The chemicals did not kill outright; they built up in fatty tissue of predatory birds to cause reproductive failure from thin eggshells in eagles, falcons, and other flesh-eating birds. *Silent Spring* was met with much criticism by the chemical industry and with much interest by the general public and officials of the Kennedy administration (1961–1963). Carson's testimony at two congressional hearings helped set environmental policy that led to the ban on domestic use of DDT in 1972 (Griswold 2012). Once set in motion, environmentalism became a massive social movement in the cultural climate of political activism inspired by civil rights and the anti-war movement in the 1960s.

Membership in established conservation organizations, such as the Sierra Club, Wilderness Society, and Defenders of Wildlife, grew. New organizations formed, including the National Resource Defense Council (NRDC) (1970), Green Peace (1971), and Earthjustice (1971). The first Earth Day on April 22, 1970, galvanized public attention on threats to the environment and sent a message to politicians to take action. The public was further stimulated to action by a series of environmental crises. In 1969, an oil well platform blew out on the coast of Santa Barbara, California, and covered the beaches, shore, and wildlife with oil; in addition, the Cuyahoga River near Cleveland, Ohio, caught fire from the amount of sewage and trash it contained (Geary 2003).

There was also a new interest in habitat preservation. As wilderness became scarce, its value became more appreciated. The Wilderness Act of 1964 established the Wilderness Preservation System to protect permanently, in a natural state, road-free federal lands from commercial or economic development. The act defined wilderness as "an area where the earth and its community of life are untrammeled by man, where man himself is a visitor who does not remain." The Wilderness Act prohibits permanent roads and commercial enterprises. Although no roads, motorized equipment, vehicles, or mechanical transport are allowed, there is ample opportunity for recreation such as hiking, backpacking, rafting, canoeing, camping, climbing, horseback riding, cross-country and downhill skiing, swimming, fishing, hunting, and wildlife viewing. Today, there are over 765 wilderness areas in 44 states and Puerto Rico consisting of over 109 million acres in forests, swamps, tundra, and deserts. Protected wilderness consists of about 5 percent of the entire area of the United States with only 2.7 percent in the contiguous U.S and the remaining areas in Alaska (Wilderness. net 2016). These wilderness areas are important water sheds and refuges for plants and animals and the homes to many endangered and threatened species.

By the 1960s, so many rivers were impaired by dams, dredging, pollution, and diversion that pristine, free-flowing rivers were becoming rare. In response, Congress established the National Wild and Scenic River System in 1968 to preserve rivers with outstanding scenic features, fish and wildlife, and geological, cultural, and recreational value in their free-flowing condition. As of December 2014, 12,709 miles of 208 rivers in 40 states (0.25% of American's rivers) have been protected. In contrast, 75,000 large dams have modified 600,000 miles comprising 17 percent of the country's rivers (National Wild and Scenic River System 2014).

The 1970s was a decade of unprecedented, bipartisan federal legislation with Democrats and Republicans working together to enact sweeping environmental laws to curb pollution: the Clean Air Act (1970), the Pesticide Control Act (1972), the Ocean Dumping Act (1972), the Federal Water Pollution Control Act (1972), the Safe Drinking Water Act (1974), and the Toxic Substance Control Act (1976). To regulate national environmental quality standards, the Environmental Protection Agency (EPA) was established in 1970. This independent federal agency is responsible for regulation and enforcement of air and water pollution, pesticides, and solid waste.

Concern about population declines of marine mammals led to the passage of the Marine Mammal Protection Act (MMPA) in 1972. The "whole ecosystem" approach in the act was novel for the time and became a standard provision in later legislation. The MMPA protects all marine mammals from being taken from their habitat, including cetaceans (whale and dolphins), pinnipeds (seals, sea lions, and walrus), sea otters, manatees, and polar bears. It also controls import and export of marine mammals and any products taken from them. Both the FWS and the National Oceanic and Atmospheric Administration (NOAA) Fisheries are responsible for management of the MMPA (Mills 2011). In 1973, Congress passed the strongest environmental legislation to protect all imperiled species, the ESA of 1973.

A bipartisan Congress continued to pass major environmental laws during the next decade. One important act for endangered species was the 1980 Alaska National Interest Lands Conservation Act (ANILCA). This sweeping act designated 79.5 million acres of federal lands in Alaska into national parks, national wildlife refuges, wild and scenic rivers, national wilderness, and national forest. In the wake of the 1980 Love Canal toxic waste tragedy, Congress passed the Comprehensive Environmental Response Compensation Liability Act (CERCLA), a tough pollution control and liability law that established a superfund to clean up sites contaminated with hazardous pollutants. In 1990, George H. W. Bush sought to fulfill his promise to be an "environmental president" by championing key amendments to the Clean Air Act. While not known at the time, this was the last large bipartisan environmental law to come out of Congress (Lazarus 2013).

Why Protect Endangered Species?

Reasons to protect endangered species range from aesthetic to practical. Wild plants and animals have an irreplaceable aesthetic value and contribute to the beauty and diversity of the world. Nature and wildlife may serve as philosophical and spiritual resources to inspire religious experiences and creative expression. Nature is beautiful, and the aesthetic value of species is important to the quality of human life. Morally, humans have an obligation to preserve species that share the Earth with them. Biologically, species are an important part of biodiversity and the functioning of healthy ecosystems. Practically, species provide "services" via agricultural, industrial, and medical benefits.

The view of species as integral components of "ecosystem services" provides an added incentive to prevent their extinction. A tiny obscure animal may not directly benefits humans, but it supports an ecosystem. Often the contribution of a single species is subtle and poorly understood, but its role in species' interactions and the stability of the ecosystem may be important. For instance, mussels, oysters, and clams filter pollutants out of seawater; large fruit-eating birds disperse seeds of hardwood trees that smaller birds are unable to crack; and woodland salamanders consume carbon-emitting insects (Gascon et al. 2015).

Rare and endangered species are an important part of the growing business of ecotourism, which generates local revenue and jobs. A recent scientific analysis of ecotourism using population models found that ecotourism can provide the critical difference between survival and extinction for some endangered animals, depending on population variables, predation, and ecotourism scale (Buckley et al. 2016). In 2011, 46.5 million people visited national wildlife refuges to generate $2.4 billion of sales in regional economies. As this spending flowed through the economy, over 35,000 people were employed to generate $793 million in employment income (Carver and Caudill 2013).

Key Provisions of the 1973 Endangered Species Act (ESA)

Prior to 1973, Congress passed two laws related to endangered species. The Endangered Species Preservation Act of 1966 authorized the secretary of interior to list native species of fish and wildlife as endangered and to acquire habitat in the NWFS. In 1969, Congress passed the Endangered Species Conservation Act to extend protection to animals threatened worldwide. Despite these advances in legislation to protect endangered species, the two acts were inadequate and did not provide enough comprehensive protection to endangered species to prevent extinction.

In 1973, Congress passed one of the toughest and most comprehensive environmental laws in its history. The Endangered Species Act:

• Defined "endangered" and "threatened";
• Made plants and all invertebrates eligible for protection;

- Expanded on prohibitions for all endangered animal species;
- Allowed the prohibitions to apply to threatened animal species by special regulation;
- Required federal agencies to use their authorities to conserve listed species;
- Prohibited federal agencies from authorizing, funding or carrying out any action that would jeopardize a species, destroy its critical habitat or modify its critical habitat;
- Made matching funds available to states with cooperative agreements;
- Provided funding authority for land acquisition for foreign species;
- Implemented CITES protection in the United States (Bradford 2016).

The law, therefore, has become the best legal tool available for dealing with biodiversity loss from species extinctions. The legislation, signed by President Richard Nixon, was the product of a bipartisan Congress with a unanimous Senate vote and a vote of 390–12 in the House of Representatives. The law, broad in scope, provides wide-ranging protection for listed animals. It consists of 18 sections that strengthen elements of prior legislation, regulate commerce of both listed and economically valuable species, and provide a formal process to list species as endangered or threatened.

Sections 2 and 3 of the ESA state the purpose of the act and define an endangered species as "any species which is in danger of extinction throughout all or a significant portion of its range." Threatened species are "any species which is likely to become an endangered species within the foreseeable future throughout all or a significant portion of its range." A proposal for a species to be listed as endangered or threatened originates from experts employed by the FWS and NOAA Fisheries Service. A formal process ensues with notices printed in the *Federal Register*. Members of the public or environmental organizations can also petition for a species to be listed (FWS 2004).

Section 4 explains the five criteria for listing species: (1) "the present or threatened destruction, modification, or curtailment of a species' habitat or range; (2) overutilization for commercial, scientific, or educational purposes; (3) disease or predation; (4) the inadequacy of existing regulatory mechanisms; and (5) other natural or manmade factors affecting its continual existence" (FWS 2004). To warrant protection and become a candidate species, a listing must be based on the best scientific evidence available about whether the species is declining in population numbers. There is no formal protection for candidate species, and they may remain on the candidate list for an indeterminate duration because of low priority numbers. For instance, it is not uncommon to see that a species has been accepted for listing but remains unlisted because its priority number is too low. As of September 15, 2017, 30 species remain on the FWS candidate list (ECOS 2017a).

Critical habitat is considered essential to species' recovery and must be considered at the time a species is proposed for listing under the ESA. Critical habitats are those with the particular physical or biological features the listed species requires for survival and protection. These features include space for individuals and populations to grow, mate, and rear offspring. They include cover, shelter, food, water, air, and light. Protection from harassment and disturbances is also an important consideration. A critical habitat has to be a specific area within the geographical area of the species and formally designated under the ESA.

Section 6 provides for cooperation between federal agencies and the states. An amendment established the Cooperative Endangered Species Conservation Fund to provide funding to states and territories for species and habitat conservation actions on nonfederal lands. States and territories must contribute a minimum nonfederal match of 2 percent for the estimated program costs of approved projects, or 10 percent when two or more states or territories implement a joint project. A state or territory must currently have, or enter into a cooperative agreement with the FWS to receive grant funds.

Section 7 prohibits federal agencies from any action that jeopardizes the continued existence of critical habitat of a listed species. All federal agencies are required to consult with the FWS and the NOAA Fisheries Service before beginning a federal project to make sure that any authorized, funded action does not jeopardize the continued existence or critical habitat of a listed species. The consultation process includes land that is presently occupied by the listed species and land that is important for its continued and future existence. Consultations between agencies are commenced to ensure that actions do not violate ESA prohibitions.

One of the strictest provisions in the ESA, least liked by critics, is found in Section 9. No listed animal can be legally "taken" unless issued a special permit. ("Take" is defined as any action that harasses, harms, pursues, hunts, shoots, wounds, kills, traps, captures, or collects an endangered species.) The restrictions on "take" of an endangered or threatened species apply to private property as well as state and federal lands. Individuals, corporations, or government agencies are all subject to violations of the act. A criminal violation may result in imprisonment and a fine of up to $50,000. A civil violation of a major provision may result in a $25,000 fine (knowingly killing or harming an endangered species) or a $12,000 fine. A violation of a minor provision, permit, or regulation may incur a $500 fine. Fish, wildlife, and plants illegally taken, possessed, sold, or purchased may be confiscated (the most usual outcome). If there is a criminal conviction, equipment and vehicles used to violate the ESA may also be confiscated.

Provisions of the ESA are also enforced through "citizen suits," as well as through civil and criminal penalties. Section 11 states that "any person" may commence a civil suit against any person, including government agencies, who may be in violation of the law. The citizen suits provision authorizes action against the secretary of interior and NOAA Fisheries Service where there is failure to perform an act or duty. Environmental groups file legal challenges when the FWS denies listing of a species the scientific evidence supports or when a species is delisted before there has been sufficient recovery. Citizen suits are also used when there are direct violations of ESA requirements, such as complying with specific timelines for making listing decisions. The FWS has 90 days after it receives a petition to add or remove a species from the list of endangered and threatened species. If the FWS concludes in the 90-day finding that the petitioned action is warranted, the ESA requires the FWS to issue a finding within 12 months (Glitzenstein 2010, 261).

The ESA not only seeks to prevent extinctions but also to bring the species back to a healthy population level. A recovery plan, therefore, becomes the guide used by the government to develop and implement the recovery of an endangered or threatened species. The recovery plan is written by the governmental agency involved, and it must specify how a listed species will be recovered and the critical habitat improved if necessary for a self-sustaining population. A recovery plan must have a goal of when recovery might be achieved, a description of on-site management plans, and a schedule with priorities and cost estimates. The FWS or NOAA appoints a recovery team representing state and federal agencies, academic institutions, nongovernmental organizations, and commercial enterprises.

The Snail Darter, Tellico Dam, "God Squad," and 1978 ESA Amendment

Soon after the passage of the ESA, development-minded individuals began to realize the strength and the restrictions in the law if endangered species were found in a critical habitat. Opponents of the ESA began to lobby Congress to amend the act, but it was a small, snail-eating fish native to the Tennessee River, the snail darter (*Percina tanasi*), that became the focus of one of the nation's most significant environmental battles.

In 1975, the FWS listed the three-inch snail darter as an endangered species and designated 17 miles of the Little Tennessee River as critical habitat for the fish. The Tennessee Valley Authority (TVA), however, was already in the process of building the Tellico dam on that last undammed stretch of the river in the Tennessee River basin. The TVA had been building dams in the area since the Great Depression to stimulate the economy and provide electricity and flood control. The Tellico dam, considered marginal for flood control, electric power, and navigation, was the last of 69 dams. Local farmers, sportsmen, residents, environmental groups, and the Tennessee Game and Fish Commission opposed the dam because it would destroy 33 miles of the last free-flowing river in the valley, displace 300 families from their farms, and eliminate places of historical and archeological interest. In 1972, a group of local citizens and environmentalists filed a lawsuit under the National Environmental Protection Act (NEPA), activated on January 1, 1970, to halt construction of the dam until an environmental impact statement was prepared. This action delayed construction of the Tellico dam by over two years. During the delay, a biologist from the University of Tennessee discovered the endangered snail darter in the section of river that was to be dammed. The ESA then became the basis for *TVA v. Hill*, and the snail darter as an endangered species became a strong legal basis for an injunction to stop the dam (Garrett 2009).

TVA v. Hill (1978) went all the way to the Supreme Court that ruled in a six to three decision to uphold the ESA and stop the dam based on "no exceptions" in the law. Congress responded to the Supreme Court decision and amended the ESA in 1978 to establish a mechanism to circumvent the decision. They established the Endangered Species Committee known as the "God Squad," because it has the power to determine what species could go extinct. The committee was empowered to grant exemptions to the ESA's absolute ban on any harming of listed species for nonscientific purposes. Its seven members include heads of the EPA, NOAA, the Council of Economic Advisers, and the Secretaries of Agriculture, Army, and Interior as well as a representative from the state(s) in which the project would take place. This committee reviewed the Tellico dam project and ruled unanimously to halt the dam construction to save the river and the snail darter. The benefits of completing the partially built dam did not outweigh the benefits of the last free-flowing river. Development of the undammed river and its valley for agriculture, light industry, and tourism would save an endangered species and produce far more economic benefits for the region.

The decision to stop the Tellico dam was a short-lived win, however, because the dam was finished anyway. Legislators from Tennessee attached a rider to an appropriations bill that directed the TVA to finish the project. President Jimmy Carter, reluctant to veto an appropriation bill, signed the bill. The snail darter was transplanted and established some small populations elsewhere, but the free-flowing river and its riparian habitats and farmland along the river were gone forever (Plater 2004, Garrett 2009).

The story of a little brown fish halting a multimillion dollar project received much media attention. Congress members were shocked when they realized that the ESA not only protected large, charismatic mammals but also could include species of fish, insects, and spiders. Although the snail darter case clearly won on the law and economics, it ultimately lost to pork barrel politics and the media. Law Professor Zygmunt J. B. Plater, who spent six years on the snail darter case, thinks that the media misrepresented the case and got the story wrong. The presentation to the public as a noneconomic little fish blocking an important hydroelectric dam affected the outcome of the case and opinion about the ESA in a negative way. Foes of environmental regulation were able to shift endangered species from a position of broad public support to a targeted wedge issue (Plater 2004, 302). How could a small brown fish get in the way of progress? This case illustrated that protection of endangered species is political.

The Mission Blue Butterfly and Habitat Conservation Plans (HCPs)

Private landowners and developers found the definition of "take" in the 1973 ESA much too restrictive. They feared investment in projects could be thwarted at any time by the discovery of an endangered species. Discovery of the mission blue butterfly, *Icaricia icarioides missionensis,* did just that; the insect, a listed endangered species, halted a housing development project on San Bruno Mountain south of San Francisco. The narrow restrictions on "take" in the original ESA had been amended by Congress in 1982 to allow more flexibility. As specified by the amendment, projects could proceed if the parties involved developed a Habitat Conservation Plan (HCP) that specifies how the development alters habitats to minimize and mitigate the impact of incidental takings on threatened or endangered species as much as is practical. Once the HCP is approved, the FWS issues an Incidental Take Permit (ITP) for a designated amount of time, and the applicant is then absolved from liability under the ESA for harm to the species (Wheeler and Rowberry 2010, 222–223).

Working together, citizen groups, developers, and government officials formulated a HCP for San Bruno Mountain that protected the endangered species but still allowed lawful development. The FWS awarded its first HCP permit to the San Bruno Mountain project in 1983, and it became a model for future habitat plans. The HCP protected 3,000 acres, 87 percent of the habitat, for three listed species: the mission blue butterfly, the callippe silverspot butterfly (*Speyeria callippe callippe*), and the multicolored San Francisco garter snake (*Thamnophis sirtalis tetrataenia).* The developers supported the HCP because the greater spacing of the residential units made them more expensive. Opponents of the plan had been concerned about difficulty in replacing the degraded habitat and an increase in invasive species (Lamar 2010), but in 2016, the Golden Gate National Parks Conservancy (2016) estimated populations of the mission blue butterfly to consist of 18,000 adults.

In 1988, Congress further amended the HCP to specify regulations for monitoring the recovery and protection of plants. The amendment required HCP to undergo public notice and comments (which must be given consideration by federal agencies), five years of monitoring recovered species, and biennial reports on the recovery and status of all species. The FWS is required to monitor candidate and recovered species and to adopt emergency listings when there is evidence of significant risk. Protection for endangered plants includes a prohibition on malicious destruction on federal land and other "take" that violates state law (FWS 2013).

No Surprise and Safe Harbor Agreements

Many landowners were still wary of any participation in conservation of imperiled species after establishment of HCP and receiving an ITP; they were fearful of future, unforeseen limitations on what they can do with their land. Bruce Babbitt, secretary of the interior in the Clinton administration, recognized that involvement by private landowners was essential, because about 80 percent of endangered species occur on private property. In 1999, Secretary Babbitt implemented the "No Surprise" policy and Safe Harbor Agreement (SHA) to address the concerns (Wheeler and Rowberry 2010, 224).

The "No Surprise" policy was aimed at creating incentives and assurances for the private sector to participate in sponsorship of HCP. Landowners would not be held liable for endangered species if unforeseen circumstances occurred that had not been negotiated in the HPC. ITP permit holders who adhered to the terms of the HCP would not be required to expend additional resources to conserve the endangered species in the HCP, even if unforeseen developments warranted an adjustment. Additional expenses would be borne by the federal government or other entity, not the landowner. These additional assurances had a positive effect, leading to the approval of 177 HCP during Babbitt's tenure. From 2001 to 2009, the FWS approved 424 HPC of over 22 million acres of land to total 48 million acres in HCP agreements (Wheeler and Rowberry 2010, 225). The SHA is a voluntary program for private landowners to contribute to the recovery of imperiled wildlife on their land in exchange for formal assurances that the FWS will not require additional or different management of the species without the owner's consent or impose additional restrictions on land use (FWS 2011).

The Role of States in Endangered Species Protection and Conservation

Many states have developed their own endangered species program that plays a vital role in the protection and conservation of plants and animals within their borders. The laws in place vary greatly from state to state, however, and range from a prohibition on "taking" or trafficking to provisions for listing, management, and protection. There is no mechanism for recovery, consultation, or critical habitat designations in 32 states; 5 states have no act at all and rely on the federal act or nongame programs. The California Endangered Species Act is the more comprehensive of the state acts; Kansas and Hawaii also have substantial measures. Forty-one state acts prohibit in some form the import, export, transportation, sale, or take of listed species, but there is great variety in the meaning of the term "take." Only Massachusetts interprets "take" similar to the federal interpretation as including alteration of habitats (George and Snape 2010, 344–359).

In recognition of the role of the states and local government, the FWS and NOAA Fisheries issued updated policies in

February 2016 to reaffirm federal-state collaboration in implementing the ESA. The federal agencies recognize that the states have developed expertise in resource management that is especially relevant in listing decisions and the designation of critical habitat. There is a commitment for engagement and collaboration between the FWS, NOAA, and state fish and wildlife agencies on many aspects of ESA implementation, with the understanding that this collaboration is undertaken in the context of the ESA's statutory timelines.

The updated policy includes proactive conservation of imperiled species before they require protections of the ESA. The expertise and information of state agencies will be used in determining which species should be listed as candidate species. The federal agencies will work collaboratively with state agencies to engage proactive conservation of species (FWS 2016).

Criminal Liability under Wildlife Laws

In reality, few individuals are prosecuted under the ESA, and when prosecuted, few cases result in jail time and large fines. A major loophole is a 1998 policy, established under the Clinton administration, that a suspect must know the species identity at the time an endangered or threatened species was killed or harmed. The "McKittrick Policy" originated from the court case of Chad McKittrick who illegally killed "wolf number ten" near Yellowstone National Park. Wolf Ten was one of the original wolves released in Yellowstone and was wearing a radio collar around his neck. McKittrick claimed he thought he was shooting a wild dog and could not be prosecuted because he did not know the biological identity of the animal or that it was an endangered species. A jury found McKittrick guilty, and he also lost on appeal. Shortly thereafter, the Department of Justice (DOJ) adopted the policy that it will not prosecute unless the violator "knowingly" commits the act. It is unclear why the DOJ made this concession, unless it was political, but the policy has restricted enforcement and become an easy way to escape prosecution when killing or harming an endangered species (Schoch 2003, Linder 2016).

Environmental groups became increasingly distressed by the lack of prosecutions under the ESA and took the DOJ to court over the McKittrick policy. The groups charged that the DOJ was abdicating its responsibility to enforce the ESA under the rule that "takers" of endangered species must know they are killing a protected animal. The suit was in response to the high numbers of endangered Mexican wolves that were illegally shot to cause the deaths of more than half of the animals released in the wild since the beginning of the reintroduction program (Cart 2013). In June 2017, a federal judge struck down the DOJ McKittrick policy. Individuals who kill or harm an endangered species are no longer freed from prosecution by claiming they did not know the biological identity of the species (George 2017).

Oil spills are another example of how the McKittrick policy restricted prosecution for killing endangered species. The 2010 BP Deepwater Horizon oil spill in the Gulf of Mexico killed hundreds of animals that probably included threatened or endangered species, but because it was an accident and not done knowingly, prosecution under the ESA was restricted. The same stipulation of "knowingly violate" restricts the MMPA. The MBTA of 1918, however, allows for prosecution based on strict liability. Prosecutors have used this act to charge a crime whenever birds are killed, including the 1989 Exxon Valdez oil spill in Alaska. Exxon ended up paying a $25 million criminal fine and $100 million in restitution. Many Alaska residents and environmentalists considered this amount embarrassingly small for a corporation worth billions of dollars (Alexander 2010).

The ESA also makes it unlawful to "take" by habitat modification. Enforcement here is important because when a habitat is modified many species could be destroyed. There are no criminal penalties for accidentally killing listed species during farming and ranching activities if the farmer and rancher did not know the species was present. The subject must know the species is present and endangered, actively harass or harm it, and has not obtained the required permits. The permit process often allows for mitigation and the planned activity to go forward, except in cases when the conduct cannot be approved or mitigated. Criminal prosecutions involving habitat modification, therefore, are uncommon. Cases of cutting down trees in endangered red-cockaded woodpecker habitat, diverting water from a stream and killing fish, and erosion from a pipeline are some examples that could lead to prosecution (Colbourn and Birchell 2015).

Legal Challenges to ESA Policy

During its tenure, the ESA has been the target of numerous legal actions. Decisions in most of these cases have helped to clarify the law. One area that was clarified by the courts was the definition of "take" in Section 9 of the ESA. In *Palila v. Hawaii Department of Land and Natural Resources*, the Hawaiian Department of Natural Resources was ordered to remove herds of sheep and goats from the habitat of the palila (*Loxioides bailleui*), a Hawaiian honeycreeper. The palila's critical habitat included the existing mamane-naio forest, essential for the bird's survival on Mauna Kea on the big island of Hawaii. The court found that sheep and goats grazing in the area were contributing to a significant modification and degradation of the palila's critical habitat. Therefore, "take" can include habitat modification that harms the wildlife but does not cause either actual or proximate injury or death. The case established the important and controversial precedent that protecting endangered species includes their critical habitat. The case also showed that states do not have exclusive control over endangered and threatened wildlife residing within their borders, even those species solely indigenous to one state. The ESA favors uniform federal legislation for protection of endangered species rather than the vagaries of each state's perception (Nelson 1982).

Babbitt v. Sweet Home Chapter of Communities for a Better Oregon (1995) challenged the palila decision. A number of small landowners, logging and timber companies, and individuals who depend on logging in the Pacific Northwest brought the case alleging that restriction on timber harvesting because of the northern spotted owl was illegal. In a six to three decision, the Supreme Court held that habitat modification is a legitimate application of the word "harm." "Take" does not have to involve direct contact with endangered animals. Lower courts now cite the *Sweet Home* decision when modification of an endangered species' critical habitat becomes an issue (Stone 1997).

Status of the ESA Today

Today, the ESA has become intensely political and subjected to yearly denouncements on the floor of Congress. In the 114th Congress (January 6, 2015–January 4, 2017), legislators introduced over 130 bills, amendments, or riders to omnibus bills to reform or weaken protections for at-risk wildlife in the ESA, more than in any other time in the past two decades. Investments in natural resources have been falling for decades from a 2.5 percent of the federal budget in 1975 to just 1 percent in 2015 (Green Investments 2016, Figures 1, 2, 5, and 6). The FWS Endangered Species program had an 11 percent reduction in real dollars from fiscal year 2010 to 2015, and the average dollar amount per species has decreased every year since 2010 for both recovery and listing. Many species have no or outdated recovery programs. Budget cuts have restricted implementation of HPC, because the FWS does not have the staff or resources to help prepare and review them (Green Investments 2016, 18–19). Although funding is yet to be determined for the fiscal year 2018, if Congress accepts Trump's budget proposal, resources for protection of endangered species will drop 17 percent, and the fund to compensate private land owners, the Cooperative Endangered Species

Conservation Fund, will be cut by 64 percent. NOAA grants and educational programs would sustain a decrease of $262 million (Akpan and Santhanam 2017).

The American public historically has shown broad support for the ESA and protection of at-risk species. In repeated polls, the public indicates that the extinction of species is of concern, and species survival is a human value. A 2015 poll, conducted on behalf of Defenders of Wildlife, found a broad-based national consensus on the ESA with 90 percent of voters supporting the law. There was wide agreement that the ESA is necessary to prevent extinctions and that saving endangered species does not have to hurt the economy. The economy can grow while protecting wildlife. Seventy-one percent preferred science-based decisions about species protection made by biologists, rather than by politicians. Voters favored legislators who support environmental protection with large majorities of voters of all political persuasions saying they would be more likely to vote for a member of Congress who supports environmental safeguards like the ESA (Tulchin et al. 2015). A 2011 Harris poll showed similar support for the ESA; but in another poll, 63 percent favored updating and modernizing the ESA, while 49 percent believed state or local authorities rather than the federal government should lead the recovery of endangered species (American Farm Bureau 2015).

Listing under the ESA continues yearly, although sometimes slowly. The George W. Bush administration (2001–2009) averaged only 8 listed species a year for a total of 60 species, with a majority of these species a result of litigation by environmental groups. The Bush administration also leased millions of acres of public land for private extraction of oil and gas without regard for the ESA (Gibson 2009). In contrast, the Obama administration listed 390 species. There are 502 animals and 774 plants listed as endangered and 209 animals and 168 plants threatened in the United States. Active recovery plans are in place for 482 animals and 677 plants. Foreign listings include 585 endangered and 87 threatened animals and one plant endangered and two threatened. There are 30 candidate species (ECOS 2017b).

International Threatened and Endangered Species

The International Union for Conservation of Natural Resources (IUCN), established in 1948, is the world's largest and most diverse environmental network composed of both government and civic organizations. IUCN is considered the global authority on the status of the natural world and the measures necessary to safeguard it. Its organization consists of six commissions: species survival, environmental law, protected areas, social and economic policy, ecosystem management, and education and communication (IUCN 2016).

The IUCN publishes the *Red List of Threatened Species*. Founded in 1964, it is the world's most comprehensive inventory of the global conservation status of biological species. Each year, thousands of scientists around the world assess or reassess species and update the IUCN Red List with new data checked for accuracy. This up-to-date information provides a continuous focus on the status of the world's at-risk plants, animals, and other organisms. As a result, national governments and conservation organizations may use the information in the Red List to prioritize their own species-protection efforts. More than 85,000 species on the Red List have been assessed; 24,307 are threatened with extinction, including 42 percent of amphibians, 40 percent of conifers (evergreen trees), 33 percent of reef-building corals, 25 percent of mammals, and 13 percent of birds (IUCN 2017a, Table 1, Figure 3). The goal of the IUCN is to double the number of species assessed to 160,000 by 2020.

Critically endangered is the highest risk category assigned by the IUCN Red List for wild species other than extinct. It includes species that have declined 90 percent over 10 years (or three generations) and are facing a very high risk of extinction in the wild. The most recent Red List documents 5,210 total species in this category worldwide. Species undergoing a 50 percent decline over the same period are classified as endangered (7,781 total), and a species experiencing a 30 percent reduction over the same time frame would be considered vulnerable (11,316 total). Taken together, all of these species are classified as threatened. Two other categories include near threatened (5,736 total) and of least concern (40,920). During each year's assessment a species may change categories, depending on whether its populations have increased or decreased (IUCN 2017b).

The IUCN Red List includes the number of species threatened in each country. Developed countries with better assessment efforts may exhibit proportionately higher numbers compared with developing countries. Nevertheless, these countries stand out: Madagascar 1,274; Tanzania 1,084; China 1,080; India 1,052; Indonesia 1,282; Malaysia 1,271; Ecuador 2,356; Mexico 1,159; and the United States 1,514 (IUCN 2017a, Table 5).

International Trade in Endangered Species

Trade in endangered species and their parts (elephant ivory, exotic woods, and leather goods) is a lucrative business estimated to be worth billions of dollars. It includes huge numbers of animals and plant specimens, and when unregulated it can have devastating effects on population numbers. To ensure that international trade in endangered species does not threaten survival, the Convention on International Trade in Endangered Species (CITES) was conceived. Signed in 1973 and into force on July 1, 1975, CITES is a voluntary international agreement of 182 countries ("parties") that provides varying degrees of protection to more than 35,000 species of animals and plants. Many wildlife species in trade are not endangered, but the CITES agreement helps to ensure sustainability to safeguard the resources into the future.

CITES regulates wildlife trade through controls and regulations on species listed in three appendices. Appendix I lists species endangered from international trade, and trade is permitted only in exceptional circumstances. Elephant ivory is in this category. Appendix II species may become endangered if trade is not regulated. Their controls are aimed at preventing unsustainable use, maintaining ecosystems and preventing species from entering Appendix I. Appendix III species are subject to domestic regulation, but cooperation in their control in international trade is requested (CITES 2016).

CITES sets policy in the regulation of marine species, except for the great whales (humpback, blue, gray, sperm, minke, etc.). The International Whaling Commission (IWC) is the global body charged with conservation of great whales and management of whaling. The IWC, established in 1946, has 88 member governments. The United States officially banned whaling in 1971, and the IWC agreed on a moratorium on commercial whaling in 1986, but Norway and Iceland objected; they still harvest several hundred minke, fin, and Bryde's whales a year, setting their own take limits over the objections of the IWC. Japan continues to hunt and kill whales for scientific research. During their most recent whaling season, Japan killed 333 minke whales. Conservationists view Japan's hunt as a way to skirt international rules, rather than for science. Much of the whale meat is sold commercially. The United Nations International Court of Justice has ordered Japan to halt their whaling program, because research claims do not justify the killing (Izadi 2016).

The IWC is involved in many other aspects of whale conservation; it also sponsors research and coordinates and funds conservation work on many species of aquatic marine mammals. They work to prevent ships striking, injuring, and killing whales, whale strandings, and entanglements. Entanglement in fishing gear is a growing problem, and although difficult to quantify, a recent report estimated that 308,000 whales and dolphins die annually entangled in fishing gear and marine debris. The commission has also adopted a Strategic Plan for Whale Watching to facilitate the further development of this activity in a responsible and consistent way (International Whaling Commission 2016).

Ecosystem Services

The concept of "ecosystem services" is a pragmatic approach to conservation. This human-directed approach stresses the value of natural ecosystems to human well-being. Ecosystems provide humans with products they cannot live without: food, fiber, fresh water, medicine, recreation, and climate and disease control. The more diverse an ecosystem, the better it functions and the more services it offers (Millennium Ecosystem Assessment 2005).

In the late 1990s and early 2000s, a growing number of naturalists began to recognize the appeal of raising awareness by framing ecological concerns in economic terms. The rationale of directing ecosystem function toward humans was to increase awareness of decision makers about how the disappearance of biodiversity affects human well-being and the need to include it in international conservation policy (Gomez-Baggethun et al. 2009).

The monetary benefits of ecosystem services supplied by endangered species are difficult to calculate. The estimated costs of saving endangered species worldwide are huge. Saving land animals is estimated to cost $76.1 billion a year, and saving marine species will likely cost much more (Cossins 2012). On the other hand, the monetary benefits of ecosystem services such as green plants providing oxygen to breathe, insects for pollination of crops, and forests that absorb carbon, if they could be accurately calculated, would be substantial. Although pricing nature's benefits could be a fool's errand, a recent estimate in a scientific paper by a group of ecologists suggests that the biosphere provides services worth around $33 trillion a year, and the benefits from conserving biodiversity outweigh the costs by a factor of 100 to 1. Unchecked species loss could remove 18 percent off the global economic output. If these values are close to being correct, the cost to conserve the world's species is a small price for all the benefits they provide (Marshall 2015).

Payment for ecosystem services (PES) consists of direct and conditional payments to local landholders and users in return for adopting practices that conserve and restore ecosystems and protect endangered species. Hundreds of PES schemes have been implemented around the world since the early 1990s with mixed results. An analysis of 40 cases of PES in Latin America found that 23 cases were classified as successful, 12 as partially successful, and 5 as unsuccessful. The researchers linked success to four factors: (1) livelihood improved from receiving a critical resource such as water, (2) projects were local and regional lasting 10–30 years, (3) payment was in nonmonetary goods and services, and (4) private organizations implemented the project (Grima et al. 2016).

There are, however, serious doubts about viewing species and ecosystems as commodities with cash value. How can we place a price on nature? The traditional economic approach of market price and tourist dollars will always underestimate the true value of nature. Biologists balk at the anthropomorphism that places human needs in the center of why biodiversity is important, rather than for its intrinsic value of diversity in nature. Besides, ecosystems are not necessarily benign and beneficial to humans. Processes such as fire, drought, disease, and floods work against the goals of humanity but could be vital for ecosystem function. Implementation of ecosystem services may not always lead to biodiversity, because introduced species may do the job just as well as natural species, and artificial systems and bioengineering of nature could impact biodiversity. Finally, many services are not amenable to pricing. Just because a monetary price cannot be established does not mean that a species has no value. All species contribute to the services of an ecosystem in some way or other (Redford and Adams 2009, Schröter et al. 2014).

A big concern about ecosystem services is that a monetary emphasis separates consumers from nature. Instead of biodiversity, economics becomes the conservation goal. By pricing the natural world and establishing a market for ecosystem services, the biosphere could become a subsidiary of the economy. George Monbiot (2013), a British writer, worries that putting a price on nature will not solve our environmental problems and could make them worse. He writes, "Forests, fish stocks, biodiversity, hydrological cycles become owned, in effect, by the very interests—corporations, landlords, banks—whose excessive power is most threatening to them."

References

Akpan, Nsikan, and Santhanam, Laura. 2017, May 23. "What Trump's Budget Proposal Means for Science, Health, and Tech." *PBS Newshour.* http://www.pbs.org/newshour/rundown/trumps-budget-proposal-means-science-health-tech/. Accessed September 14, 2017.

Alexander, Kristina. 2010, June 28. "The 2010 Oil Spill: Criminal Liability under Wildlife Laws." *Congressional Research Service.* https://www.fas.org/sgp/crs/misc/R41308.pdf. Accessed July 9, 2016.

American Farm Bureau. 2015, September 29. "Poll Shows Strong Support for Endangered Species Act Reform." *The Voice of Agriculture.* http://www.fb.org/newsroom/news_article/353/. Accessed July 11, 2016.

Barnosky, Anthony D., Brown, James H., Daily, Gretchen C., Dirzo, Rodolfo, Ehrlich, Anne H., Ehrlich, Paul R., Eronen, Jussi T., Fortelius, Mikael, Hadly, Elizabeth A., Leopold, Estella B., Mooney, Harold A., Myers, John Peterson, Naylor, Rosamond L., Palumbi, Stephen, Stenseth, Nils Chr, and Wake, Marvlee H. 2014. "Introducing the Scientific Consensus on Maintaining Humanity's Life Support Systems in the 21st Century: Information for Policy Makers." *The Anthropocene Review* 1: 78–109.

Boivin, Nicole L., Zeder, Melinda A., Fuller, Dorian Q., Crowther, Alison, Larson, Greger, Erlandson, Jon M., Denham, Tim, and Petraglia, Michael D. 2016. "Ecological Consequences of Human Niche Construction: Examining Long-Term Anthropogenic Shaping of Global Species Distributions." *Proceedings of the National Academy of Science* 113: 6388–6396. http://www.pnas.org/content/113/23/6388.full.pdf. Accessed September 16, 2016.

Bradford, Alina. 2016. "Facts about the Endangered Species Act of 1973." *Live Science*, http://www.livescience.com/54707-endangered-species-act.html. Accessed March 19, 2017.

Briggs, John C. 2016. "Global Diversity Loss: Exaggerated versus Realistic Estimates." *Environmental Skeptics and Critics* 5: 20–27. http://www.iaees.org/publications/journals/environsc/articles/2016–5(2)/global-biodiversity-loss-exaggerated-versus-realistic-estimates.pdf. Accessed March 17, 2017.

Brinkley, Douglas. 2009. *Wilderness Warrior*. New York: Harper Collins.

Buckley, Ralf C., Morrison, Clare, and Castley, J. Guy. 2016, February 17. "Net Effects of Ecotourism on Threatened Species Survival." *PLOS One*. http://journals.plos.org/plosone/article?id=10.1371/journal.pone.0147988. Accessed July 9, 2016.

Cart, Julie. 2013, May 29. "U.S. Sued over Policy on Killing Endangered Wildlife." *Los Angeles Times*. http://articles.latimes.com/2013/may/29/local/la-me-0530-endangered-species-lawsuit-20130530. Accessed July 16, 2016.

Carver, Erin, and Caudill, James. 2013, October 2013. "Banking on Nature: The Economic Benefits to Local Communities of National Wildlife Refuge Visitation." *U.S. Fish and Wildlife Service*. https://www.fws.gov/

uploadedFiles/Banking-on-Nature-Report.pdf. Accessed
June 21, 2016.

Ceballos, Gerado, Ehrlich, Paul R., Barnosky, Anthony D.,
García, Andrés, Pringle, Robert M., and Palmer, Todd M.
2015. "Accelerated Modern Human-Induced Species
Losses: Entering the Sixth Mass Extinction." *Science
Advances* 1: 1–5. http://advances.sciencemag.org/
content/1/5/e1400253.full. Accessed September 16,
2016.

CITES. 2016. "What Is Cites?" https://www.cites.org/eng/
disc/what.php. Accessed September 3, 2016.

Colbourn, Elinor, and Birchell, Jill. 2015. "Home, Sweet
Home: Prosecuting Endangered Species Act Habitat
Modification Cases." *Wildlife Tracking II* 63: 1–22. https://
www.justice.gov/usao/file/770921/download. Accessed
September 3, 2016.

Corn, M. Lynne, Ratner, Michael, and Alexander, Kristina.
2015. "Arctic National Wildlife Refuge (ANWR): A Primer
for the 114th Congress." *Congressional Research Service.*
https://www.fas.org/sgp/crs/misc/RL33872.pdf. Accessed
July 10, 2016.

Cossins, Dan. 2012, October 12. "Conservation Will Cost
$76 Billion." *The Scientist.* http://www.the-scientist.com/?
articles.view/articleNo/32827/title/Conservation-Will-
Cost—76-Billion/. Accessed September 15, 2016.

Curtin, Charles G. 1993. "The Evolution of the U.S.
National Wildlife Refuge System and the Doctrine of
Compatibility." *Conservation Biology* 7: 29–38.

Czech, Brian, and Krausman, Paul R. 2001. *The Endangered
Species Act: History, Conservation Biology and Public Policy.*
Baltimore: Johns Hopkins University Press, p. 262.

Daly, Matthew. 2017, September 18. "Interior Chief
Urges Shrinking 4 National Monuments." *Washington*

Post. https://www.washingtonpost.com/politics/ interior-secretary-recommends-shrinking-6-national-monuments/2017/09/17/c9a82d5e-9c1d-11e7-b2a7-bc70b6f98089_story.html?utm_term=.6367a6501894. Accessed September 18, 2017.

Dirzo, Rodolfo, Young, Hillary S., Galetti, Mauro, Ceballos, Gerardo, Isaac, Nick, J. B., and Collen, Ben. 2014. "Defaunation in the Anthropocene." *Science* 345: 401–406. (Review paper.) http://science.sciencemag.org/ content/345/6195/401.full. Accessed May 30, 2016.

Dobzhansky, Theodosius. 1973. "Nothing Makes Sense in Biology Except in the Light of Evolution." *American Biology Teacher* 35: 125–129.

Duncan, Dayton, and Burns, Ken. 2009. *National Parks: America's Best Idea*. New York: Knopf.

ECOS 2017a. "Species Reports." *U.S. Fish and Wildlife Service*. https://ecos.fws.gov/ecp/report/table/candidate-species.html. Accessed September 15, 2017.

ECOS 2017b. "Species Reports." *U.S. Fish and Wildlife Service*. https://ecos.fws.gov/ecp0/reports/box-score-report. Accessed September 13, 2017.

Fimrite, Peter. 2017. "Swaths of Wildlands Face New Scrutiny." *San Francisco Chronicle*. http://digital.olive software.com/Olive/ODN/SanFranciscoChronicle/Default .aspx. Accessed April 27, 2017.

Fretwell, Holly. 2015. "The NPS Franchise: A Better Way to Protect Our Heritage." *The George Wright Forum* 32: 114–122. http://www.georgewright.org/322fretwell.pdf. Accessed September 15, 2016.

FWS. 2004. "Endangered Species Act of 1973 as Amended through the 108th Congress." https://www.fws.gov/ endangered/esa-library/pdf/ESAall.pdf. Accessed September 3, 2016.

FWS. 2011, July. "Safe Harbor Agreements for Private Landowners." USFWS Endangered Species Program. https://www.fws.gov/endangered/esa-library/pdf/harborqa .pdf. Accessed July 11, 2016.

FWS. 2013. "Endangered Species Act: A History of the Endangered Species Act of 1973—1988 ESA Amendment." https://www.fws.gov/endangered/laws-policies/esa-1988.html. Accessed September 3, 2016.

FWS. 2015. "National Wildlife Refuge System." Department of Interior. https://www.fws.gov/refuges/whm/endangered .html. Accessed September 2, 2016.

FWS. 2016. "Laws & Policies: Regulations and Policies— Interagency Policy Regarding the Role of State Agencies in ESA Activities." Department of Interior and Department of Commerce. https://www.fws.gov/endangered/laws-policies/ policy-state-agencies.html. Accessed September 3, 2016.

Garrett, Elizabeth. 2009. "The Story of the *TVA v. Hill*: Congress Has the Last Word." *University of Southern California Law*. http://law.usc.edu/assets/docs/contribute/ TVAvHillssrn.pdf. Accessed September 3, 2016.

Gascon, Claude, Brooks, Thomas M., Contreras-MacBeath, Topiltzin, Heard, Nicolas, Konstant, William, Lamoreux, John, Launay, Frederic, Maunder, Michael, Mittermeier, Russell A., Molur, Sanjay, Mubarak, Razan Khalifa Al, Parr, Michael J., Rhodin, Anders G. J., Rylands, Anthony B., Soorae, Pritpal, Sanderson, James G., and Vie, Jean-Christopher. 2015. "The Importance and Benefits of Species." *Current Biology* 25: 431–438.

Geary, Daniel. 2003. "Environment Movement." *Dictionary of American History*. http://www.encyclopedia.com/topic/ Environmental_Movement.aspx. Accessed March 13, 2016.

George, Gerald. 2017, June 27. "Court Rules DOJ Enforcement Directive Arbitrary and Capricious."

Energy & Environmental Law Blog. http://www.energy environmentallaw.com/2017/06/27/court-rules-doj-enforcement-directive-arbitrary-and-capricious/. Accessed September 15, 2017.

George, Susan, and Snape, William J. III. 2010. "State Endangered Species Acts." In *Endangered Species Act Law, Policy, and Perspective*, second edition, edited by Donald C. Baur and William Robert Irvin, 344–359. Chicago, IL: American Bar Association.

Gibson, James William. 2009. "Cleaning Up Bush's Mess on Public Land." *Los Angeles Times.* http://articles.latimes .com/2009/apr/02/opinion/oe-gibson2. Accessed September 17, 2016.

Glitzenstein, Eric R. 2010. "Citizen Suits." In *Endangered Species Act Law, Policy, and Perspective*, second edition, edited by Donald C. Bauer and William Robert Irvin, 261–291. Chicago, IL: American Bar Association.

Golden Gate National Parks Conservancy. 2016. "Mission Blue Butterfly." http://www.parksconservancy.org/ conservation/plants-animals/endangered-species/ mission-blue-butterfly.html. Accessed September 3, 2016.

Gomez-Baggethun, Erik, de Groot, Rudolf, Lomas, Pedro L., and Montes, Carol. 2009. "The History of Ecosystem Services in Economic Theory and Practice: From Early Notions to Markets and Payment Schemes." *Ecological Economics.* http://www1.montpellier.inra.fr/lameta/ articles/5.3.2_ESS_HISTORY.pdf. Accessed March 19, 2017.

Green Investments. 2016. "How Budget Cuts Are Impacting Our Communities and the Environment: The Case for Reinvestment in FY17." http://wilderness.org/sites/default/ files/2016%20Green%20Investments.pdf. Accessed September 3, 2016.

Grima, Nelson, Singh, Simron J., Smetschka, Barbara, and
Ringhofer, Linda. 2016. "Payment for Ecosystem Services
(PES) in Latin America: Analysing the Performance of
40 Case Studies." *Ecosystem Services* 17: 24–32.

Griswold, Eliza. 2012, September 21. "How 'Silent Spring'
Ignited the Environmental Movement." *New York Times.*
http://www.nytimes.com/2012/09/23/magazine/how-
silent-spring-ignited-the-environmental-movement.html.
Accessed March 17, 2017.

International Whaling Commission. 2016. "Conservation
and Management." https://iwc.int/welfare. Accessed
September 3, 2016.

IUCN. 2016. "About." https://www.iucn.org/secretariat/
about. Accessed September 3, 2016.

IUCN. 2017a. *The IUCN Red List of Threatened Species.
Version 2016–3.* http://www.iucnredlist.org/about/
summary-statistics. Accessed March 19, 2017.

IUCN. 2017b. *The IUCN Red List of Threatened Species.
Version 2016–2.* http://www.iucnredlist.org. Accessed
March 19, 2017.

Izadi, Elahe. 2016, March 25. "A Japanese Fleet Killed
333 Whales for 'Research'." *Washington Post.* https://
www.washingtonpost.com/news/speaking-of-science/
wp/2016/03/24/a-japanese-fleet-killed-333-whales-for-
research/. Accessed September 3, 2016.

Keiter, Robert B. 2011. "Revisiting the Organic Act: Can It
Meet the Next Century's Conservation Challenges?" *The
George Wright Forum* 28: 240–253.

Koberstein, Paul. 2015, April 7. "Will the Northwest Forest
Plan Come Undone?" *High Country News.* http://www.hcn
.org/articles/will-the-northwest-forest-plan-come-undone.
Accessed September 23, 2016.

Lamar, Chad W. 2010. "Habitat Conservation Plans:
Balancing the Endangered Species Act's Protection of

Threatened and Endangered Species While Providing
Landowners with Options for the Development of Land
Containing Critical Habitat." Dickinson School of Law,
Pennsylvania State University.

Lazarus, Richard J. 2013. "Environmental Law at the
Crossroads: Looking Back 25, Looking Forward 25."
Michigan Journal of Environmental & Administrative Law 2:
267–284. http://repository.law.umich.edu/cgi/viewcontent
.cgi?article=1012&context=mjeal. Accessed March 18, 2017.

Linder, Ann. 2016, Winter. "*Mens Rea* and McKittrick: An
Unraveling of the Endangered Species Act." *Law & Paws*
4: 4–17. https://www.law.uh.edu/financialaid/Laws%20
and%20Paws%20(winter%202016).pdf. Accessed July 16,
2016.

Lovejoy, Thomas. 2000. "Biodiversity." *BBC REITH Lectures
2000.* http://news.bbc.co.uk/hi/english/static/events/
reith_2000/lecture2.stm. Accessed March 19, 2016.

Marshall, Michael. 2015, July 14. "What Is the Point of
Saving Endangered Species?" *BBC Earth.* http://www
.bbc.com/earth/story/20150715-why-save-an-endangered-
species. Accessed July 6, 2016.

Mayr, Ernst. 1982. "The Growth of Biological Thought:
Diversity, Evolution and Inheritance." Cambridge, MA:
Harvard University Press.

McCann, Nick. 2017. "9th Circuit Oks Logging Project in
Alaska's Tongass Park." https://www.courthousenews
.com/9th-circuit-oks-logging-project-alaskas-tongass-park/.
Accessed September 23, 2017.

McManamon, Francis P. 2014. "The Antiquities Act and
How Theodore Roosevelt Shaped It." *The George
Washington Forum* 31: 324–344. http://www.georgewright
.org/313mcmanamon.pdf. Accessed March17, 2017.

Meretsky, Vicky J., Fischman, Robert L., Karr, James R.,
Ashe, Daniel M., Scott, Michael J., Noss, Reed F.,

and Schroeder, Richard L. 2006. "New Directions in Conservation for the National Wildlife Refuge System." *BioScience* 56: 135–143.

Millennium Ecosystem Assessment. 2005. "Ecosystems and Human Well-Being: Synthesis: 2005." Washington, DC: Island Press (http://www.millenniumassessment.org/en/Index-2.html).

Mills, Georgiana. 2011. "Marine Mammal Protection Act-Marine Bio.org." *MarineBio Conservation Society.* http://marinebio.org/oceans/conservation/laws/marine-mammal-protection-act. Accessed September 17, 2016.

Monbiot, George. 2013, July 15. "The Downside of Valuing Nature." *Corporate Knights.* http://www.corporateknights.com/channels/natural-capital/the-downside-of-valuing-nature-13738968/. Accessed July 10, 2016.

Mora, Camilo, Tittensor, Derek P., Adl, Sina, Simpson, Alastair G. B., and Worm, Boris. 2011. "How Many Species Are There on Earth and in the Ocean?" *PLoS Biology* 9. http://journals.plos.org/plosbiology/article?id=10.1371/journal.pbio.1001127. Accessed June 6, 2016.

National Academy of Science Steering Committee on Science and Creationism. 1999. "Evidence Supporting Biological Evolution." *Science and Creationism: A View from the National Academy of Science,* second edition. http://www.nap.edu/read/6024/chapter/4. Accessed June 6, 2016.

National Geographic. 2016. "Top 10 Issues Facing National Parks." http://travel.nationalgeographic.com/travel/top-10/national-parks-issues/. Accessed September 2, 2016.

National Park Service. 2017. "Theodore Roosevelt and Conservation." https://www.nps.gov/thro/learn/historyculture/theodore-roosevelt-and-conservation.htm. Accessed September 14, 2017.

National Wild and Scenic River System. 2014. "A National System." https://www.rivers.gov/national-system.php. Accessed September 2, 2016.

Nelson, Jack R. 1982. "*Palila v. Hawaii Department of Land and Natural Resources*: State Governments Fall Prey to the Endangered Species Act of 1973." *Ecology Law Quarterly* 10: 281–310. http://scholarship.law.berkeley.edu/cgi/viewcontent.cgi?article=1219&context=elq. Accessed August 11, 2016.

Olson, Jeffrey. 2016. "Happy Birthday National Park Service." *National Park Service Press Release*. https://www.nps.gov/aboutus/news/release.htm?id=1775. Accessed September 2, 2016.

Pimm, Stuart L., Russell, Gareth J., Gittleman, John L., and Brooks, Thomas M. 1995. "The Future of Biodiversity." *Science* 269: 347–350.

Pitcaithley, Dwight T. 2007. "On the Brink of Greatness: National Parks and the Next Century, the National Park Service Centennial Essay Series." *The George Wright Forum* 24: 9–20. http://www.georgewright.org/242pitcaithley.pdf. Accessed March 17, 2017.

Plater, Zygmunt J. B. 2004. "Endangered Species Act Lessons Over 30 Years, and the Legacy of the Snail Darter, a Small Fish in a Pork Barrel." *Environmental Law* 34: 289–308. http://lawdigitalcommons.bc.edu/cgi/viewcontent.cgi?article=1173&context=lsfp. Accessed September 2, 2016.

Redford, Kent H., and Adams, William A. 2009. "Payment for Ecosystem Services and the Challenge of Saving Nature." *Conservation Biology* 23: 785–787.

Rein, Lisa. 2016, May 9. "Yosemite, sponsored by Starbucks? National Parks to Start Selling Some Naming Rights." *Washington Post*. https://www.washington post.com/news/powerpost/wp/2016/05/09/yosemite-national-park-brought-to-you-by-starbucks/. Accessed September 4, 2016.

Rozan, Kristina. 2014. "Detailed Discussion on the Migratory Bird Treaty Act." *Animal Legal and Historical Center.* https://www.animallaw.info/article/detailed-discussion-migratory-bird-treaty-act. Accessed September 2, 2016.

Sahagun, Louis. 2016, February 11. "Volcanic Spires and Joshua Trees: Obama Protects 1.8 million Acres in California's Desert." *Los Angeles Times.* http://www.latimes.com/science/la-me-monuments-20160212-story.html. Accessed June 23, 2016.

Schoch, Deborah. 2003, June 22. "Policy Limits Endangered Species Act Prosecutions." *Los Angeles Times.* http://articles.latimes.com/2003/jun/22/nation/na-species22. Accessed July 10, 2016.

Schröter, Matthias, van der Zanden, Emma H., van Oudenhoven, Alexander P. E., Remme, Roy P., Serna-Chavez, Hector M., de Groot, Rudolf S., and Opdam, Paul. 2014. "Ecosystem Services as a Contested Concept: A Synthesis of Critique and Counter Arguments." *Conservation Letters* 7: 514–523. http://onlinelibrary.wiley.com/doi/10.1111/conl.12091/full. Accessed March 19, 2017.

Shands, William E. 1992. "The Lands Nobody Wanted: The Legacy of the Eastern National Forests." In *The Origins of the National Forests*, edited by Harold K. Steen, The Forest History Society. http://www.foresthistory.org/Publications/Books/Origins_National_Forests/sec3.htm. Accessed March 17, 2017.

Souder, William. 2013, March. "How Two Women Ended the Deadly Feather Trade." *Smithsonian Magazine.* http://www.smithsonianmag.com/science-nature/how-two-women-ended-the-deadly-feather-trade-23187277/?no. Accessed March 15, 2016.

Steffes, David. 2013. "Darwin and the Environment" In *The Cambridge Encyclopedia of Darwin and Evolutionary Thought*, edited by Michael Ruse, 391–396. Cambridge, UK: Cambridge University Press.

Stone, Laurie M. 1997. "Harm Means Harm: Babbitt v. Sweet Home Chapter of Communities for a Great Oregon." *Pepperdine Law Review* 24: 695–723. http://digitalcommons.pepperdine.edu/plr/vol24/iss2/5. Accessed August 11, 2016.

Tulchin, Ben, Krompak, Ben, and Brunner, Kiel. 2015, July 6. "Poll Find Overwhelming, Broad-Based Support for the Endangered Species Act among Voters Nationwide." *Tulchin Research.* http://www.defenders.org/publications/Defenders-of-Wildlife-National-ESA-Survey.pdf. Accessed July 10, 2016.

USDA Forest Service. 2014. "Field Guide to the Forest Service—Chapter 2." U.S. Forest Service. http://www.fs.usda.gov/Internet/FSE_DOCUMENTS/stelprd3813392.pdf. Accessed September 2, 2016.

Vignieri, Sacha. 2014. "Vanishing Fauna." *Science* 345: 392–395.

Vincent, Carol Hardy. 2016, September 7. "National Monuments and the Antiquities Act." Congressional Research Service. https://fas.org/sgp/crs/misc/R41330.pdf. Accessed March 17, 2017.

Wheeler, Douglas P., and Rowberry, Ryan M. 2010. "Habitat Conservation Plans and the Endangered Species Act." In *Endangered Species Act: Law, Policy, and Perspective*, edited by Donald C. Baur and William Robert Irvin, 220–245. Chicago: American Bar Association.

Wilderness.net. 2016. "Fast Facts." University of Montana. http://www.wilderness.net/NWPS/fastfacts. Accessed September 2016.

Williams, Gerald. 2008. "Controversy over Clearcutting." *U.S. Forest Service History.* http://www.foresthistory.org/ ASPNET/Policy/Forest_Management/Clearcutting/ 1988-1992_policy.aspx. Accessed September 23, 2017.

Wilson, Edward O. 1992. *The Diversity of Life.* New York: W.W. Norton, 424 p.

Introduction

Chief Seattle from the Duwamish tribe said in the 19th century: "Humankind has not woven the web of life. We are but a strand within it. Whatever we do to the web, we do to ourselves. All things are bound together. All things are connected" (California Indian Education 2008). He understood that the loss of a single species in a natural community of plants and animals, no matter how small its role, can set off a chain reaction affecting other species and disrupt the whole system.

Instead of cherishing biodiversity and recognizing the benefits it provides, humans continue to use the Earth's resources without regard for the damage they create. The biggest drivers of global biodiversity decline and endangered species have been overexploitation from harvesting species at a rate they are unable to sustain and agriculture from production of food and fiber and fuel crops, livestock farming, and cultivation of trees. Other sources include urban development, invasive species, pollution, human disturbance, transportation, and energy production. Global climate change as a result of the buildup of greenhouse gases (GHG), especially carbon dioxide (CO_2), in the atmosphere from the burning of fossil fuels is a threat that will only grow larger in the future (Vignieri 2014).

A Cook Inlet Beluga whale, washed ashore near Anchorage, Alaska. Oil and gas extraction underneath Cook Inlet from hydraulic fracturing is a potential threat to this endangered species of only 328 individuals considered by NOAA at risk of extinction. (AP Photo/Al Grillo)

61

The International Union for Conservation of Natural Resources (IUCN) Red List database reveals two disturbing trends in the United States. A large portion of identified plants and animals are in decline and threatened with extinction, and an even higher proportion of species the IUCN classifies as low risk of extinction are declining. Eighteen percent of all animal species and 30 percent of all plant species are classified as threatened in the United States. The IUCN list shows that more than one-fifth of amphibians, one-third of insects, and two-fifths of salmon, trout, and other salmonid fish are threatened. Of mammals, 35 species are threatened, and more than two-thirds show declining populations (Lee-Ashley and Gentile 2015, 2–3).

Roadblocks to Action: Environmental Skepticism in the 21st Century

Today's Congress makes bipartisan legislation of environmental laws a distant memory. Rather than acting to prevent losses of biodiversity, the U.S. Congress has grown polarized and cooperation has become so minimized that very little is accomplished. Richard Lazarus (2013), a Harvard law professor, laments: "Congress is a legislative body that has essentially abdicated its lawmaking responsibilities in environmental law. And it is not as though new laws and amendments are needed less now than before. Today, new information and new challenges warrant statutory attention. The whole world around us is changing . . . economically, politically, and now with climate change, ecologically." This lapse in environmental legislation is especially troubling, because some of the regulatory measures designed to address environmental problems of the 20th century are ill equipped to address the more complex challenges of the 21st century (Adler 2013).

Congress has been unable to agree on any comprehensive energy legislation or to address climate change. National climate change legislation did look hopeful in 2009. Newly elected president Obama spoke positively about climate legislation and made key administration appointments of people who placed climate change as a top priority. Congress also seemed ready to act with Democrat control and some bipartisan support. Groups for and against the legislation geared up to lobby Congress. Environmental groups spent a record $22.4 million for passage compared with about $179 million spent by the oil and gas industry to defeat it. Exxon spent $27.4 million alone. A climate bill did pass the House of Representatives but stalled in the Senate (Mackinder 2010). After the 2010 mid-term election of ultraconservative "Tea Party" members, national climate change legislation became toxic, and many conservatives who had favored climate change legislation reversed their positions (Lazarus 2013).

President Obama took the initiative when Congress failed to act and used the Antiquities Act to protect important public lands and water and established environmental policy on climate change by issuing rules via executive orders. After the 2016 election in a reversal of policy, President Trump directed the Environmental Protection Agency (EPA) to start the legal process of withdrawing the Obama era directives on climate change and environmental pollution. Scott Pruitt as the new EPA head quickly moved to undo, delay, or block more than 30 environmental rules on climate, pesticide use, water pollution, and chemicals. Steps were taken to overturn the "Clean Power Plan" rule that was designed to close hundreds of polluting coal-fired power plants, freeze construction of new plants, and replace old plants with vast new wind and solar farms. Mr. Pruitt also delayed requirements that fossil fuel companies monitor and decrease leakage of methane, a major GHG emission. Pruitt made many of these decisions without the council of EPA scientists and career staff members who have decades of experience. Instead, his main source of council appears to be from the fossil fuel industries (Davenport 2017).

Whatever happened to conservative support for the environment? After all, Teddy Roosevelt and Richard Nixon were

Republicans, and Republican Congresses passed many of the strongest environmental laws in the history of the nation. After gains in environmental legislation in the 1960s and 1970s, conservatives began to view these large regulator laws as incompatible with their principles of limited government, free enterprise, and constitutional constraints. Environmental policies became suspect because they were considered threats to industrial activity, economic growth, and job creation. Environmentalists became viewed as "radicals" and "job-killers" who distort evidence, exaggerate problems, and want to shut down uses of America's public and private lands.

Conservatives argue there are too many job-killing environmental regulations that raise the costs for firms and manufacturers. President Trump favors business and development. He believes that government regulations are bad for the economy and that climate and environmental policies put the U.S. economy at risk. His political appointees share this thinking. They have low environmental ratings and do not accept climate change. Scott Pruitt as attorney general of Oklahoma sued the EPA multiple times and is a climate change denier. The EPA is staffed with industrial lobbyists and climate change skeptics. Former CEO of ExxonMobil Rex Tillerson as secretary of state, Ryan Zinke, secretary of interior, and Rick Perry, secretary of energy, are all skeptics of climate change and favor decreasing environmental regulations.

Conservatives are also skeptical of central government authority outside the context of national security, and they consider big government inefficient. They favor minimizing the regulatory burden on the private sector and would rather see responsibility for regulation closer to the people in the hands of state and local governments (Adler 2013). The 115th Congress with its conservative majority in the House and Senate is pushing hard for states to take over federal functions and even federal lands. Recently, lawmakers in the western states offered bills and resolutions seeking to take control of federal lands inside their state borders, and the Republican National

Committee (RNC) adopted resolutions to support the transfer of public lands to willing states. Some western Republicans are at odds with the federal government over mining and water quality controls and advocate abolishing the EPA (Yardley 2015).

Conservatives, because of their concern about national security, show strong support for building a wall along America's southern border to prevent illegal immigrants and terrorists from crossing into the United States. They supported George W. Bush when he built much of the existing wall under waivers of environmental laws. Within days of taking office, President Trump sought to fulfill his campaign promise about a "big, beautiful wall" and directed the Homeland Security secretary to secure the border with a contiguous and impassable physical wall. Naturalists and environmental advocates, however, consider a border wall very harmful to endangered species. The wall puts an insurmountable barrier through the corridors animals (jaguars, ocelots, bears, wolves, pronghorn antelope, and low-flying pigmy owls to name a few) have used for millennia and cuts through at least six national wildlife refuges. Using the FWS database, Greenwald et al. (2017) identified 93 endangered, threatened, or candidate species that could be harmed by the wall either directly or indirectly by associated infrastructure of roads and buildings. The wall would also degrade and destroy critical habitat for 25 species within 50 miles of the border. Preparations are already underway to build part of the wall through the species-rich Santa Ana wildlife refuge in the Rio Grande valley of Texas, a top birding location that brings in hundreds of millions of dollars to the local economy (Hardy 2017).

In another campaign promise, Trump vowed to minimize environmental regulations and give more power to the states through dismantling the EPA. EPA head Scott Pruitt, a proponent of states' rights, is in the process of radically remaking the agency to become smaller and more industrial oriented. Several agency scientists have been fired and replaced with people sympathetic to industry. Proposed budgets reduce funding to the EPA by over 30 percent with a majority of the cuts going to areas involved in climate change and environmental regulations. Especially targeted is the Office of Science and Technology. Chances are that Congress will refrain from passing a budget with such drastic cuts to the EPA. The reality is, however, that the EPA is destined to become much weaker under the Trump administration (Davenport 2017, Dennis and Eilperin 2017).

Environmental advocates are extremely opposed to the rollback of federal regulations on climate change, endangered species, pollution, and weakening of the EPA. They argue that strong federal regulations are necessary for public safety and health, to safeguard the environment from overexploitation, and for efficient regulation of the economy. Uniform federal standards are preferable to state-by-state regulations, including when endangered species are involved. Species, air, and water are not confined to state boundaries, and local control subjects them to political pressures. Voluntary regulation does not work, as seen in the damage done by oil spills. Although regulations may have significant compliance costs, these costs are warranted if they provide even larger economic and social benefits.

The staggering cost to society of unregulated use of the environment often outweighs the compliance cost from the regulations. An example is the British Petroleum (BP) Deepwater Horizon oil spill in the Gulf of Mexico in 2010 that caused billions of dollars of damage and cleaning costs and seriously disrupted fishing, tourism, and energy production in the Gulf States. Furthermore, the initial oil rig explosion killed 11 people, injured 17, and continued to pollute for months. The commission to investigate the spill documented serious lapses in regulation by the government agency charged with oversight, the Minerals Management Service (MMS). The MMS lacked both the resources and technical expertise to monitor the offshore oil industry, and meaningful reviews were lacking.

Government officials relied too much on assertions by the oil extractors, Halliburton, Transocean, and BP, of the safety of their operations (Shapiro and Irons 2011, 6–7).

Although the cost-benefit of environmental regulation is difficult to assess, there are estimates that show the benefits are greater than the cost. A cost-benefit analysis by the Federal Office of Management and Budget (OMB) for the period of October 1, 2004, to September 30, 2014, found that benefits from environmental regulation significantly exceeded costs. The OMB estimated the annual benefits in 2010 dollars to be between $261 and $981 billion and costs between $68 and $103 billion. The large ranges reflect the uncertainty in calculating the benefits and costs of environmental rules at any one time (Shapiro and Irons 2011, 8–9). Jobs shift from traditional manufacturing position to more bureaucratic ones or to new types of energy. Environmental regulations can cost a particular company significant sums of money, but overall employment may remain the same.

Global Warming, Climate Change, and Species Extinction

The planet is becoming hotter with more days of higher maximum temperatures recorded each year. India and Iran experienced record temperatures in May and July 2016: 123.8° and 127.4°F, respectively, and in June 2017, a city in Iran recorded a temperature of 129°F. Heat waves are becoming more common and longer in the United States. In June 2017, Las Vegas, Nevada, experienced nine consecutive days of 110°F, and Redding, California, had five consecutive days of record high temperatures with a peak of 113°F (Masters 2017). NOAA's heat index is in the red at 125°F, indicating extreme danger for heat stroke in humans. Both NASA and NOAA, in independent analyses, reported 2016 as the third year in a row as the warmest year on record globally, and 2017 is on track to becoming the second hottest year on record. Average global temperatures have increased almost 2°F since the late 19th century (Mooney 2017, Waldman 2017).

Scientists consider climate change the greatest threat to biodiversity in the 21st century. The Earth is warming from the "greenhouse gas" effect. Heat normally emitted from the Earth's surface is trapped in the atmosphere by greenhouse gases (GHG) such as carbon dioxide and methane from the burning of coal, petroleum, and natural gas to cause an increase in atmospheric concentrations of GHG by the unprecedented amount of about 40 percent since 1970. When heat is unable to escape, the Earth's surface begins to warm. The result is a rise in global average temperatures of 1.44°F (0.8°C). This increase may not seem like much, but the effects are enough to warm oceans, raise sea levels, and melt ice in the Arctic (National Academy of Sciences: The Royal Society Report 2014, 2–4, B1).

For at least 50 years, climate scientists have issued frequent warnings about the buildup of GHG and a warming and unpredictable climate that threatens the well-being of living creatures. They show that indicators of climate change, both direct and indirect and experienced now and in the future, affect global health. Heat waves, drought, fires, floods and storms have become more frequent and intense. In 2017, the United States experienced several extreme climate events consisting of unusually intense hurricanes and record flooding in Texas and Florida to heat waves and record fires in the western United States. Although global warming does not cause hurricanes, the warm water in the Atlantic most likely fueled the storms to cause them to grow stronger, larger, and more severe. Rising temperatures increase evaporation to result in increased precipitation and flooding while areas away from storm tracks experience less precipitation and drought (Union of Concerned Scientists 2011). A multidisciplinary commission (organized by the British medical journal *The Lancet*) predicts the frequency of extreme weather events will increase; the number of people exposed to extreme rainfall will be four times higher than in the 1990s, and those exposed to droughts will triple. Record high temperatures in the Mediterranean and Middle East may make these areas uninhabitable by the end of this century as temperatures approach the level at which animals, including humans, are unable to maintain their body temperatures (Watts et al. 2017).

Alaska is already hit hard by climate change. Alaska has warmed twice as fast as the rest of the country with melting permafrost, loss of sea ice, and more threatening fire seasons. Native villages are being washed away. To help finance adaptations to climate change, the governor of Alaska proposes to open the Arctic National Wildlife Refuge (ANWR) to oil drilling. The state has financial problems because of the drop in oil prices, a main source of revenue for the state because it has no income or sales taxes. In addition, opening of ANWR to oil and gas drilling is a top priority of the Trump administration with provisions included in the 2018 budget request.

Environmentalists oppose opening ANWR, one of the last totally pristine areas in the state, because of the potential negative effects on wildlife. In addition, climate scientists warn that drilling in the Arctic could have serious consequences for climate change. The oil extracted from the Arctic may in the short-term boost Alaska's revenues, but the increase in global warming would have a more serious negative impact on the state in the long term (Geiling 2015).

Sea level is rising from melting glaciers and ice sheets and expansion of volume as water warms. Increased rain is falling into seas swollen by melted ice caps. With higher background levels of water, dangerous and destructive storm surges push farther inland. Southern Florida, Louisiana, and most of the coastal areas of the United States and around the globe will endure inundation and increased flooding. Florida, barely above sea level, already experiences severe "king tides." Millions of people and countless numbers of plants and animals could be displaced. Already "Sunny Day" flooding from higher tides has increased along the Atlantic coast from Boston to Key

West, Florida. The average number of flood days in Washington, D.C., increased from 6 in the 1950s to 32 in the 2010s. Wilmington, North Carolina, experienced 49 flood days in the 2010s compared with 0.9 in the 1950s (Corum 2016; EPA 2017). Coastal cities require tens of billions of dollars to install flood control measures. A potential national security threat is the rising seas at the Naval Station at Norfolk, Virginia, and other coastal bases. Congress, however, has resisted any action on either climate change or the flooding problem. If the ocean continues to rise, there will be huge economic consequences as parts of large cities like Miami and New York City become uninhabitable.

Climate change threatens some of our most cherished and diverse locations, the national parks. To obtain a measure of how climate change is affecting the parks, National Park Service (NPS) scientists compared climate data for 289 national parks over the past 10 to 30 years with the historical range of variability from 1901 to 2012. They found that "parks are overwhelmingly at the extreme warm end of the historical temperature distributions." Eighty-one percent of the parks studied have experienced extreme heat in the past three decades, and 27 percent have seen extreme drought (Monahan and Fisichelli 2014). Glaciers in Glacier National Park are melting and may be gone by 2030 or less. Joshua Tree National Park may lose all its Joshua trees from California droughts. Rising sea levels in the Everglades National Park will submerge large areas (Cafaro 2012). Drought and dead trees increase the threat of uncontrollable fires as experienced in northern California in October 2017.

Based on concern about warming temperatures and their projected effects, the World Meteorological Organization (WMO) and the United Nations Environment Programme (UNEP) established the Intergovernmental Panel on Climate Change (IPCC) in 1988. Through the IPCC, climate experts from around the world synthesize the most recent climate science every five to seven years and present their report to the world's political leaders. The IPCC issued comprehensive assessments in 1990, 1996, 2001, 2007, and the Fifth Assessment Report (AR5) released in 2014 (IPCC 2014). These reports are statements of scientific consensus of the progression of increasing GHG leading to global warming and climate change.

Each IPPC report has issued the same basic message since the beginning: the risk from GHG is increasing, and human burning of fossil fuels is the dominant cause of global warming over the past several decades. As climates shift, entire ecosystems will be forced to move, colliding with one another. Many plants and small animals will not be able to move quickly enough to keep up and will go extinct (IPCC 2014).

How Does Global Warming Endanger Species?

Endangered species are often on the brink of extinction, and added stressors such as the events associated with climate change may be the final factor that pushes a species already stressed from habitat loss, pollution, and invasive species over the edge. At present, about 2.8 percent of global species are estimated at risk of extinction from climate change. The number increases to 5.2 percent at 2°C, and at 3°C the extinction risk increases to 8.5 percent. If temperatures increase on the present trajectory, up to one in six species (16 percent) will disappear (Urban 2015, Figure 2).

New studies show that the current warming of just 1°C is already leaving a discernible mark on ecosystem processes and biodiversity. Scheffers et al. (2016) found that 77 of 94 different ecological processes are affected such as species genetics, seasonal responses, distributions, and physical traits. Another study found that 47 percent of land mammals (of 893 species) and 23 percent of birds (of 1,272 species) have already suffered negative impacts from some form of climate change. In all, nearly 700 species in these two groups are affected negatively (Pacifici et al. 2017).

As the Earth warms and climate becomes more varied, living organisms must respond by shifting their geographic ranges, seasonal activities, migration patterns, and species interactions. Migratory birds are nesting earlier, and butterfly species have shifted their migration timing to arrive earlier. This mismatch in timing of migration and breeding can have serious effects on growth and survival when migrants arrive before or after food sources are present. For instance, the red knot (*Calidris canutus canutus*) is an avian, long-distance migrant that is experiencing warming temperatures at its breeding grounds in the Arctic from snow melting at least two weeks earlier. Because of limited food when the adult birds arrive, the offspring are smaller. These smaller birds with shorter bills are unable to obtain the deeply buried clams in their tropical wintering grounds causing their survival rates to drop (van Gils et al. 2016).

The ranges of many North American species move northward in latitude and upward in elevation as temperatures increase. As the mountain pine beetle (*Dendroctonus ponderosae*) in the Northern Rocky Mountains moves up to higher elevations, it attacks the whitebark pine (*Pinus albicaulis*), a high altitude species. The trees are also vulnerable to an invasive pathogen, blister rust (*Cronartium ribicola*), that can devastate the trees weakened from the beetle. Threatened grizzly bears (*Ursus arctos horribilis*) depend on the pine seeds as a high-calorie food source to build fat for winter hibernation. When the bears do not have the rich pine seeds, they migrate to lower elevations to find food, causing more bear-human conflicts. The Fish and Wildlife Service (FWS) declared the whitebark pine in danger of extinction and placed the species on the Candidate list with a low priority designation (Platt 2011).

The America pika (*Ochotona princeps*) is a small, charismatic rabbit that inhabits the colder areas of western U.S. mountain ranges. The warming climate causes pikas to heat stress and die as they move up the mountain as far as they can go to escape the summer heat. Despite a petition by environmental groups to list the American pika under the ESA, the FWS found in 2010 that listing the species as threatened or endangered was not warranted based on the assertion that pikas were adapting to changing temperatures (Platt 2016). A recent scientific study from the U.S. Government Survey confirmed, however, that pika populations are shrinking in much of their range from the negative effects of climate change (Beever et al. 2016).

Warming water temperatures create stress on fish, ranging from brook trout in Appalachia to salmon in the Pacific Northwest. The warming waters in rivers, lakes, and streams allow warmwater fish to expand into areas previously inhabited by cold-water fish. More extreme weather events of droughts, heat waves, wildfires, and floods increase fish mortality, and higher average temperatures and change in precipitation enable invasive species to expand into new ecosystems. Warm waters also stress fish and make them more susceptible to disease and death. A deadly bacterial disease that is normally not a problem in cold-water systems can cause large fish kills when water temperatures rise. Already 147 freshwater fish are listed under the Endangered Species Act (ESA) as threatened or endangered, and an estimated 37 percent of freshwater animals are considered at risk (Staudt et al. 2013).

Severe weather patterns of drought in some regions and excessive rainfall leading to flooding in other regions take their toll on endangered species. Florida will be battered in the coming decades by extreme weather conditions of dry seasonal drought and rainy season deluges (Cafaro 2012). The region is vulnerable to rising sea levels, storm surges, and increased salinity. The rise in sea level will reduce the amount of habitat available to endangered species such as the Key deer (*Odocoileus virginianus clavium*) and the critically endangered Florida panther (*Puma concolor coryi*) (Early et al. 2010).

Polar regions of the Earth are showing the most visible effects of climate change. The Arctic's top predator, the polar bear (*Ursus maritimus*), was listed as threatened under the ESA in 2008. Because the bears use sea ice in the summer as a platform for hunting, ice-free areas mean the bears have to rely on stored fat and foraging on land. This leads to a poorer diet, the bears starving, and increased contact with humans when the bears hunt for food on land. Whether polar bears will be able to sustain their populations under the warming conditions and continued loss of sea ice remains to be seen, but environmentalists and scientists are concerned and have lobbied to change the listing of the polar bear to endangered; even that listing is insufficient to save the bears if climate temperatures continue to rise. The FWS cites Arctic warming as the biggest threat to the bears in a final plan to save the animal. Without action to address the causes of diminishing sea ice, 80 percent of the polar bear population will collapse (Fears 2017).

Climate Change Controversy

In view of the accumulated scientific evidence, how did climate change and global warming become a controversy rather than an accepted body of scientific information? There is a broad misunderstanding of climate science by the American public and skepticism about the causes of climate change and the amount of scientific agreement to support it. This skepticism originates from an organized counter-movement backed by conservative donors and think tanks, media, and fossil fuel companies to confound public understanding of climate science to delay meaningful government policy to address the issue (Brulle 2014). A similar strategy was used by the tobacco companies to generate skepticism about the overwhelming medical and scientific evidence that smoking cigarettes was addictive, caused lung cancer, and could be lethal. Big tobacco fabricated a debate that helped cast doubt on the scientific evidence, and they suppressed evidence from their own scientists about the harmful effects of cigarette smoke. These efforts delayed public policy and control measures on smoking for years (Oreskes and Conway 2010, 10–35).

The misrepresentation of climate science is of great concern to those worried about climate change, especially in view of the high amount of agreement among scientists that human-emitted GHG are causing the Earth's atmosphere to become warmer and moister. An analysis of peer-reviewed publications and citations of 1,372 climate researchers showed that 97 to 98 percent support human causes of climate change (Anderegg et al. 2010). In an even larger study based on 11,944 climate abstracts published from 1991 to 2011, 97.1 percent of abstracts stating a position endorsed the consensus position (Cook et al. 2013). These studies have been criticized, however, because results were obtained by interpreting abstracts rather than direct surveys of climate scientists themselves. Direct surveys of climate scientists found similar results. Ninety percent of those who had published over 10 peer-reviewed publications on climate change agreed that GHG were the dominant drivers of global warming (Verheggen et al. 2014). A survey of non-climate scientists across biophysical disciplines found that 94 percent accept that average temperatures have risen, and 92 percent believe that the rising temperatures have a negative influence on nature (Carlton et al. 2015).

Some of the perpetuators of skepticism about the causes of climate change are from conservative think tanks with links to fossil fuel companies and industrial billionaires. Conservative donors fund the think tanks and other organizations to misdirect the public discussion and distort the understanding of climate science (Brulle 2014). Similar to the strategy used by the tobacco companies, climate change deniers promote a distrust of science and the reliability of climate models with the aim to prevent or weaken environmental regulation on the extraction and burning of fossil fuels. Ninety-two percent of English language books that express doubt about climate change published between 1972 and 2005 are linked to conservative think tanks (Jacques et al. 2008).

The biggest fossil fuel producer, Exxon (now ExxonMobil), knew of the dangers of CO_2 emissions on climate 40 years ago, but the company suppressed the information and spent millions to promote confusion and misled investors, policy makers, and the public by asserting that the uncertainty of climate science was sufficient to cast doubt on the effects of greenhouse gases on climate (Oreskes 2015). Besides denying their own science, ExxonMobil channeled money to the American Enterprise Institute and other conservative think tanks over nine years to fund their denial of climate change. Efforts are now underway to hold energy companies liable for the warming planet. The Rockefeller family, whose family fortune came from Exxon, has denounced Exxon's climate policies, and state attorney generals have joined forces in an investigation of ExxonMobil (Schwartz 2016).

The credibility of climate scientists themselves has also been questioned. A series of hacked e-mails from climate researchers in the United Kingdom in 2009 seemed to support the claim that climate scientists manipulated data for personal gain. Seven commissions in the United States and United Kingdom, including the U.S. National Science Foundation, examined the e-mails and concluded there was no evidence of misconduct and that the climate data were accurate. Those who represent themselves as scientific experts with the counter-movement are often not scientists, and if they are scientists, their area of scientific expertise is not in climate science, and they do not publish peer-reviewed papers on the subject (Governor's Office of Planning & Research 2012).

Climate deniers have their talking points. They point to severe winter weather as proof that global warming is not real. Senator James Inhofe of Oklahoma, who calls climate change a "hoax," famously brought a snowball into the Senate chambers to make his point during a particularly severe winter in Washington, DC. Senator Inhofe of course was talking about weather, not climate. Climate is long-term changes in the physical environment, while weather means the short-term daily and yearly fluctuations. Another argument is that global warming is from natural causes such as sunspots, but direct measurements by satellite show no net increase in the sun's output while global surface temperatures have increased (National Academy of Science: Royal Society Report 2014, 7). Climate skeptics consider the satellite data unreliable, and they point to the gains in sea ice in Antarctica as evidence to dispute global warming. Ice is increasing in the eastern part of the continent from increased precipitation in the interior, but ice is melting in western Antarctic and the Antarctic Peninsula to generate a large crack in the ice shelf.

Some opponents of limits to CO_2 emissions do accept that climate change is occurring. They believe, however, that the current economic and political costs to mitigate CO_2 are too high, place too large a burden on society and the U.S. economy, and present too little benefit for the American people (Lane 2014). Other skeptics use the uncertainty in climate projections to justify policy inaction. In their opinion, the magnitude of risk is just not high enough to justify the cost to control and lower GHG emissions and risk the potential loss of jobs in the fossil fuel industries (Stern et al. 2016). Instead, they favor inaction on reduction of GHG and increased energy production of fossil fuels.

There are costs to reducing GHG pollution, but new technologies and smart regulatory policies can decrease emissions while allowing the economy to thrive. According to the U.S. Energy Information Administration (EIA), the source of official energy statistics from the U.S. government, between 2005 and 2015 carbon emissions declined steadily, with some fluctuations related to weather, to fall to 12 percent below 2005 levels in 2015 while the economy grew an average of around 2 percent, a value considered too low for the economy by many conservatives. In 2015, when adjusted for inflation, the economy was 15 percent larger than it was in 2005 while the United States used 15 percent less energy per unit of GDP (Energy Information Administration 2016). Through a pairing of its industrial sector and international trade with progressive climate and environmental policies, Germany was able to increase its GDP while reducing its GHG emissions to 21 percent below 1990 levels (Alexander-Kearns and Cassady 2015).

Although there is significant uncertainty about the costs to curb GHG, inaction is predicted to have a strong negative effect on the world's economy. Developing countries are especially at risk for reduced agricultural yields, sea level rise, extreme weather events, and the greater prevalence of some infectious diseases. The economic and welfare costs of policy inaction could cause as much as a 14 percent loss in average world consumption per capita. On the other hand, mitigation of climate change would slow world economic growth by 0.11 percent to result in the world GDP lower by about 4 percent in 2050. Substantial human and capital resources will have to be reallocated to GHG mitigation, thus reducing the resources available for producing other goods and services, but world GDP would still be expected to grow, even if significant action to lower GHG is undertaken (Organization for Economic Cooperation and Development 2009, 11).

Climate Action

Can anything be done to control CO_2 and increasing global temperatures? The answer is yes, but action requires international cooperation, fast action, and binding agreements by all countries, including the biggest emitters: China, India, and the United States. Despite attempts for over 25 years to formulate an international agreement on curbing GHG, progress has been slow and limited.

The first attempt to get all the nations to agree on the problem of global warming was an international treaty in 1991, the UN Framework Convention on Climate Change (UNFCCC), known as the Rio Earth Summit. Regular meetings by parties to the convention (Conference of the Parties, COP) monitored voluntary implementation of obligations under the treaty to lower emissions to 1990 levels by 2000, a goal most countries did not meet. By 1995, countries realized that the reduction in emissions outlined by the convention was inadequate, and in December 1997 the third COP (COP3) adopted the Kyoto Protocol that obliged industrialized countries and countries of the former Soviet bloc to cut their emissions of GHG by an average of 5 percent below 1990 levels by 2012 (Center for Climate and Energy Solutions 2016).

After George W. Bush became president in January 2001, the United States rejected the Kyoto Protocol and opted out of participation in Kyoto-related negotiations. The reported deal breaker for the United States was the lack of standards for major emitters of GHG like China and India while creating mandates for the United States that might harm its economy. Furthermore, there was strong resistance to any action or acceptance of climate change among key members of the Bush administration, including Vice President Richard Cheney, former head of Halliburton. The European Union (EU) nations and others expressed deep concern and dismay at this new U.S. position (Sanger 2001). A majority of countries of the EU and the Russian Federation ratified the treaty, and it finally entered into force as a legally binding document on February 16, 2005.

Disagreements at international COP meetings subsequent to Kyoto demonstrated the inability of governments to bring climate change under control. Finally, at COP21 in Paris in December 2015, goals were established to prevent global temperatures from increasing more than 2° Centigrade (3.6° Fahrenheit) and to transfer $100 billion to poorer countries to help them adapt to the consequences of climate change. Although agreements are nonbinding and still must be ratified by the participating countries, they were endorsed by major business leaders and policy makers around the world. The legal requirement that countries monitor, verify, and report updated plans creates pressure for countries to follow through (Center for Climate and Energy Solutions 2015).

A major step was taken toward success of the Paris accord when the biggest polluters, the United States and China, ratified the agreement on September 3, 2016, and submitted plans to the UN to reduce carbon emissions. President Obama acted on the plan by an "executive agreement" and, therefore, did not require Senate approval for the ratification (Liptak 2016). President Trump, however, announced in June 2017 that the United States would not honor its commitment to the Paris agreement and was withdrawing for unspecified economic reasons.

Not all climate scientists are optimistic about international progress on climate change Climate scientist James Hansen considers the Paris agreement "just worthless words. There is no action, just promises. As long as fossil fuels appear to be the cheapest fuels out there, they will continue to be burned." Hansen favors a carbon tax as the best means to curb emissions, because it is the only incentive that puts a direct monetary price on the real costs imposed on the economy and planet by GHG and the global warming they cause. Fees levied against polluters would be powerful incentives to encourage companies and households to invest in cleaner technologies and greener practices (Milman 2015).

An alternative incentive to curbing GHG is the cap-and-trade system where allowances for polluting with GHG can be bought and sold to facilitate emission reduction. Some polluters favor this system over a carbon tax because it is market-based and provides more flexibility of economic activity. California became the first state to implement a comprehensive cap-and-trade system in January 2013. Despite warnings that cap-and-trade would kill the California economy, the program worked well without a drag on the economic growth of the state. In 2014, the program generated almost a billion dollars in revenues, and there was a decrease in CO_2 emissions between 2014 and 2015 (Hiltzik 2016). The state's emissions have fallen 9.5 percent since their peak in 2004, and the goal of reaching 1990 levels by 2020 is within reach. Governor Jerry Brown signed two new climate laws on September 8, 2016. One requires California to slash its GHG emissions 40 percent below 1990 levels by 2030 and the other prioritized efforts to cut GHG in low-income and minority communities. The new laws did not include Brown's request to continue the cap-and-trade system after 2020 (Baker 2016, A1, A10). In July 2017, however, California governor Jerry Brown signed bipartisan legislation to extend the cap-and-trade program to 2030. California has become a leader on climate change as the federal government retreats from any action on global warming (Megerian 2017).

Despite an early success, California's cap-and-trade market for greenhouse gases showed a sharp decline in purchases of pollution allotments with only 11 percent of available permits sold in May and 35 percent sold in August 2016. The November 2016 auction, however, showed a rebound with about 88 percent of the available credits purchased. The decline in purchases of allotments may actually indicate the program's success. Emissions have fallen faster in California than anticipated, which reduces the demand for allowances. Another cause for the reduced sales was the legal uncertainty generated by a lawsuit filed by the California Chamber of Commerce about whether revenues from the cap-and-trade auction are a tax or a regulatory fee. The Chamber alleged that the emission permits were an illegally levied tax that imposed a financial burden on a segment of California's businesses. In California, revenues categorized as a tax require a two-thirds vote of members of the state legislature, and the cap-and trade legislation was passed by a majority vote as a regulatory fee (Hiltzik 2016). In April 2017, California courts ruled in favor of the cap-and-trade program. The Chamber plans to appeal the ruling to the state Supreme Court (Megerian 2017).

Besides decisive action on global emissions more can be accomplished to counteract the effects of climate change on a more local scale. Planned adaptation will be necessary to cope with the challenges of climate change. For instance, a proactive response to climate change could be to designate critical habitat of an endangered species outside its historic range in anticipation of movements toward cooler conditions.

Individuals can take action to help reduce emissions, with the bonus of saving money at the same time. Energy efficiency is the best and easiest way to reduce the energy demand for household and transportation uses of energy. The EPA suggests these simple actions: switch to energy efficient light bulbs and fixtures, insulate and seal homes, replace old heating and cooling equipment, use water efficiently, reduce consumption and recycle, and purchase green power. Going solar with panels on private homes is expensive initially, but they save money and the environment in the longer term. Some states offer grants and rebates to reduce the costs and to encourage the use of solar panels for private electricity production (EPA 2016).

Species in Rapid Decline

Extinctions in most cases result from multiple causes linked together: climate change, habitat loss, pollution, pesticides, overexploitation, and poaching. The beginning of the 21st century has seen these linkages come together in a number of systems to threaten biodiversity and endanger species at an unprecedented rate. In some cases, action has been taken to mitigate declines, but in others the fast rate of decline and a lack of understanding the causes restrict what actions are available.

Fungi in Amphibians and Bats

Much to the alarm of scientists, amphibians are dying world-wide and quickly becoming the most endangered group of animals on the planet. Historic data reveal sudden disappearances of amphibians in pristine habitats in Puerto Rico, Costa Rica, Ecuador, and Venezuela beginning in the 1980s. Initially scientists viewed the reports with skepticism, because amphibian populations are known to fluctuate, but a global assessment by the IUCN-Global Amphibian Assessment found the declines are real, and amphibians are far more threatened than any other taxon. Of the 6,300 described species of amphibian, 32 percent are globally threatened with extinction, and 43 percent are experiencing some form of population decrease (Wake and Vredenburg 2008). This decline is harmful to ecosystem stability because frogs and salamanders are important links in food webs as predators of insects in moist forests, freshwater streams, and wetlands.

Why are amphibians disappearing? Habitat destruction and disease are considered major causes with climate change a contributing factor. Pollutants also threaten amphibian species, and exotic species outcompete them. Because amphibians are thermo-conformers (they do not regulate their internal body temperature like birds and mammals), they are particularly sensitive to extreme changes in air and water temperatures. Another threat is the physical alteration of aquatic habitats from impoundments, dredging, and water diversion. Recreation from off-road vehicles, and overutilization for commercial, scientific, and educational purposes take their toll. The most alarming and damaging cause of amphibian population declines, however, is the recent uncontrolled spread of a fungal disease.

Scientists have now learned that a virulent fungal infection (chytridiomycosis) is the source of an unexplained epidemic causing extinctions in frog populations throughout the world. This chytrid fungus feeds on the skin of the frogs. Because frogs breathe through their skin, they die of suffocation. The decline of frogs is especially serious in the tropics where fungi flourish and small ranges make frogs susceptible to extinction. Climate change exacerbates the effects of the fungus. Increased precipitation and temperatures associated with climate change act together to favor growth of the infectious fungus (Wake and Vredenburg 2008). To make matters worse, a similar fungus is now attacking salamanders. Extinction rates of amphibians are now four orders-of-magnitude higher than background rates (Alroy 2015). So far, scientists have been unable to stop the spread of the fungus.

A devastating fungus called the "white-nose" syndrome is causing hibernating bats to experience one of the most rapid declines in wildlife populations ever observed in the northeastern and central United States. Since the winter of 2007–2008, millions of these insect-eating bats in 25 states and 5 Canadian provinces have died from the disease, with the mortality estimated at 80 percent. This sudden and widespread mortality is unprecedented in bats, and once infected with the disease recovery of a population is unlikely because of the bats' low reproductive rate of a single pup a year. The fungus grows on the bat's skin causing irritation. The irritated bats wake up during hibernation, deplete their deposits of fat, and eventually starve to death (USGS 2016).

Bats play a significant role in controlling insect populations by consuming up to half their body weight in insects each night. Fewer bats mean more pesticides that cost agriculture billions of dollars and increase the threat of damage to beneficial species. The fungal disease has not been specifically linked to climate change, but the disease is worse in caves with increased humidity and temperatures, and the coldest and driest areas provide refuges from the disease (Langwig et al. 2012). The good news is that scientists may have found a remedy in a bacterium that kills fungi, but employment of the remedy is still in its early stages (Lee 2015).

Poaching of Megafauna

Elephants, rhinoceroses, lions, tigers, chimpanzees, and gorillas are just a few examples of charismatic megafauna fighting for survival. Large-bodied mammals are at higher risk than smaller ones because they require larger ranges, often exist in lower densities, and have a slow reproductive rate because their large body size requires a longer period of development. Many mammalian megafauna are experiencing dramatic contractions in their ranges and population declines, despite conservation efforts.

Although habitat loss and environmental degradation have traditionally been major factors in the decline of megafauna, the recent increase in poaching is pushing some species to the edge. Poaching is so intense in some parts of Africa and Asia that even in protected areas populations are declining under the onslaught of poachers with automatic guns. For instance, despite a ban on the ivory trade instigated by CITES in 1989, a recent scientific study verifies that ivory-seeking poachers are killing African elephants (*Loxodonta africana*) at an unsustainable rate. Three of four local populations are declining, and in just three years 100,000 elephants were killed. Central Africa has sustained a decline of 64 percent in 10 years (Wittemyer et al. 2014).

The high rate of poaching has stimulated debate about whether a limited legal ivory trade would help satiate the demand for ivory, especially in China. Others argue that the 1989 ban must be kept in place because legal trade would only generate an even greater demand for ivory, and illegal ivory could be sold as legal. Corruption among government officials who accept bribes to overlook illegal activities is thought to be too prevalent for enforcement of wildlife-related legislation. Even a one-time sell of confiscated ivory is discouraged. The sale of stockpiled ivory in 2008 in an effort to flood the market and decrease poaching was unsuccessful. Instead, elephant poaching skyrocketed (Russo 2014).

A near total ban on commercial trade in African elephant ivory went into effect in the United States on July 6, 2016. A total ban was necessary because venders selling ivory products (such as stores in Chinatown in San Francisco) could claim legality, and there was no way of sorting out the legal from the illegal ivory. The FWS is charged with enforcement of the ban under the ESA and CITES. The National Rifle Association (NRA), however, opposes the ban because firearms that contain ivory could not be sold unless they are more than 100 years old. The NRA also objects to limits on the number of trophies that can be brought into the United States (Russo 2014).

The rhinoceros is seriously imperiled. The growing demand for rhino horn for use as a pharmaceutical with no known medical advantage in Chinese medicine is fueling a poaching crisis. The rhino horn is ground into a powder and used as a treatment for everything from cancer to hangovers. Once abundant, all five species of rhino are now listed in the IUCN Red List of Threatened Species. The northern white rhino (*Ceratotherium simum cottoni*) is almost extinct, with less than five individuals surviving in captivity. The western race of the black rhino

(*Diceros bicornis longipes*), once a symbol of African wildlife, is officially extinct. Southeast Asia's Sumatran rhino (*Dicerorhinus sumatrensis*) numbers are extremely low, and around 50 Java rhinos (*Rhinoceros sondaicus*) are sheltered in a national park in Indonesia (Wilson 2016, 29–33). There are roughly 20,400 southern white rhinos (*Ceratotherium simum simum*) and 5,250 critically endangered black rhinos (*D. bicornis*) in Africa with the majority in South African national parks. Kruger National Park in South Africa is home to the largest population of rhinos in the world, around 9,000, but poachers kill on average two to three there every day. The soaring demand for rhino horn has caused a rapid rise in prices and an escalation in poaching. South Africa reported losing just 13 rhinos in 2007 and 83 in 2008. In 2014, despite patrols of armed guards, poachers killed 1,175 rhinos using AK-47s. The chief ranger at Kruger admits that protecting the rhinos is no longer a conservation challenge: "It's a war" (Christy 2016).

The best solution to stop poaching is to quell the demand for elephant ivory and rhino horns by making them unprofitable, a huge task that requires education, cooperation, and changes in the culture of the main consumers of the product, China and Thailand (Martin 2013). Until that happens, wildlife law enforcement must be considerably strengthened both at the site and nationally. An immediate approach is an aggressive enforcement of anti-poaching laws, better security at country borders to detect when there is illegal trade in animal products and by increasing armed guards. A common suggestion is the removal of horns and tusks from animals. This method does not always work. Elephants and rhinos are killed anyway to retrieve the stumps left behind and out of vengeance. Because animals use the tusks and horns for social interactions, their removal makes the animal vulnerable in other ways (Argall 2014).

The use of technology is becoming an important aid to apprehend poachers. Drones with night vision and thermal imaging help to detect poachers in the field. In the laboratory, investigations of wildlife crimes are aided by the latest DNA and other forensic technologies. The FWS Forensic Laboratory in Ashland, Oregon, analyzes over 600 cases annually. The lab works with around 200 federal wildlife agencies and fish and game agencies in all 50 states and more than 170 foreign countries (Neme 2009).

Bleaching of Coral Reefs

Global warming of oceans is pushing coral to extinction. Coral reefs are beautiful and productive habitats of high biotic diversity of marine fish, lobsters, clams, sponges, and many other organisms. They are living structures of a symbiotic relationship (a relationship in which both participants benefit) between colorful marine algae (zooxanthellae) and tiny marine animals (polyps), relatives of jellyfish and sea anemones. The coral derives 90 percent of its energy from the algae, and their stony calcium structures provide a home for the algae. Corals stressed by warm temperatures expel the beneficial algae and turn white in a process called coral bleaching. The coral can recover, but if stressed too often the entire coral reef may starve and die. When the corals die, the ecosystem around them transforms. Fish that feed on the coral or use it as shelter die or move away. The bigger fish that feed on the reef fish also disappear, and birds that eat fish lose their energy source. People are negatively affected because they lose their food resource. Unless ocean temperatures decline, the coral dies and becomes covered by a blanket of seaweed (Slezak 2016).

The rising temperature of the world's oceans has become a major threat to coral reefs. They show the most dramatic decline of any other group of animals in the IUCN Red List Index (IUCN 2016, Figure 1). There have been three major instances of coral bleaching of the world's reefs in the past 12 years. In 2005, the United States lost half of its coral reefs in the Caribbean from massive bleaching. Satellite data confirmed that thermal stress in 2005 was greater than the previous 20 years combined. In 2010, coral bleaching was observed in every ocean and major sea from the Persian Gulf to the Caribbean, where 80 percent of the coral surveyed was bleached. There were unusually high temperatures in 2010 from El Niño weather patterns and overall warming from climate change. With base ocean temperatures higher, increased temperatures from weather patterns push coral beyond their limits (Gaskill 2010).

The 2015–2016 El Niño was especially hard on the world's coral reefs spanning from Australia to Indonesia and across the Indian Ocean to Africa's east coast. Water already warmed from global warming caused 620 miles of the pristine Great Barrier Reef off the coast of Australia to show the worst coral die-off ever. Bleaching has caused 67 percent of the corals to perish. The Great Barrier Reef is one of the most complex ecosystems on the planet. It supports 1,600 species of fish, 130 types of sharks and rays, and more than 30 species of whales and dolphins. When the damaged coral die, fish and other marine life disappear. Millions of people depend on the reefs for fish for their livelihoods and protein. The only way to stop the bleaching is an immediate decrease in the emissions of GHG to slow ocean warming (Innis 2016).

The buildup of CO_2 in the atmosphere also affects coral negatively by increased acidification of the ocean. Carbon dioxide is absorbed and combined with water to produce carbonic acid. This action causes a reduction in concentrations of carbonate, a substance the reef-building corals must have to produce their skeletal structures. When the rate of carbonate saturation in the ocean decreases, the corals build structures of decreased density that make them brittle and subject to damage in storms. As a result, reef-protected coastlines become vulnerable to erosion and the loss of beaches (Hoegh-Guldberg et al. 2007).

The Pollination Crisis

For the first time in the United States, the FWS added seven species of Hawaiian yellow-faced bees (*Hylaeus* spp.) to the endangered species list (Wang 2016). Wild bees as pollinators have declined and may be reaching a "pollination crisis," because one-third of food consumed by humans requires pollination, and the bees do the majority of the work. Pressures on bees include habitat loss, exposure to a mixture of agrochemicals, and infections by novel parasites and pathogens accidently spread by humans. Climate change will further exacerbate these problems in the future. Managed honeybee stocks have declined in North America and Europe, but the demand for insect pollination of crops has tripled. To maintain sustainable farming methods, steps must be taken to reduce stress on bees. These include incorporation of flower-rich habitats into farmlands, reduction of pesticide use, and prevention of the spread of pathogens (Goulson et al. 2015).

Bumblebees, however, worry scientists the most. In North America, the relative abundances of four species have experienced up to a 96 percent decline, with a 23 to 83 percent contraction in their geographic ranges (Cameron et al. 2010). The IUCN Red List reports that 24 percent of Europe's bumblebees are at risk of extinction and 46 percent are in decline. Of the five most important insect pollinators in Europe, three are bumblebees. Climate change seems a major cause as well as intensification of agriculture and pollution from agricultural waste. Europe has already banned and restricted pesticides known to be harmful to bees. In addition to stopping GHG emissions, the IUCN suggests increasing margins around agriculture fields and preserving grasslands (IUCN 2014).

The ESA Works

The ESA is the best line of defense against species extinctions in the United States. Scientists and naturalists view the act as a success and are fighting hard to keep the law intact. They recognize the broad and diverse influence the ESA has had on species recovery at the federal and state level. Although removing species from the endangered species list is slow, proponents of the ESA stress that delisting species is not the only measure of success. There are many other measures of success that include preventing extinctions and conservation efforts that help stabilize species' status and eliminate the need for federal listing. Instead of focusing on how many species have been delisted, proponents of the ESA stress how many species have not become extinct and are in the process of recovery.

There has been steady progress in species recovery under the ESA as illustrated by the prevention of extinction of more than 99 percent of the over 1,500 protected species. When judged by plan timelines for recovery, the ESA is remarkably successful, and species with dedicated recovery plans and critical habitat for two or more years are likely to show improvement. The longer a species is listed, the more likely its populations are to increase. Scientists and auditors assert that the great majority of species, about 80 percent, have not been listed long enough to warrant an expectation of recovery, but 90 percent of species are recovering at the rate specified by their federal recovery plans. Species have been listed for an average of just 32 years, while their recovery plans require an average of 46 years of listing (Taylor et al. 2005).

Opponents of the ESA must understand that recovery of endangered species is a complicated process with the potential for setbacks. At-risk species often have extremely small populations in areas of limited habitat. Many endangered species lack strong recovery trends, and they may not reach full recovery for several decades. An analysis of 110 threatened or endangered species advancing toward recovery since being protected revealed that 90 percent were meeting their delisting deadlines (Suckling et al. 2012). For instance, whooping cranes (*Grus americana*) had a population of 54 birds when listed in 1967 and 599 in 2011. Their population, according to their recovery plan, is not expected to have full recovery until at least 2050, 80 years from listing. The American Bird Conservancy reports that 70 percent of all listed U.S. birds are on the road to recovery and being delisted, while 21 percent are in decline (Holmer 2016).

There are many success stories of species brought back from near extinction under the ESA (Suckling et al. 2012, Holmer 2016). One species is the Aleutian Canada goose (*Branta hutchinsii leucopareia*) that was listed in 1967 and then delisted seven years earlier than projected in 2001. The goose was nearly driven to extinction by foxes introduced into their nesting habitat. Protected from foxes on a remote Alaskan island, a small population grew from 750 birds in 1975 to more than 60,000 in 2005. The Steller sea lion (*Eumetopias jubatus*) is another species that was almost extinct from exploitation and decline of their prey. Following an emergency listing as an endangered species in 1993, its populations increased to 63,488 by 2009. The eastern population of the species was delisted in 2013. The once abundant Lake Erie water snake (*Nerodia sipedon insularum*) almost disappeared, and the FWS listed it as threatened in 1999. Through federal, state, and local efforts the snake populations increased to over 11,000 by 2008, and in 2011 the snake was delisted and considered recovered (Stanford 2013). The California condor (*Gymnogyps californianus*) is one of the most endangered birds in the world. The FWS and conservation partners removed 22 remaining birds from the wild and bred them in captivity with the goal to release them back into the wild. By 2014, 228 condors inhabited the wild, and another 193 condors resided in zoos (Suckling et al. 2012). A total of 19 species have been delisted from the ESA in the past 7 years.

The ESA plays an important role as a stimulus to respond to threats before species become endangered. The FWS is forming partnerships with landowners, state wildlife managers, and other groups to implement conservation measures and prevent the need to list species (FWS 2013, 2016). There are numerous examples of cooperation and partnerships among state and federal agencies, nongovernmental organizations, industry, and private citizens to restore species. The swift fox (*Vulpes velox*) and black-tailed prairie dog (*Cynomys ludovicianus*) are two examples. The greater sage-grouse (*Centrocercus urophasianus*) is another promising example of cooperation among government groups in 10 states and the federal government to designate and manage critical habitat on private and public lands with the goal to recover the grouse to prevent the necessity of listing them under the ESA (Haubold and Branciforte 2013).

An example of working toward recovery before listing under the ESA is the bog turtle (*Glyptemys muhlenbergii*). Listed as endangered in the IUCN Red List, the small turtle lost the majority of its suitable habitat, a rare type of wetland, in its range from New York and western Massachusetts south to Maryland. Until a few years ago the species was thought to be unrecoverable, but a partnership between the Natural Resource Conservation Service (NRCS) and the FWS initiated in 2010 seems to be leading the species to recovery. The voluntary program offers private land-owners compensation to protect, restore, and enhance wetlands on their property. As of spring 2013, 30 permanent bog turtle sites covering more than 747 acres were permanently protected, and 17 sites were enrolled for 2013 (Dershem 2013).

The ESA is accused of being a killer of jobs and economic development, but the data fail to support this accusation. Under Section 7 of the ESA, all federal projects must consult with the FWS to ensure that the project does not jeopardize listed species or their critical habitat. Because these projects are often large industrial developments that involve lots of money and provide many jobs (building a dam, for instance), there is great interest in the local community to have the project approved. A project delayed or halted after consultations receives much publicity, although it is a small percentage of all the projects in the thousands of consultations that have occurred under Section 7 since passage of the ESA. Before 2008, the FWS often required modifications to projects to minimize harm to endangered species, but few projects were denied (Parenteau 2011). The FWS may have gained efficiency in the consultation process in recent years. An analysis of data from over 88,000 consultations from January 2008 to April 2015 found no project stopped or extensively altered and only two projects advanced with modifications for wildlife (Malcom and Li 2015).

Proponents of endangered species consider the "citizen-suit" provision of the ESA an important tool to ensure that congressional priorities are implemented when other factors may limit federal or state enforcement of those priorities. Far fewer endangered species would be listed and protected if environmental groups had not been able to force the issue in court. A majority of the lawsuits challenge a failure of the FWS and NOAA to meet deadlines. In 2011, a large listing backlog led to a court settlement between the FWS and environmental groups. The FWS agreed to make final listing determinations for over 757 species by 2018 and to make concurrent critical habitat designations. In addition, the FWS was required to review 251 candidate species and either propose listing or make a final finding (Center for Biological Diversity 2011). Many species languish for years on the Candidate List without protection after receiving a warranted for listing but lower priority designation. (As of March 21, 2017, 30 species are on the FWS Candidate List.) In exchange, the FWS received a reprieve from listing litigation that has dominated its workload. The agreements include provisions intended to reduce the amount of litigation regarding listing decisions to allow the FWS to focus its resources on species protection under the ESA.

Developers, homebuilders, and farmers, however, have the same opportunity to seek economic relief in the courts as the conservation groups have to sue for endangered species protection. In 1997, the U.S. Supreme Court ruled in *Bennett v. Spear* that citizens who have experienced economic damage from actions related to the ESA have jurisdiction to sue (Evans 1997).

The ESA Is Not Working

Is the ESA a failure? Some private property owners, conservative politicians, the fossil fuel industry, developers, and representatives of commercial interests claim the ESA is not working because few species have been delisted, and the act has become radicalized, politicized, too bureaucratic, and is no longer effective. It violates property rights and fails to consider the tremendous cost to industry and commerce associated with it by direct prevention of energy development, ranching, farming, timber, mining, and other productive uses of the land. The 114th Congress introduced dozens of amendments, bills, and riders aimed at stripping away provisions of the ESA, including citizen lawsuits, as a means to minimize protections for species and to limit the number of species that can be protected.

Opponents point to the low number of species that have been delisted in over 40 years of the ESA's existence. Depending on how the number is counted, only 1 to 2 percent of listed species have been removed. Moreover, onerous restrictions and lack of incentives in the ESA have soured relations with private landowners to the point where there is little cooperation with federal and state regulators. Landowners consider the process by which the federal government determines harm to a habitat as arbitrary and unpredictable, and federal regulatory agencies use the ESA to lock up vast amounts of public land and resources (Seasholes 2015).

The ESA is viewed as a penalty-based act, rather than one with incentives, that violates landowners' property rights. Restrictions on land use require private property owners to absorb undue costs because of the negative impact on property values and the ability to earn income from the land. This has created enormous hostility and actually harmed species in some cases. Rather than comply with regulations imposed by the ESA, landowners have undertaken preemptive habitat destruction before a listing occurs to imperil further the species requiring protection (Seasholes 2007).

Uncompensated regulatory "taking" under the ESA creates an incentive for landowners to do precisely what the law is intended to prevent: rid the property of endangered species. Species are removed directly by killing them ("shoot, shovel, and shut-up") or indirectly by making actual or potential habitat unsuitable through plowing, prematurely cutting trees, or clearing bush. A well-cited example of this action is a landowner in North Carolina who preemptively cut trees and clear-cut timber to deny the red-cockaded woodpecker (*Picoides borealis*) habitat (Seasholes 2015, 4). The ESA is ineffective if landowners deny wildlife researchers access to their land and destroy potential habitat for fear of an endangered species turning up there. A system of easements and subsidies to reward property owners would be a more effective approach (Adler 2013).

Opponents of the ESA especially dislike the citizen-suit provision of the ESA. They think the lawsuits divert resources away from actual species recovery and set policies that run counter to larger public interests. Environmental groups overload the FWS with listing petitions and then sue for missing the deadlines. The U.S. Chamber of Commerce, an advocate of pro-business policies, created the catchphrase "sue and settle" to describe the use of the citizen-suit provision in the ESA to bring lawsuits against federal agencies. The legally mandated settlements typically favor the goals of the environmental groups bringing the lawsuit, and the process is a way for environmental groups to demand the enactment of their preferred policies (Johnson 2014). The Western Energy Alliance, an organization representing the oil and natural gas industries, accuses "radical environmental groups" of undermining the ESA by overwhelming the FWS with a sue and settle strategy. They claim expenses in legal fees to the FWS are excessive and take a large portion of the budget, especially since the courts usually mandate the FWS to pay the legal fees of environmental groups bringing the law suits (Western Energy Alliance 2016).

States' Rights and Local Control of Wildlife

Those who dislike the ESA are often advocates of state rights, small government, and local control. There has been a long history of resentment in the western United States over federal control of land. Of the 28 percent of all U.S.-owned land, 52 percent is in 12 western states ranging from a high of almost 80 percent of land in Nevada to about 29 percent in Washington State. By contrast, the federal government owns only 4 percent of area in the other states. This western concentration of federally owned land has contributed to a higher degree of controversy over land ownership and use than in other parts of the country. There is the belief that federal control of western public lands strips residents of their state rights to control the public domain for economic gain and to generate taxes. Passage of the ESA and other legislation in the 1960s and 1970s added restrictions on land use. As a result, ranchers protested restrictions on grazing on public lands in acts of defiance against the Bureau of Land Management (BLM), the agency that controls the grazing rights on public lands. Although this "Sagebrush Rebellion" ran its course in the 1980s, resentment of the federal government and the desire to take control of federal lands persists among residents in the western states today (Vincent et al. 2017).

Inspired by the conservative American Legislative Exchange Council (ALEC) and Americans for Prosperity, legislatures in several western states have promoted legislation demanding that federal property be turned over to their states' jurisdictions. In 2012, Utah passed the Transfer of Public Lands Act demanding that the federal government relinquish millions of acres of federal land to Utah by the end of 2014. The federal government did not oblige, and Utah is filing an expensive lawsuit to force the issue. In the meantime, the land transfer movement is gaining ground in other western states. New Mexico, Nevada, Idaho, Washington, and Wyoming have passed, introduced, or explored legislation for federal land transfer (Goad and Kenworthy 2013).

Different administrations have periodically proposed to sell public lands. The auctioning of public lands to reduce the national deficit was included in President George W. Bush's 2006 budget. Since 1990, the BLM has lost 8.7 percent of its land and the Department of Defense 44.5 percent, while the NPS and FWS gained 7.4 percent (Vincent et al. 2017). The Cato Institute, a libertarian think tank, developed a model to replace federal control with private interests. In 2000, Congress implemented one of the Cato Institute ideas as an experiment in New Mexico and transferred the Caldera National Preserve to a private trust. The Trust, mandated to become self-sufficient by 2015, was never self-supporting and transferred the preserve to the NPS in 2014, thus ending an unsuccessful experiment (Ribe 2015).

The land rights movement and the ESA finally clashed in 2014. The listing of a threatened species, the Mojave desert tortoise (*Gopherus agassizii*), stimulated the standoff between Cliven Bundy and the BLM at the Bundy Ranch in Nevada. Bundy, like most ranchers, depends on federal allotments to graze his cattle on public lands. When conservation priorities for the desert tortoise altered the terms of his grazing allotment, Bundy stopped paying grazing fees and continued grazing his cattle on the conservation area that was permanently closed to grazing, despite two court orders to remove the cattle and nearly $1 million in unpaid fees and fines. The BLM decided to confiscate the cattle herd to pay the delinquent fees, which led to the standoff and release of the cattle in the face of an armed protest (Allen 2014). Bundy, however, did not escape justice. He and 18 other defendants in the confrontation with government officers have been indicted and are going to trial.

The strong feeling about state's rights in the management of endangered species has also made its way to the U.S. Congress. An example is the Endangered Species Management Self-Determination Act, introduced into the 114th Congress in May 2015 by Senators Rand Paul (R-KY) and Dean Heller (R-NV). The act would require state consent and congressional approval before any listing as an endangered or threatened species. After five years, a species would be delisted automatically, regardless of its status of recovery, and states could block federal protections for species that occur in just one state.

(That would include all species in Hawaii.) (Clarke 2013). Although this and similar bills have not gained approval, similar legislation is being introduced in the 115th Congress, and the Trump administration is reviewing national monuments for transfer of land back to the states.

The "Taking" of Private Property

Probably the most contentious part of the ESA is Section 9 that contains the prohibition on "taking" endangered species. The broad definition of "take" includes any type of harm to an endangered species on private land as well as state and federal lands by individuals, corporations, or government agencies. The courts have established that this definition of harm applies both directly through harming animals and indirectly by changing or destroying critical habitat.

The courts in the majority of cases have upheld a long-standing legal tradition of broad government authority to regulate private property to protect wildlife. Property owners, therefore, were not very successful when they challenged the "taking" provision under the ESA in court (Echeverria and Sugameli 2010, 297). The proposal by opponents of the ESA to transfer ownership of wildlife to land owners and local governments for a more effective management of endangered species goes against legal tradition and would be difficult to win in court (Seasholes 2007).

However, there are mandates in the ESA designed to generate flexibility so that conservation goals can be met without taking private property. The ESA requires consideration of economic effects on landowners and contains alternative ways available for the landowner to avoid a legal challenge. A main alternative is to construct a Habitat Conservation Plan (HCP) and obtain an Incidental Take Permit (ITP). There are also Safe Harbor and Candidate Conservation Agreements with Assurances (CCAA). An alternative is to petition the secretary of interior to invoke a "special rule" to allow some impact on the species in exchange for the landowner's agreement to enter into a regional conservation plan. A last resort might be the "God Squad" committee established during the Tellico dam controversy (Parenteau 2011).

The Good and the Bad of HCP

Development of HCP can work as a solution for private landowners to use their property for economic gain, while protecting an endangered species. Developing a HCP, however, can be time consuming and expensive, which could discourage many landowners from considering one. For instance, a HCP is too expensive for most small farmers and ranchers. HCP often require extensive planning and costly biological surveys and data collection that take several years to accumulate and process. Farmers are also unable to afford the mitigation fees that can be paid by large developers. The mitigation fee per acre is the same for developers and farmers. Developers can pass the fees to a purchaser, but farmers cannot (Pauli 1999).

"Mitigation" is the offset of habitat loss of an endangered species. The FWS can require mitigation in the HCP via five steps from the least to the most invasive: (1) avoid by no harmful action, (2) minimize by limiting the magnitude of the action, (3) rectify by eliminating the impact over time through restoration, reduction, or elimination, (4) reduce or eliminate the impact over time through maintenance during the life of the action, and (5) compensation by placing or providing substitute habitats. This last action is often used by developers who mitigate by ensuring the conservation in perpetuity of a compensating amount of "equivalent" habitat elsewhere. The problem with mitigation is the difficulty of returning a damaged ecosystem to a more natural condition and to find equivalent habitats. Compensation sites may never replace natural ones, and the time to reach functional equivalency may take much longer than the monitoring periods. Often monitoring is insufficient and the ecology of areas poorly understood.

The absence of data causes important gaps in the quality of information that underlies mitigation proposals in HCP. Plans based on poorly understood species lack the data to describe accurately the current status of a species. Both proponents and critics agree that HCP should be based on a strong foundation of scientific data and ecological principles, but reviews of HCP for the northern spotted owl (*Strix occidentalis caurina*) and other species indicate that mitigation solutions are often arbitrary and lack an empirical foundation in the species' life history requirements (Bingham and Noon 2002). Monitoring is critical for effective management to determine whether HCP meet their objectives. For many reasons, there has been inadequate funding and resources devoted to monitoring (Camacho et al. 2015).

The FWS recognized the financial burden and established the HPC Assistance Grants' program to help states and landowners to plan and implement projects to conserve species. A recent FWS program plans to allocate approximately $4.7 million in grants to states and local governments. Some of the funding is awarded to larger, multispecies projects. For instance, the state of Florida will receive $750,000 for a statewide plan for Florida's beaches (Shire 2015).

The traditional approach to development of a HCP was to concentrate on a single species, but the single species model does not always work well. It leads to habitat fragmentation and is ill-suited for working landscapes. Many states and jurisdictions are turning to multispecies and ecosystem plans. California is an example of a state that is developing cross-jurisdictional, ecosystem-based planning over large areas of the state. The program uses cooperative agreements to create large habitat reserves for multiple species. Enrollment is voluntary by private landowners in conservation banks that are purchased over time and funded by land developers. So far 8 conservation plans cover 3.4 million acres with 18 more planned. The programs have not existed long enough to determine whether they will reverse the decline of listed species.

Many habitats are degraded and fragmented, and conservation plans are mainly for mitigation rather than species recovery (Evans et al. 2016).

A More Effective Endangered Species Program and Act

The inability of government to empower fully the agencies to implement the law has been one of the more notable problems with the ESA. Although the ESA consists of strong laws to protect biodiversity, scientists and environmentalist have long been concerned with the law's poor implementation and enforcement. Problems have occurred because of long delays in listing of species, failure to designate critical habitat, excessive allowance of "take," and poor implementation of recovery plans. Furthermore, funding for endangered and threatened species is grossly insufficient. Much of the spending does not go directly to species recovery but rather for bureaucratic requirements to pay staff, fund law enforcement, listings, and consultations. Total spending over the past 15 years has covered only about a third of recovery requirements (Evans et al. 2016).

Besides greater funding, a more balanced program for species recovery should be implemented. There has been a taxonomic bias in disproportionate government spending. The FWS has shown a taxonomic bias by focusing on large, charismatic species while spending little on other, sometimes more ecologically important, species. Animals are favored over plants, vertebrates over invertebrates, and mammals over fish and reptiles. Although the law requires protection for all species, the political reality is that the charismatic species receive more attention. The FWS has limited resources and must somehow assign priorities to various species. There is a prioritization system for analyzing trade-offs, but it is rarely used. Instead, FWS allocations are often driven by political and social factors. Priorities must be based on the best science, rather than political pressure and which species is more charismatic or politically expedient (Evans et al. 2016).

Endangered species listing is usually an option of last resort for a species with declining populations. A more successful approach would be to protect species before they are on their "deathbeds." Earlier and more effective conservation of imperiled species would reduce pressure on the ESA and lower the financial costs of recovery. In 2002, the Society for Conservation Biology sought to promote more effective recovery planning for species listed under the ESA. They sponsored a systematic review of a large sample of ESA recovery plans in collaboration with the FWS, the National Center for Ecological Analysis and Synthesis, and 19 universities (Clark et al. 2002). The main recommendation was to start earlier and acknowledge that some species may require protection under the ESA for many decades, if not permanently. The Center for American Progress suggests a new category of wildlife designation, "at-risk," to apply to declining species that do not yet merit the protection as a threatened or endangered species under the ESA. An at-risk designation would encourage voluntary conservation, provide earlier and more effective conservation of imperiled species, and reduce economic costs of ESA listing (Lee-Ashley and Gentile 2015, 9–13).

Many species that deserve endangered species protection may languish on the Candidate list for years without legal protection. Candidate species warrant listing, but because of resource constraints or other species having priority, they are not given a final endangered or threatened species listing. A program designed for private property owners, the CCAA, authorizes a variety of activities designed to help conserve species on the Candidate List of the ESA. The goal is to preclude the need for federal listing as threatened or endangered before the species status has become so dire that listing is necessary. If a landowner agrees to protect a candidate species, the FWS provides assurances that the landowner will not be subject to additional restrictions if the species becomes listed. There are different categories of protection in the CCAA. The most limiting agreement is the conservation only agreements. Another category covers activities designed to restore species to their former range in reintroductions when landowners allow species to be released onto their property. A third category, and the one used most frequently, is a combined nonconservation and conservation approach. Nonconservation activities such as ranching and farming can be coupled with certain conservation activities. Because participation in CCAA is low, the program has not reached its full potential and the FWS should be encouraged to evaluate more closely how the agreements are meeting conservation objectives (Li and Male 2013).

Options Available to Private Land Owners

Species conservation in the future will depend on effective programs for private lands, where the majority of endangered species reside. It is important that property owners, therefore, have incentives that align them with species protection. Private and public compensation funds could prevent endangered species from being a liability to landowners. An example is a program funded by the Nature Conservancy (TNC), a well-known environmental organization that concentrates on buying land for conservation. The TNC pays rice growers in the Sacramento valley in California to keep their fields flooded during bird migration on the Pacific Flyway. The farmers submit bids with their price for flooding their fields, and the TNC selects which properties it wants to fund (Evans et al. 2016).

Conservation banks are an option. The banks are lands permanently protected, conserved, and managed for at-risk species. The banks allow landowners to offset adverse impacts to species on their own land by contributing to protection of species in the banks. In exchange for permanently protecting the land and managing it for these species, the FWS approves a specified number of habitat or species credits. A conservation bank benefits landowners because they can profit by selling habitat or species credits. Conservation banks benefit species by the establishment of large reserves that function as mitigation for multiple projects (FWS 2012).

The Conservation Reserve Program (CRP) in the Department of Agriculture pays farmers a yearly rental payment in exchange for removing environmentally sensitive land from agricultural production and the planting of species that improve environmental quality. By compensating landowners, there is less incentive to destroy habitat and a positive incentive for better management to coincide with the needs of endangered species. Landowners may agree to increase the number of protected species on their property or give up or postpone development and potentially undertake conservation actions. Contracts for rental payments are 10–15 years in length and payments are based on the landowners' success at meeting the conditions of the contracts (Simmons 2002).

Conservation easements can work for endangered species under some circumstances. A conservation concession easement is when a resource is purchased from a landowner, but instead of exploiting it (by logging the trees, for instance) the land is left intact for the endangered species. The more common conservation easement is a voluntary legal agreement between a landowner and a land trust or government agency that permanently limits uses of the land in order to protect its conservation values. For example, an easement on property containing rare wildlife habitat might prohibit any development, while one on a farm might allow continued farming. The conservation easement protects land for future generations while allowing the owner to retain property rights and to live on the land and use it, but at the same time gain tax benefits (Simmons 2002).

Politics and Problems at the FWS

The FWS in the Department of Interior has a huge job to do: enforce federal wildlife laws, protect endangered species, manage migratory birds, restore fisheries, conserve and restore wildlife habitats, help with international conservation efforts, and manage National Wildlife Refuges. Responsibilities for endangered species alone include: listing, reclassifying and delisting, enforcement of species protection, protection of habitats, assist states in conservation efforts, conduct consultations with other federal agencies, and writing reports.

Environmental organizations have been critical of the FWS for not doing its job well enough and for being too susceptible to political influences. The revelation that of 88,000 consultations under Section 7 of the ESA from 2008 to 2015 no projects were stopped and only two were modified indicates the FWS has either become more efficient or is not following through when species are jeopardized from government projects. In comparison, from 1979 to 1981, the FWS evaluated 10,762 proposed actions and found that 173 would jeopardize a species, and they cancelled two of the projects. From 1987 to 1991, the FWS completed 73,560 consultations and found that 350 projects were likely to threaten a species' survival (Malcom and Li 2015).

The FWS is accused of using Rule 4(d) in the ESA to circumvent stronger prohibitions of at-risk species to accommodate industry interests. Several species, such as the polar bear, the northern long-eared bat (*Myotis septentrionalis),* and the lesser prairie chicken (*Tympanuchus pallidicinctus*) have been listed as threatened, while scientists and environmentalists want stronger protection for the species with an endangered species designation (Rodriguez 2015). Rule 4(d) allows the FWS to provide special regulations for threatened species and to change some or all of the strong protections in Section 9 that automatically apply to species listed as endangered. The FWS claims it uses Rule 4(d) to streamline the regulatory process for "minor impacts" and to clarify or simplify what forms of "take" of a threatened species are prohibited. For instance, allowed activities under the 4(d) rule for the threatened Preble's meadow jumping mouse (*Zapus hudsonius preblei*) seem to include some rather invasive activities of limited rodent control, ongoing agricultural activities, landscaping, noxious weed control, and ditch maintenance (FWS 2014).

Scientific integrity and political interference at the Department of Interior and FWS have been an ongoing problem. A senior George W. Bush political appointee in the Department of Interior, Julie MacDonald, resigned after she revised scientific reports to minimize protection of endangered species. Two supervisors of the FWS ignored staff concerns in order to shrink the habitat by 4.5 million acres of the endangered American burying beetle (*Nicrophorus americanus*). They used a flawed method to create a smaller and more industry-friendly range for the insect in path of a major and controversial oil pipeline, the Keystone Pipeline System. The two officials were found guilty of misconduct. While the whistle-blowers faced retaliation in reduced pay, some doubt exists about whether the guilty officials were punished. They quickly left the FWS for other jobs (Halpern 2014).

The Union of Concerned Scientists (UCS) (2015) has conducted surveys to evaluate the state of scientific integrity at the FWS and NOAA and two other federal agencies after an initial review in 2005. They found that the FWS did improve after 2005 on a number of metrics: agency morale, the ability to publish, the consideration of expert advice in decision-making, and whistle-blower protection awareness (UCS 2015, Figures 10 and 12, pp. 15, 17). The 2015 survey also found, however, there were still areas where the agency must improve, especially in political influence and morale.

The 2015 survey found that problems were widespread across agencies and scientific disciplines, but the FWS seemed to have the most problems. Scientists at the FWS had the lowest job satisfaction of the four agencies in the survey. Of 826 FWS scientists, 73 percent responded that consideration of political interests was "too high and too responsive to political pressure." At NOAA, 56 percent of 973 respondents agreed that too much weight was given to political interests (UCS 2015, Figure 4, p. 8). A considerable number of scientists said they were unable to communicate their scientific work to the public and the media, lack of resources constrained them, and respect for the scientific process was lacking. On the other hand, 52 to 59 percent of the scientists across agencies thought they could express concerns about the mission-driven work of the agency without retaliation (UCS 2015, Figure 12, p. 17). The UCS developed a set of recommendations for federal agencies to improve scientific integrity and stressed that much more work is necessary to protect science and scientists from outside political interference in decision-making. The UCS recommended that the FWS and NOAA improve their scientific integrity and work better with scientists. The White House should take a stronger leadership role in promoting government-wide integrity.

Although morale within the FWS was better in 2015 than in 2005, it was still low. Only 7 percent of respondents to the survey rated morale excellent and 32 percent good. Thirty-one percent said morale was fair and 21 percent had extremely poor morale (UCS 2015, Figure 10, p. 15). The greatest barrier to timely decisions for FWS and NOAA was limited staff capacity with inefficient decision-making processes within the agency. Although the FWS budget increased from 2012 through 2015, the number of full-time equivalent staff positions decreased by 13 percent (UCS 2015).

The Gray Wolf: The Intersection of Science, ESA, and Politics

Love them, hate them, no one seems neutral about the gray wolf (*Canis lupus*). In the United States, wolves were killed almost to extinction by the 1930s and then protected by being listed as endangered under the ESA in 1974. Reintroduced into Idaho and Wyoming in 1995 and 1996, wolves were delisted over the objections of wolf scientists in 2008. They were relisted as endangered by court order in 2010 and finally delisted by action of a rider on a budget bill in Congress in 2011. Removal of the listing became the subject of several court cases with varied decisions. As a result, gray wolf policy and management became inconsistent, controversial, and a prime example of how politics can override science to the possible detriment of an endangered species.

Reintroduction of Gray Wolves as Apex Predators

In 1974 in a noncontroversial action, because there were practically no wolves remaining in the United States outside of Alaska, gray wolves were provided full protection as an endangered species under the ESA throughout the contiguous 48 states, except for Minnesota where they were listed as threatened. Changing attitudes and a better understanding of the role of predators in an ecosystem led to proposals to reintroduce wolves into Yellowstone National Park and the Frank Church–River of No Return Wilderness in central Idaho (Fischer 2003, 24–54). It took years of discussion, an environmental impact statement, action of environmental groups, and lots of politics to gain final approval for an introduction of an "experimental population" of 15 gray wolves from Canada into Yellowstone National Park in 1995 and 1996. At the encouragement of a Republican senator from Idaho, James McClure, 15 wolves were also introduced into the 2.4 million acre wilderness in central Idaho (Fischer 2003, 143–197). To the amazement and joy of tourists and scientists, and the dismay of livestock owners, the introductions were successful and wolves began to thrive and disperse.

From a scientific point of view, wolves play an important role in the biotic stability of the ecosystems they inhabit. They are apex predators at the top of the food web. They selectively eat the plant eaters that are old, sick, and young, and in the course of doing so strengthen the genetics of the prey and prevent these primary consumers from overpopulating and overconsuming plants in the habitat to the detriment of other species. The carrion remains from wolf kills provide important food for scavengers such as eagles and grizzly bears. Wolves are highly social animals and live in groups (packs) of relatives that cooperatively take care of the young. Of the several members of a pack, the only animals to reproduce are usually the alpha male and female ("alpha" is a term for the most dominant animals in a social group.) Because many social interactions revolve around the alpha animals, removal of an alpha animal disrupts the stability of the pack.

Shortly after the wolf reintroductions, the positive effects of an apex predator were seen in the Greater Yellowstone ecosystem. Without wolves, elk (*Cervus canadensis*) had overpopulated and overbrowsed the trees along rivers and streams during the harsh winters when most forage was buried under snow. The stream banks became exposed and degraded, and beaver (*Castor canadensis*) and the ponds behind their dams disappeared. Upon return of the wolves, the elk population decreased, and the elk avoided browsing in some of the high-risk areas. Without the heavy consumption by elk on aspen, willows, and cottonwoods, the streams began to recover. Recovery of streamside vegetation correlated with the appearance of beaver. Beaver dams helped to restore the stream banks to provide pools for fish. Species of songbird also began to appear in the restored trees and shrubs. Although this cascade effect triggered by the wolves is still in the early stages of an ongoing process, the positive influence of an apex predator on the health and biodiversity of an ecosystem is becoming well established in the greater Yellowstone ecosystem (Ripple and Beschta 2012).

Controversy Surrounding Delisting Gray Wolves

As gray wolf populations increased, livestock owners, hunters, and politicians levied political pressure for the FWS to delist the wolves from the ESA and give management to the western states where the wolves resided. Over the objections of scientists, in March 2008 the FWS delisted the wolves in the Northern Rockies and turned over management to the states of Idaho, Montana, and Wyoming. Environmental and animal-rights groups immediately challenged the delisting in court. A federal judge agreed with the environmental groups and blocked the delisting in time to stop the fall 2008 hunting season. In March 2009, the FWS once again affirmed the delisting decision. A September 2009 to March 2010 wolf-hunting season proceeded with the death of over 500 wolves in the Northern Rocky Mountains. In August 2010, a federal district court judge reinstated ESA protection, but in April 2011 Congress capitulated to political pressure and took the unprecedented action of attaching a rider in the budget bill to delist wolves in Montana, Idaho, Washington, Oregon, and Utah. This action not only circumvented the science-based process of the ESA, but a last-minute rider to a bill allowed Congress to avoid committee hearings and debate (Cohn 2011).

The delisting of wolves in the Northern Rockies placed them in harm's way. State wildlife agencies in Idaho and Montana rushed to establish hunting seasons. The state of Idaho has been especially active in killing wolves. Idaho Fish and Game (IDFG) even hired a professional trapper/hunter to remove by lethal means wolves in two packs deep within the Idaho wilderness. The reason was to decrease wolf predation to inflate elk populations for hunting and recreation. After environmental organizations challenged the wolf removal with a lawsuit, the IDFG backed down and ended this wolf extermination program, but nine wolves had already been killed (Missoulian 2014).

The IDFG was not finished with killing wolves. In keeping with the game management plan calling for the removal of 60 percent of wolf populations in the River of No Return Wilderness to boost elk populations, 23 wolves were hunted and killed from helicopters at great expense in winter 2014 and 19 in the winter of 2015. In January 2016, the U.S. Forest Service authorized the IDFG to land helicopters in the River of No Return Wilderness to capture and place radio telemetry collars on wild elk. IDFG also captured and radio-collared four wolves during these operations—an action not authorized by the Forest Service. Environmentalists sued the Forest Service to challenge the use of helicopters in a designated wilderness. They also feared the IDFG placed collars on wolves to locate them to implement the wolf-killing management plan. The judge ruled that the 120 helicopter landings in a designated wilderness violated the Wilderness Act and attaching the collars was unlawful. Therefore, the data are illegal, cannot be used for future proposals, and must be destroyed (Chaney 2017).

According to the IDFG Wolf Management Status Timeline (2016), by the end of 2015 a total of 1,885 Idaho wolves met human-caused mortality from legal hunting and control measures by Wildlife Services since losing ESA protection in 2011. (Data were derived from adding together documented human-caused mortalities for each year. There are no data for wolf numbers and mortality in Idaho after 2015.) IDFG documented the highest densities of wolves in Idaho in 2009 at 856 wolves in 94 packs with 49 breeding pairs. By 2013, wolf populations were down to 659 wolves in 107 packs with only 20 breeding pairs. Populations rebounded somewhat by the end of 2015 to 786 wolves in 108 packs with 33 breeding pairs (IDFG Timeline 2016, Figures 4 and 5, pp. 6–7). Of most concern to scientists, however, are the number of breeding pairs and total pack sizes. The high mortality, lower number of breeding pairs, and smaller pack sizes (6.5 wolves per pack compared with 8.1 from 2005 to 2008) led wolf scientists to express concern about the ability of the gray wolf to maintain viable population sizes in Idaho at the current rate of mortality (Creel et al. 2015).

What happened to the wolves in Wyoming? The FWS rejected the state's management plan for being inadequate and opted to keep the wolves on the ESA list. In August 2012, the FWS reversed its decision and transferred control of the gray wolf to state officials in Wyoming, but in September 2014, a federal judge vacated the delisting of the wolves in Wyoming and reinstated ESA protection in response to legal action by environmental groups, who considered the Wyoming management plan open season on wolves. The plan referred to wolves as vermin and allowed unregulated killing in 80 percent of the state and sport hunting (Wolf Trophy Management Area) in the remainder of the state (Winter 2014). Wolves, however, are now back under Wyoming control after the U.S. Court of Appeals reversed the lower court's judgement and ruled that the state management plan was adequate. The state plans to open a 2017 hunting season to reduce wolf populations. Because sightings of wolves become significantly reduced when they are trapped and hunted, tourism in Yellowstone could be affected (Robbins 2017).

Gray wolves also inhabit the western Great Lakes area of Minnesota, Wisconsin, and Michigan. The FWS discontinued endangered species protection of these wolves at the beginning of 2012 and gave management to the states. Lawmakers in these states soon established hunting programs. The Humane Society objected to the number of wolves killed (1,500) and filed a lawsuit to protect the Great Lake wolves. In December 2014, a federal judge issued an order to relist the wolves as endangered because the rule revising the endangered listing was "arbitrary and capricious" and violated the ESA of 1973. Pro-hunting groups collected signatures to place two proposals on the November 2014 ballot in Michigan to reinstate the state's ability to manage wolves for hunting, but voters rejected both measures (Flesher 2014).

The FWS in the Obama administration took the ultimate step in June 2013 and proposed a rule in the *Federal Register* to remove all gray wolves from federal protection in the remaining states where they are still protected by the ESA, except the highly endangered Mexican wolf (*Canis lupus baileyi*). This action would mean wolves that disperse into new ranges would lack federal protection. The FWS came under extreme criticism for this ruling, especially by scientists, for using faulty science to support the decision. Scientists were nearly unanimous that the gray wolf was only about 6 percent recovered in its historic range, and it was too soon for delisting, because there are many areas where gray wolves might thrive. Sixteen scientists submitted a letter to Secretary of Interior Sally Jewell protesting the ruling. The decision for the proposed delisting was made without input from the key scientists responsible for the research referenced in the draft rule. The rule did not reflect conclusions of the scientists' research or the best available science concerning the recovery of wolves. The FWS sought an independent peer review of the science behind the decision and enlisted the National Center for Ecological Analysis and Synthesis to conduct an unbiased review. In a unanimous result, the panel concluded that the FWS rule to delist the gray wolf throughout its range was not supported by the available science and was based on a flawed taxonomic paper unsupported by recent science (Cohen 2014). On July 1, 2015, the Obama administration withdrew the petition.

Scientists also disagree with the FWS that wolf harvests in the western United States are having no negative effects on population dynamics and demography of wolves. A FWS review considered wolf populations secure under state management and concluded that harvesting of wolves in the Northern Rockies "has not increased any risk" to wolf populations (Jimenez 2014). This position of the FWS runs counter to ecological theory and data (Creel et al. 2015, Vucetich 2016). Creel et al. (2015) took issue with the sampling methods used to account for wolf populations. For instance, Idaho overestimates their wolf count 1.75 times with the method they use to adjust for pack size. There is also concern that disruption of pack size will have long-term effects on wolf survival and reproduction. Wolves may be unable to withstand human-caused mortality of 28-50 percent without declining in nature (Creel et al. 2015). If wolves are hunted too intensively, their ecological value is diminished and range expansion is significantly curtailed. Intensive hunting of wolves impairs their genetic connectedness (Vucetich 2016).

Mexican Gray Wolves

The Mexican gray wolf (*Canis lupus baileyi*) is a genetically distinct lineage of wolves that historically lived across the southwestern part of the United States into Mexico. Although they numbered in the thousands, the same fate that the gray wolf encountered in other parts of the United States happened to them. The livestock industry, ranchers, and government agents killed them almost to extinction. The FWS listed them as endangered in 1976, and between 1977 and 1980 surviving Mexican gray wolves in the wild were captured to become part of a captive-breeding program.

In 1998, the FWS, Arizona Game and Fish Department, New Mexico Department of Game and Fish, and U.S. Department of Agriculture (USDA) Wildlife Services released 3 family groups consisting of 11 Mexican wolves into the primary recovery zone on public lands within the Apache National Forest in eastern Arizona. Additional wolves were released in subsequent years into southern Arizona and New Mexico. These wolves were released as a nonessential experimental population which meant that, although listed as endangered, the wolves could be legally harasses or killed in self-defense and in defense of livestock or when there is an unacceptable impact on wild ungulate populations of deer, elk, and sheep.

Despite recovery efforts, the wild population of Mexican gray wolves remains on the brink of extinction. The February 2016 count found only 97 wolves in the wild. Escalating mortalities and illegal killing (18 percent increase in 2015) with reduced pup survival caused a population decline of 11 percent from the previous year. The lack of genetic diversity in the inbred population may also be a factor in lower pup survival.

Why isn't the Mexican wolf doing better? Environmental groups and scientists want the FWS to commit to better management with more wolf releases to increase the genetic diversity of the population, a science-based recovery plan, and more wolf populations in suitable habitats. The FWS has been operating on a short-term recovery plan since 1982. A draft recovery plan in 2012 recommended establishing two additional Mexican gray wolf populations, one in the Grand Canyon and another in the southern Rocky Mountains of New Mexico. The overall goal was to create three self-sustaining subpopulations totaling 750 wolves. The plan also suggested several areas of suitable habitat for reintroduction efforts including land in northern Arizona and New Mexico, and southern Utah and Colorado. That plan, however, was never published, and the recovery team that produced it never reconvened to review the proposal.

A coalition of wolf conservation groups, environmental organizations, and a retired federal wolf biologist viewed the FWS action as caving to demands of the anti-wolf states, especially since governors from the four states involved sent letters to the secretary of interior protesting wolf releases. Environmental groups, therefore, went to court to demand that the FWS implement an updated, scientifically based, recovery plan. In April 2016, the groups settled and the FWS is required to prepare a long-term recovery plan by November 2017 (Earthjustice 2016).

Although a FWS rule in 2015 expanded the range of where Mexican wolves could be released, the rule limited the area to south of Interstate 40 in Arizona and New Mexico. Several environmental groups have protested limiting the wolves to below the interstate because there is suitable range for the wolves above it, and the draft recovery plan of 2012 recommended expansion of the wolves in areas north of Interstate 40. The reason given for the limitation is that the historic range of the Mexican wolf was limited below I-40. Recent DNA

evidence, however, shows that the Mexican wolf was historically in southern California and probably ranged over a greater
distance than the current limitation (Hendricks et al. 2016).

Lethal and Nonlethal Control of Wolves

Since the arrival of the Pilgrims, wolves have been shot, trapped,
and poisoned until almost all the wolves in the contiguous
United States disappeared by 1930. The deep-seeded hatred
and fear of wolves (the "big bad wolf"), losses of untended livestock, the notion that wolves compete with hunters for game
animals, and a lack of understanding of the biological role of
wolves in a balanced ecosystem led to government-sanctioned
programs for wolf extermination. As settlers depleted bison,
elk, moose, and deer in the western states, wolves turned to
predation on livestock, and landowners turned to predator
control by the U.S. government (Fischer 2003, 10–23).

The Division of Predator and Rodent Control was established in 1915 under the Biological Survey, which became
part of the FWS. The government paid official hunters to kill
wolves, including in Yellowstone and Yosemite National Parks,
until almost none remained (Boitani 2003). Today, predator
and rodent control still exists under the USDA Wildlife Services. Opposite of the purpose of the ESA, Wildlife Services
uses lethal means to kill animals that interfere with human
activities; in 2014, the federal agency killed 322 wolves, 580
black bears, 61,702 coyotes, 2,780 foxes, and 305 mountain
lions (Goldfarb 2016a). In response to hundreds of gray wolves
killed by Wildlife Services using foothold traps, wire snares,
and aerial gunning from helicopters, five environmental organizations filed a lawsuit in federal court on June 1, 2016, to
challenge the activities.

Wolves at times do prey on livestock, and individual livestock owners suffer financially from the losses. Several sources
are available to livestock owners to compensate for livestock
deaths. The 2014 Farm Bill authorized the Livestock Indem-
nity Program (LIP) to provide benefits to livestock producers

for deaths of livestock in excess of normal mortality, including attacks by animals reintroduced into the wild by the federal government (USDA 2016). There are grants from the federal government to the states for compensation to livestock owners for losses from wolf predation. Idaho was awarded $100,000 from the federal government for depredation compensation for 2014 losses. Idaho lawmakers also approved $400,000 in state money matched by $220,000 from cattle and sheep groups and sportsman for Wildlife Services to use for lethal control of wolves in 2014, but there has been no money allocated for nonlethal control (O'Connell 2014).

Although lethal control of wolves is the traditional choice of managers, its effectiveness is open to question, and there are less costly alternatives. In a scientific review of over 100 peer-reviewed predation studies, only 12—5 nonlethal methods and 7 lethal methods—met the accepted "gold" standard of scientific testing with unbiased sampling, treatment, measurement, and reporting. Of those 12, prevention of livestock predation was demonstrated in 6 tests (4 nonlethal and 2 lethal controls), whereas increases in predation were shown in 2 tests using lethal control. The remaining four (one nonlethal and three lethal) showed no effect on predation. The authors recommend suspension of lethal methods until there are studies with acceptable scientific standards that demonstrate effectiveness of lethal controls (Treves et al. 2016). Killing wolves may even increase the odds of depredation the next year. The indiscriminate killing of wolves by hunters and trappers fragments and destroys the social cohesion of the pack. When older wolves are killed, young ones have to fend for themselves and may turn to easier prey, thus increasing predation rates of domestic sheep and cattle (Wielgus and Peebles 2014).

A less costly alternative to lethal wolf management is to use nonlethal methods that are both more economical and also viewed by the public as more humane (Slagle et al. 2017). Some nonlethal procedures are very simple, such as removing any decomposing carcasses or sick animals that might attract wolves. Other measures include guard dogs, herders, patrols of livestock on horseback, fencing, fladry barriers (line of ropes with strips of colored fabric that flap in the breeze), spotlights, loud noises, telemetry, and avoidance of areas of high risk from wolves (Stone et al. 2017, Table 1). Nonlethal control of wolves, however, is not yet part of the policy for state fish and game commissions, and funds to provide compensation for livestock losses do not include funds to help livestock owners implement nonlethal control methods.

Are nonlethal control methods effective against wolves? The answer is yes. A scientific study comparing predation by gray wolves on sheep over seven years in an area protected with nonlethal control methods and an area of no protection found that predation loses to wolves were 3.5 time higher in the nonprotected area than in the area protected with nonlethal methods. Sheep depredation losses to wolves were just 0.02 percent of the total number of sheep present, the lowest loss rate among sheep-grazing areas where wolves range statewide (Stone et al. 2017). Oregon's wolf plan includes nonlethal, preventative measures to prevent wolf-livestock conflict as the first choice of Oregon wildlife managers. Although the wolf population in Oregon has increased over the last seven years, livestock losses have remained relatively stable (Bean 2016). A biologist in Michigan demonstrated in a study comparing predation of cattle on farms with Great Pyrenees dogs and control groups with no dogs that wolves and coyotes both stayed clear of cattle farms patrolled by dogs (Goldfarb 2016b).

Sage-Grouse Politics and Partnerships: A Different Approach

The fight to save the greater sage-grouse (*Centrocercus urophasianus*) is complicated because so many different entities have a stake in the outcome. The grouse's now fragmented range in the sagebrush plain has declined by about 44 percent and includes a vast area of 11 western states with about 50 percent on private property and the other 50 percent on land managed by the BLM. Many of these lands have vested economic interests, because they are prime areas of oil and gas extraction (fracking), mining, and cattle grazing.

As a result of an estimated 90 percent of critical sagebrush habitat destroyed or altered by human activities and a decline in greater sage-grouse populations, conservation groups pushed the FWS for an endangered species listing under the ESA. On September 30, 2015, a date mandated for a decision by the courts, the Obama administration announced that the greater sage- grouse would not be given endangered species protection. Although the bird was a candidate for listing, the FWS opted to develop management plans in partnership with ranchers, private landowners, federal agencies (the BLM and Forest Service), and the 10 states with sage-grouse populations on more than 60 million acres of critical habitat in the sagebrush plain (Lavelle 2015). The FWS would monitor all of the continuing efforts and population trends and reevaluate status of the species in five years.

The final BLM plan designates 15 areas for general management on federal lands. Within the general management areas are sagebrush core areas within priority habitats that have the highest value to maintain the species and its habitat. Habitat disturbance within these areas must be avoided or minimized because they are important landscape blocks with high breeding population densities of sage-grouse and existing high-quality sagebrush. The federal plans also propose withdrawing 10 million acres of the most critical grouse habitat from new mining claims. Additional plans to avoid further loss of habitat on federal lands limit energy development, establish buffers around mating grounds, and take steps to improve habitat and reduce fragmentation (Levelle 2015, BLM 2016).

This long-awaited decision on listing of the greater sage-grouse brought both praise and criticism. Environmental groups split on the action. Some environmentalists considered the decision political, rather than scientific. Defenders of

Wildlife called the plan "bad news," because it failed to incorporate key provisions recommended by scientists. None of the plans propose to protect sagebrush reserves as strongholds for sage-grouse, and there are no immediate actions to modify harmful grazing practices (Salvo 2014). On the other hand, the Audubon Society and National Wildlife Federation favored the plan and worked with the different entities to establish it (Lavelle 2015).

Economic interests were also unhappy with the plan. The Western Energy Alliance (2015) applauded the decision of not listing the greater sage-grouse as endangered but called the alternative plan flawed. They objected to the centralized management of the sage-grouse on public lands and believed that federal plans should defer to state plans already formulated. Furthermore, the sage-grouse restrictions in the land use could cost billions in lost economic activity and thousands of jobs because of disturbance caps on energy extraction around mating areas of the grouse.

Dissatisfaction with the plan immediately led to litigation by environmental groups, state governments, and energy developers. Only three days after the final plans were released, the Idaho governor and legislature filed a lawsuit objecting to what they considered last-minute changes in the BLM and Forest Service plan. Specifically, they objected to addition of 3 million acres of BLM land to Sagebrush Focal Areas, mating area buffers, diversion of resources away from wildfires, invasive species management, and overreaching. In April 2016, the American Explorations & Mining Association filed a lawsuit challenging restrictions on mining exploration (Taylor 2016). Environmental groups filed a lawsuit against the BLM seeking to restore science-based habitat protection with the aim to strengthen the BLM management plan by closing loopholes for oil and gas development and loose grazing restrictions (Center for Biological Diversity 2016).

Republican leaders in the U.S. Congress entered the controversy by introducing legislation to block the federal plan, place sage-grouse conservation in the hands of the respective states, and restrict the FWS from listing the species as endangered under the ESA. Governors could block federal management plans on federal lands in the state if the federal plan were considered inconsistent with the state's plan. President Trump is expected to scale back implementation measures. Secretary of Interior Zinke has appointed a task force to review the management plans with the goal to give the states more flexibility. Environmentalists are concerned that weakened plans put the grouse and the conservation program at risk (Streater 2017).

If the legislation, revisions, and lawsuits against the federal conservation plan prevail, there would be no overall plan or oversight to coordinate conservation efforts in state plans, and implementation of weak state plans would be more susceptible to pressure from local interest groups. The overturn of federal control on federal lands would set a harmful precedent for future conservation efforts. Some of the state plans fail to implement the best science. For example, greater sage-grouse leks (areas where males display to attract females for breeding) only have a 0.6 mile buffer from industrial development in Wyoming, far less than the 3.1 mile minimum buffers identified by federal scientists and applied in all other states. Inadequate protection is the main threat for the 40 percent of sage-grouse that live in Wyoming (Biondolillo 2014).

A popular federal program that seems to be working and promises results for sage-grouse preservation is the Sage Grouse Initiative (SGI) (2015), which offers incentives to private landowners to undertake voluntary sage-grouse conservation. The SGI is a partnership of private ranchers, agencies, universities, and nonprofit and businesses working together to conserve wildlife through sustainable ranching. A voluntary conservation program, the SGI, established in 2010, offers incentives to private landowners to preserve sage-grouse habitat on their land. As part of the Farm Bill's conservation program, the USDA NRCS offers money to private and public partners if they volunteer. Today 1,129 ranches across 11 western states are conserving 4.4 million acres of land. The NRCS plans to commit approximately $211 million to SGI over the life of the Farm Bill, 2014–2018. Every easement is tailored specifically for the landowner. The overall aim is to maintain the land in private ownership while limiting the amount and type of development necessary to maintain working landscapes. The agreement is attached to the land's title, regardless of ownership. Landowners may either sell or donate conservation easements.

References

Adler, Jonathan H. 2013. "The Conservative Record on Environmental Policy." *The New Atlantis* 39: 133–143. http://www.thenewatlantis.com/publications/the-conservative-record-on-environmental-policy. Accessed February 25, 2017.

Alexander-Kearns, Myriam, and Cassady, Allison. 2015. "Cutting Carbon Pollution While Promoting Economic Growth." *Center for American Progress*. https://www.americanprogress.org/issues/green/report/2015/05/27/113865/cutting-carbon-pollution-while-promoting-economic-growth/. Accessed August 28, 2016.

Allen, Jonathan. 2014. "Before Nevada Stand-off, a Collision between Ranchers and Tortoises." *Reuters*. http://www.reuters.com/article/us-usa-ranchers-nevada-tortoises-insight-idUSKBN0EA1I420140530. Accessed March 1, 2017.

Alroy, John. 2015. "Current Extinction Rates of Reptiles and Amphibians." *Proceedings of the National Academy of Science* 112: 13003–13008. http://www.pnas.org/content/112/42/13003.full.pdf. Accessed February 24, 2017.

Anderegg, William R. L., Prall, James W., Harold, Jacob, and Schneider, Stephen H. 2010. "Expert Credibility in Climate Change." *Proceedings of the National Academy of Science* 107: 12107–12109. http://www.pnas.org/content/107/27/12107.full. Accessed February 25, 2017.

Argall, Rose. 2014. "Africa's Poaching Crisis: How Do We Stop It?" *The Dodo*. https://www.thedodo.com/community/frontiergap/africas-poaching-crisis-how-do-699797004.html. Accessed September 16, 2017.

Baker, David R. 2016, September 8. "Gov. Brown Orders Big Greenhouse Gas Cuts." *San Francisco Chronicle*. http://www.sfgate.com/science/article/Gov-Brown-orders-big-greenhouse-gas-cuts-9211316.php. Accessed September 9, 2016.

Bean, Brian S. 2016. "Oversight Hearing on the Status of the Federal Government's Management of Wolves." *U.S. House of Representatives Committee on Natural Resources Subcommittee on Oversight and Investigations*. http://docs.house.gov/meetings/II/II15/20160921/105396/HHRG-114-II15-Wstate-BeanB-20160921.pdf. Accessed September 21, 2016.

Beever, Erik, Perrine, John D., Rickman, Tom, Flores, Mary, Clark, John P., Waters, Cassie, Weber, Shana S., Yardley, Braden, Thoma, David, Chesley-Preston, Tara, Goehring, Kenneth E., Magnuson, Michael, Nordensten, Nancy, Nelson, Melissa, and Collins, Gail H. 2016. "Pika (*Ochotona princeps*) Losses from Two Isolated Regions Reflect Temperature and Water Balance, but Reflect Habitat Area in a Mainland Region." *Journal of Mammalogy* 97: 1495–1511.

Bingham, Bruce B., and Noon, Barry R. 2002. "Mitigation of Habitat 'Take': Application to Habitat Conservation Planning." *Conservation Biology* 11: 127–139.

Biondolillo, Chelsea. 2014, July 10. "Conservationists Question Sage Grouse Protection Plan." *Science News*. http://www.sciencemag.org/news/2014/07/conservationists-question-sage-grouse-protection-plans. Accessed May 1, 2016.

BLM. 2016. "Sage-Grouse and Sagebrush Conservation." http://www.blm.gov/wo/st/en/prog/more/sagegrouse.html. Accessed September 13, 2016.

Boitani, Luigi. 2003. "Wolf Conservation and Recovery." In *Wolves Behavior, Ecology and Conservation*, edited by David Mech and Luigi Boitani, 317–344. Chicago: Chicago University Press.

Brulle, Robert J. 2014. "Institutionalizing Delay: Foundation Funding and the Creation of U.S. Climate Change Counter-movement." *Climate Change* 122: 681–694. http://www.climateaccess.org/sites/default/files/Brulle_Institutionalizing%20Delay.pdf. Accessed March 20, 2017.

Cafaro, Peter. 2012. "What Should NPS Tell Visitors (and Congress) about Climate Change?" *The George Wright Forum* 29: 287–298. http://www.georgewright.org/293cafaro.pdf. Accessed March 20, 2017.

California Indian Education. 2008. "Chief Seattle." http://www.californiaindianeducation.org/famous_indian_chiefs/chief_seattle/. Accessed August 27, 2016.

Camacho, Alejandro E., Taylor, Elizabeth M., and Kelly, Melissa L. March 2015. "Lessons from an Area-Wide, Multi-Agency Habitat Conservation Plans in California." *UCI Law Center for Environment, & Natural Resources.* http://www.law.uci.edu/academics/centers/cleanr/CLEANR-HCPReport-2015march.pdf. Accessed July 19, 2016.

Cameron, Sydney A, Lozier, Jeffery D., Strange, James P., Koch, Jonathan B., Cordes, Niles, Solter, Leellen F. and Griswold, Terry L. 2010. "Patterns of Widespread Decline in North American Bumble Bees." *Proceedings of the National Academy of Science* 108: 662–667. http://www.pnas.org/content/108/2/662.full. Accessed September 5, 2016.

Carlton, J. S., Perry-Hill, Rebecca, Huber, Matthew, and Prokopy, Linda S. 2015. "The Climate Change Consensus Extends beyond Climate Scientists." *Environmental Research Letters* 10. http://iopscience.iop.org/article/10.10 88/1748-9326/10/9/094025/meta. Accessed October 11, 2016.

Center for Biological Diversity. 2011. "Historic Victory: 757 Species Closer to Protection." http://www.biological diversity.org/programs/biodiversity/species_agreement/. Accessed September 7, 2016.

Center for Biological Diversity. 2016, February 25. "Lawsuit Fights Special Interest Loopholes in Greater Sage-grouse Plan." https://www.biologicaldiversity.org/news/press_ releases/2016/greater-sage-grouse-02–25–2016.html. Accessed May 3, 2016.

Center for Climate and Energy Solutions. 2015. "Outcome of the U.N. Climate Change Conference in Paris." http://www.c2es.org/docUploads/cop-21-paris-summary-02-2016-final.pdf. Accessed August 29, 2016.

Center for Climate and Energy Solutions. 2016. "History of International Negotiations." http://www.c2es.org/ international/history-international-negotiations. Accessed August 28, 2016.

Chaney, Rob. 2017, January 19. "Update: Judge Orders Destruction of Data from Illegal Elk/wolf Collaring in Wilderness." *The Missoulian*. http://missoulian.com/ news/local/update-judge-orders-destruction-of-data-from-illegal-idaho-elk/article_28645da0–16a7–5fc9-b6bd-742941e225e7.html. Accessed March 22, 2017.

Christy, Bryan. October 2016. "Special Investigation: Inside the Deadly Rhino Horn Trade." *National Geographic*. http://www.nationalgeographic.com/magazine/2016/10/ dark-world-of-the-rhino-horn-trade/. Accessed March 20, 2017.

Clark, J. Alan, Hoekstra, Jonathan M., and Boersma, P. Dee. 2002. "Improving U.S. Endangered Species Act Recovery Plans: Key Findings and Recommendations of the SCB Recovery Plan Project." *Conservation Biology* 16: 1510-1519. http://www.cfr.washington.edu/classes .esrm.458/clarketal.pdf. Accessed March 21, 2017.

Clarke, Chris. 2013, December 2. "Bill Would Gut Endangered Species Act." *KCET*. https://www.kcet.org/ redefine/bill-would-gut-endangered-species-act. Accessed March 22, 2017.

Cohen, Julie. 2014. "Panel Issues Report on Gray Wolf Science." *The UC Santa Barbara Current*. http://www .news.ucsb.edu/node/013939/panel-issues-report-gray-wolf-science. Accessed September 13, 2016.

Cohn, Jeffery P. 2011. "Wildlife Groups Opposing Congressional Delisting of Gray Wolf." *BioScience* 61: 648. https://academic.oup.com/bioscience/article-lookup/ doi/10.1525/bio.2011.61.8.17. Accessed March 21, 2017.

Cook, John, Nuccitelli, Dana, Green, Sarah A., Richardson, Mark, Winkler, Bärbel, Painting, Rob, Way, Robert, Jacobs, Peter, and Skuce Andrew. 2013. "Quantifying the Consensus on Anthropogenic Global Warming in the Scientific Literature." *Environmental Research Letters* 8. iopscience.iop.org/article/10.1088/1748-9326/ 8/2/024024/pdf. Accessed September 16, 2017.

Corum, Jonathan. 2017. September 4. "A Sharp Increase in 'Sunny Day' Flooding." *New York Times*. https://www .nytimes.com/interactive/2016/09/04/science/global-warming-increases-nuisance-flooding.html?mcubz=0. Accessed September 13, 2017.

Creel, Scott, Becker, Matthew, Christianson, David, Dröge, Egil, Hammerschlag, Neil, Hayward, Matt, W., Karanth, Ullas, Loveridge, Andrew, MacDonald, David W.,

Matandiko, Wagganson, M'soka, Jassiel, Murray, Dennis, Rosenblatt, Elias, and Schuette, Paul. 2015. "Questionable Policy for Large Carnivore Hunting." *Science* 350: 1473–1475.

Davenport, Coral. 2017, July 1. "Counseled by Industry, Not Staff, E.P.A. Chief is Off to a Blazing Start." *New York Times*. https://www.nytimes.com/2017/07/01/us/politics/ trump-epa-chief-pruitt-regulations-climate-change.html. Accessed September 14, 2017.

Dennis, Brady, and Eilperin, Juliet. 2017, May 23. "EPA Remains Top Target with Trump Administration Proposing 31 Percent Budget Cut." *Washington Post*. https://www .washingtonpost.com/news/energy-environment/wp/ 2017/05/22/epa-remains-top-target-with-trump- administration-proposing-31-percent-budget-cut/?utm_ term=.3a451079ecd1. Accessed September 16, 2017.

Dershem, Bonnie. 2013. "Partnering to Conserve Bog Turtle Habitat in Pennsylvania." *U.S. Fish and Wildlife Service Endangered Species Bulletin*. https://www.fws.gov/ endangered/news/episodes/bu-04-2013/story4/index.html. Accessed July 10, 2016.

Early, Laura M., Harvey, Rebecca G., Brandt, Laura A., Watling, James I., and Mazzotti, Frank, J. 2010. "Science Support for Climate Change Adaptation in South Florida." *University of Florida Institute of Food and Agricultural Services*. http://edis.ifas.ufl.edu/pdffiles/UW/UW33100 .pdf. Accessed September 11, 2016.

Earthjustice. 2016. "Court Settlement Provides Hope for Mexican Gray Wolves." http://earthjustice.org/news/ press/2016/court-settlement-provides-hope-for-mexican- gray-wolves. Accessed December 18, 2016.

Echeverria, John D. and Sugameli, Glenn P. 2010. "The Endangered Species Act and the Constitutional Taking Issue." In *Endangered Species Act: Law Policy, and Perspectives*, edited by Donald C. Baur and Wm. Robert Irvin, 292–315. Chicago: American Bar Association.

Energy Information Administration. 2016, May 9. "Today in Energy." *EIA*. http://www.eia.gov/todayinenergy/detail .cfm?id=26152. Accessed August 29, 2016.

EPA. 2016. "What You Can Do." https://www3.epa.gov/ climatechange/wycd/. Accessed August 30, 2016.

EPA. 2017. "Climate Change Indicators: Coastal Flooding." https://www.epa.gov/climate-indicators/climate-change-indicators-coastal-flooding. Accessed September 16, 2017.

Evans, Daniel M., Che-Castaldo, Judy P., Crouse, Deborah, Davis, Frank W., Epanchin-Niell, Rebecca, Flather, Curtis H., Fronlich, R. Kipp, Goble, Dale D., Li, Ya-Wei, Male, Timothy D., Master, Lawrence L., Moskwik, Matthew P., Neel, Maile C., Noon, Barry R., Parmesan, Camille, Schwartz, Mark W., Scott, J. Michael, and Williams, Byron K. 2016. "Issues in Ecology: Species Recovery in the United States: Increasing Effectiveness of the Endangered Species Act." *Ecological Society of America*. https://www.esa.org/esa/wp-content/uploads/2016/01/ Issue20.pdf. Accessed August 1, 2016.

Evans, Lynwood P. 1997. "Bennett v. Spear: A New Interpretation of the Citizen-Suit Provision." *Campbell Law Review* 20: 173–191. http://scholarship.law.campbell.edu/ cgi/viewcontent.cgi?article=1333&context=clr. Accessed October 10, 2016.

Fears, Darryl. 2017. "Without Action on Climate Change, Say Goodbye to Polar Bears." *Washington Post*. https:// www.washingtonpost.com/news/energy-environment/ wp/2017/01/09/without-action-on-climate-change-say-goodbye-to-polar-bears/?hpid=hp_hp-more-top-stories_ee-polarbears-910am%3Ahomepage%2Fstory&utm_term= .d43bc53410c4. Accessed January 9, 2017.

Fischer, Hank. 2003. "Wolf Wars." *Missoula Montana: Fischer Outdoor Discoveries*, LLC.

Flesher, John. 2014. "Federal Judge: Great Lakes Wolves Return to Endangered List." *Detroit Free Press*. http://www .freep.com/story/news/local/michigan/2014/12/19/great-lakes-wolves-ordered-returned-endangered-list/20655023/. Accessed September 13, 2016.

FWS. 2012. "Conservation Banking: Incentives for Stewardship." *U.S. Fish and Wildlife Service*. https://www .fws.gov/endangered/esa-library/pdf/conservation_banking .pdf. Accessed September 13, 2016.

FWS. 2013, July 12. "Defining Success under the Endangered Species Act." https://www.fws.gov/Endangered/news/ episodes/bu-04-2013/coverstory/index.html. Accessed August 26, 2016.

FWS. 2016. "FWS Funding." Fish and Wildlife Service-Department of Interior. https://www.doi.gov/sites/doi .gov/files/migrated/budget/appropriations/2016/highlights/ upload/BH063.pdf. Accessed August 1, 2016.

Gaskill, Melissa. 2010. "Coral Bleaching Goes from Bad to Worse." *Nature*. http://www.nature.com/news/2010/ 101119/full/news.2010.621.html. Accessed September 5, 2016.

Geiling, Natasha. 2015, October 13. "Alaska Governor Wants to Drill in the Arctic National Wildlife Refuge to Pay for Climate Programs." *Climate Progress*. http://thinkprogress .org/climate/2015/10/13/3711647/alaska-governor-drill-because-climate-change. Accessed July 6, 2016.

Goad, Jessica, and Kenworthy, Tom. 2013, March 11. "State Efforts to 'Reclaim' Our Public Lands." *Center for American Progress*. https://www.americanprogress.org/issues/green/ report/2013/03/11/56103/state-efforts-to-reclaim-our-public-lands/. Accessed March 21, 2017.

Goldfarb, Ben. 2016a, January 25. "Wildlife Services and Its Eternal War on Predators." *High Country News*. https://www.hcn.org/issues/48.1/wildlife-services-forever-war-on-predators. Accessed June 12, 2016.

Goldfarb, Ben. 2016b. "No Proof That Shooting Predators Saves Livestock." *Science News*. http://www.sciencemag.org/news/2016/09/no-proof-shooting-predators-saves-livestock. Accessed December 26, 2016.

Goulson, Dave, Nicholls, Elizabeth, Botias, Christina, and Rotheray, Ellen L. 2015. "Bee Declines Driven by Combined Stress from Parasites, Pesticides, and Lack of Flowers." *Science* 347: 1–9. http://science.sciencemag.org/content/347/6229/1255957. Accessed March 20, 2017.

Governor's Office of Planning & Research. 2012. "Common Denier Arguments." *California Government Web Site*. https://www.opr.ca.gov/s_commondenierarguments.php. Accessed August 27, 2016.

Greenwald, Noah, Segee, Brian, Curry, Tierra, and Bradley, Curt. 2017. "A Wall in the Wild: The Disastrous Impacts of Trump's Border Wall on Wildlife." Center for Biological Diversity. https://www.biologicaldiversity.org/programs/international/borderlands_and_boundary_waters/pdfs/A_Wall_in_the_Wild.pdf. Accessed September 18, 2017.

Halpern, Michael. 2014, February 7. "Scientific Integrity, Beetles, and the U.S. Fish and Wildlife Service." *Union of Concerned Scientists*. http://blog.ucsusa.org/michael-halpern/scientific-integrity-beetles-and-the-u-s-fish-and-wildlife-service-408. Accessed August 14, 2016.

Hardy, Michael, August 13. "In South Texas, Threat of Border Wall Unites Naturalist and Politicians." *New York Times*. https://www.nytimes.com/2017/08/13/us/in-south-texas-threat-of-border-wall-unites-naturalists-and-politicians.html?mcubz=0. Accessed September 24, 2017.

Haubold, Elsa M., and Branciforte, Brian. 2013. "Keeping Species Common in Florida, the Endangered Species Act Supports Successful Conservation." *U.S. Fish and Wildlife Service Endangered Species Bulletin*. https://www.fws.gov/Endangered/news/episodes/bu-04-2013/story5/index.html. Accessed July 10, 2016.

Hendricks, Sarah A., Sesink Clee, Paul, R., Harrigan, Ryan J., Pollinger, John P., Freedman, Adam H., Callas, Richard, Figura, Peter, J., and Wayne, Robert K. 2016. "Re-Defining Historical Geographic Range in Species with Sparse Records: Implications for the Mexican Wolf Reintroduction Program." *Biological Conservation* 194: 48–57. http://www.sierraclub.org/sites/www.sierraclub.org/files/sce/rocky-mountain-chapter/Wolves-Resources/Re-defining%20historical%20geographic%20range%20in%20species%20with%20sparse%20records%20-%20Implications%20for%20the%20Mexican%20wolf%20reintroduction%20program%20-%202016.pdf. Accessed March 21, 2017.

Hiltzik, Michael. 2016, July 29. "California Cap-and-Trade Program Has Cut Pollution. So Why Do Critics Keep Calling It a Failure?" *Los Angeles Times*. http://www.latimes.com/business/hiltzik/la-fi-hiltzik-captrade-20160728-snap-story.html. Accessed August 30, 2016.

Hoegh-Guldberg, O., Mumby, P. J., Hooten, A. J., Steneck, R. S., Greenfield, P., Gomes, E., Harvell, C. D., Sale, P. F., Edwards, A. J., Calderia, K., Knowlton, N., Eakin, C. M., Inglesias-Prieto, R., Muthiga, N., Bradbury, H., Dubi, A., and Hatziolos, M. E. 2007. "Coral Reefs Under Rapid Climate Change and Ocean Acidification." *Science* 318: 1737–1742. http://208.180.30.233/lib/reefs_endangered.071214.pdf. Accessed September 7, 2016.

Holmer, Steve. 2016. "Endangered Species Act: A Record of Success." *American Bird Conservancy.* https://abcbirds.org/wp-content/uploads/2016/07/ESA-Report-2016-FINAL.pdf. Accessed August 26, 2016.

Idaho Fish and Game. 2016. "Wolf Management/Status Timeline." https://idfg.idaho.gov/sites/default/files/idaho-wolf-monitoring-progress-report-2015.pdf. Accessed August 25, 2016.

Innis, Michelle. 2016, April 9. "Climate-Related Death of Coral Around the World Alarms Scientists." *New York Times.* https://www.nytimes.com/2016/04/10/world/asia/climate-related-death-of-coral-around-world-alarms-scientists.html. Accessed March 20, 2017.

IPCC. 2014: Climate Change. 2014. "Synthesis Report. Summary for Policy Makers." https://www.ipcc.ch/pdf/assessment-report/ar5/syr/AR5_SYR_FINAL_SPM.pdf. Accessed March 20, 2017.

IUCN. 2014. "Bad News for Europe's Bumblebees." https://www.iucn.org/content/bad-news-europe's-bumblebees. Accessed September 5, 2016.

IUCN. 2016. "The IUCN Red List of Threatened Species. Version 2016–3." *International Union for Conservation of Nature.* http://www.iucnredlist.org/about/summary-statistics#How_many_threatened. Accessed September 14, 2016.

Jacques, Peter, J., Dunlap, Riley E., and Freeman, Mark. 2008. "The Organisation of Denial: Conservative Think Tanks and Environmental Skepticism." *Environmental Politics* 17: 349–385. http://www.tandfonline.com/doi/pdf/10.1080/09644010802055576?needAccess=true. Accessed March 20, 2017.

Jimenez, Mike. 2014. "Service Review of the 2014 Wolf Population in the NRM." *United States Fish and Wildlife*

Service. https://www.fws.gov/mountain-prairie/species/mammals/wolf/post-delisting-wolf-monitoring/2014_Review.pdf. Accessed August 23, 2014.

Johnson, Steven M. 2014. "Sue and Settle: Demonizing the Environmental Citizen Suit." *Seattle University Law Review* 37: 891–937. http://digitalcommons.law.seattleu.edu/cgi/viewcontent.cgi?article=2226&context=sulr. Accessed June 9, 2016.

Lane, Lee. 2014. "Toward a Conservative Policy on Climate Change." *The New Atlantis* 41: 19–37. http://www.thenewatlantis.com/publications/toward-a-conservative-policy-on-climate-change. Accessed February 25, 2017.

Langwig, Kate E., Frick, Wilfred F., Bried, Jason T., Hicks, Alan C., Kunz, Thomas, H., and Kilpatrick, A. Marm. 2012. "Sociality, Density-Dependence and Microclimates Determine the Persistence of Populations Suffering from a Novel Fungal Disease, White-Nose Syndrome." *Ecology Letters* 15: 1050–1057.

Lavelle, Marianne. 2015. "U.S. Sage Grouse Plan Draws Divided Reaction." *Science* 348: 1304–1305. http://www.sciencemag.org/news/2015/09/us-sage-grouse-plan-draws-divided-reaction. Accessed March 22, 2017.

Lazarus, Richard J. 2013. "Environmental Law at the Crossroads: Looking Back 25, Looking Forward 25." *Michigan Journal of Environmental and Administrative Law* 2: 267–284. http://repository.law.umich.edu/cgi/viewcontent.cgi?article=1012&context=mjeal. Accessed March 20, 2017.

Lee, Jane J. 2015. "Killer Fungus That's Devastating Bats May Have Met Its Match." *National Geographic.* http://news.nationalgeographic.com/2015/05/150527-bats-white-nose-syndrome-treatment-conservation-animals-science/. Accessed March 30, 2016.

Lee-Ashley, Matt, and Gentile, Nicole. 2015, October 19. "Confronting America's Wildlife Extinction Crisis." Center for American Progress. https://cdn.americanprogress.org/wp-content/uploads/2015/10/09142515/Wildlife Extinction-report.pdf. Accessed September 2016.

Le Page, Michael. 2017, September 6. "Hurricane Irma's Epic Size is Being Fuelled by Global Warming." *New Scientist.* https://www.newscientist.com/article/2146562-hurricane-irmas-epic-size-is-being-fuelled-by-global-warming/. Accessed September 13, 2017.

Li, Ya-Wei, and Male, Tim. 2013. "Protecting Unlisted Species." *Defenders of Wildlife ESA Policy White Paper Series.* http://www.defenders.org/sites/default/files/publications/esa-white-paper-on-candidate-conservation-agreements-with-assurances.pdf. Accessed August 25, 2016.

Liptak, Kevin. 2016, September 3. "Obama, China Ratify Climate Agreements." *CNN.* http://www.cnn.com/2016/09/02/politics/obama-asia-meetings-xi-erdogan-duterte/. Accessed September 5, 2016.

Mackinder, Evan. 2010. "Pro-Environmental Groups Outmatched, Outspent in Battle over Climate Change Legislation." *Center for Responsive Politics.* https://www.opensecrets.org/news/2010/08/pro-environment-groups-were-outmatc/. Accessed December 16, 2016.

Malcom, Jacob W., and Li, Ya-Wei. 2015. "Data Contradict Common Perceptions about a Controversial Provision of the US Endangered Species Act." *Proceedings of the National Academy of Science* 112: 15844–15849. http://www.pnas.org/content/112/52/15844.full.pdf. Accessed March 21, 2017.

Martin, Keith. 2013, August 9. "To Stop Elephant and Rhino Poachers, Dissuade Buyers in China and Vietnam." *Christian Science Monitor.* http://www.csmonitor.com/Commentary/Opinion/2013/0809/To-stop-elephant-and-rhino-poachers-dissuade-buyers-in-China-and-Vietnam. Accessed July 10, 2016.

Masters, Jeff. 2017, June 23. "Summary of the Great
Southwest U.S. Heat Wave of 2017." *Weather Underground.*
https://www.wunderground.com/cat6/summary-great-
southwest-us-heat-wave-2017. Accessed September 13,
2017.

Megerian, Chris. 2017, July 25. "Gov. Jerry Brown Signs
Law to Extend Cap and Trade, Securing the Future of
California's Key Climate Program." *Los Angeles Times.*
http://www.latimes.com/politics/la-pol-ca-jerry-brown-
climate-change-law-20170725-story.html. Accessed
September 16, 2017.

Milman, Oliver. 2015, December 12. "James Hansen,
Father of Climate Change Awareness, Calls Paris Talks
'a Fraud.'" *The Guardian.* https://www.theguardian.com/
environment/2015/dec/12/james-hansen-climate-change-
paris-talks-fraud. Accessed September 2016.

Missoulian. 2014, January 30. "Professional Hunter
Eliminated Two Wolf Packs in Frank Church Wilderness."
http://missoulian.com/news/local/professional-hunter-
eliminated-wolf-packs-in-frank-church-wilderness/article_
579c30a8-8901-11e3-9949-0019bb2963f4.html. Accessed
August 22, 2016.

Monahan, William B., and Fisichelli, Nicholas A. 2014,
July 2. "Climate Exposure of US National Parks in a
New Era of Change." *PLOS One.* http://journals.plos
.org/plosone/article?id=10.1371/journal.pone.0101302.
Accessed June 26, 2016.

Mooney, Chris. 2017, January 18. "U.S. Scientists
Officially Declare 2016 the Hottest Year on Record.
That Makes Three in a Row." *Washington Post.* https://
www.washingtonpost.com/news/energy-environment/
wp/2017/01/18/u-s-scientists-officially-declare-2016-the-
hottest-year-on-record-that-makes-three-in-a-row/?utm_
term=.a97855897d86. Accessed January 20, 2017.

National Academy of Sciences: The Royal Society. 2014.
"Climate Change: Evidence and Causes." *The National*

Academy Press. http://nap.edu/18730. Accessed June 29, 2016.

Neme, Laurel, A. 2009. *Animal Investigators: How the World's First Wildlife Forensics Lab Is Solving and Saving Endangered Species.* New York: Scribner.

O'Connell, John. 2014, November 25. "Idaho Wolf Depredation Down." *Capita; Press.* http://www.capitalpress .com/Idaho/20141125/idaho-wolf-depredation-down.

Oreskes, Naomi. 2015, October 9. "Exxon's Climate Concealment." *New York Times.* http://www.nytimes .com/2015/10/10/opinion/exxons-climate-concealment .htm. Accessed May 29, 2016.

Oreskes, Naomi, and Conway, Erik M. 2010. *Merchants of Doubt.* New York: Bloomsbury Press.

Organization for Economic Cooperation and Development. 2009. "The Economics of Climate Change Mitigation." *OECD.* http://www.oecd.org/env/cc/43707019.pdf. Accessed August 28, 2016.

Pacifici, Michela, Visconti, Piero, Butchart, Stuart H. M., Watson, James E. M., Cassola, Francesca M., and Rondinini, Carlo. 2017. "Species' Traits Influenced Their Response to Recent Climate Change." *Nature.* http://www .nature.com/articles/nclimate3223.epdf?referrer_access_ token=NKWePuBmopeKY0c4p3jrs9RgN0jAjWel9jn R3ZoTv0N57SPFJrLHECuOvjklRFCCVq20TIW8 wmy1QKOnHv6BtRODHwgD70F9DkeaO7oYnKg klNDcP9YaGJACszWnAZzCChxX5tE08Z6KEm245 AqGWvlnqYsh2knPj2ylguw8Hc6PFa5dequa9XTMp DT4HaLRA201a55kZwTrkGgSJemGcWtRrF9vZM WllMjnjx1APcU0_WfbbQU75Js0hlNaj91aRRRp3Hj4 OcqvmjFmVPa3-MGb9NSNR0fnG1kjOOyZIxnV39 hiv6UENUfhT7m3dXLwDGl3RmCykS4VQYNUKV gq0w%3D%3D&tracking_referrer=www.theguardian .com. Accessed September 16, 2017.

Parenteau, Robert A. 2011. "Who's Taking What? Property Rights, Endangered Species, and the Constitution." *Fordham Environmental Law Review* 6: 619–636. http://ir.lawnet.fordham.edu/cgi/viewcontent.cgi?article=1394&context=elr. Accessed March 21, 2017.

Pauli, William. 1999, October 19. "Statement of the American Farm Bureau Federation to the Committee on Environment and Public Works Habitat Conservation Planning and the Endangered Species Act." http://www.epw.senate.gov/107th/pau_1019.htm. Accessed March 21, 2017.

Platt, John. 2011, July 21. "Whitebark Pine Turned Down for Endangered Species List." *Scientific American.* https://blogs.scientificamerican.com/extinction-countdown/whitebark-pine-turned-down-for-endangered-species-list/. Accessed September 11, 2016.

Platt, John. 2016, September 16. "Climate-Threatened American Pika Denied Protection—Again." *Scientific American.* https://blogs.scientificamerican.com/extinction-countdown/climate-pika-denied/. Accessed March 17, 2017.

Ribe, Tom. 2015, February 12. "An Experiment in Privatizing Public Land Fails after 14 Years." *High Country News.* http://www.hcn.org/articles/an-experiment-in-privatizing-public-land-fails-after-14-years. Accessed August 14, 2016.

Ripple, William J., and Beschta, Robert L. 2012. "Trophic Cascades in Yellowstone: The First 15 Years after Wolf Reintroduction." *Biological Conservation* 145: 205–213. http://www.cof.orst.edu/leopold/papers/RippleBeschta Yellowstone_BioConserv.pdf. Accessed September 13, 2016.

Robbins, Jim. 2017, May 1. "The New Threat to Wolves in and Around Yellowstone." *New York Times.* https://www.nytimes.com/2017/05/01/science/wolves-hunting-yellowstone-national-park.html?mcubz=0&_r=0. Accessed September 20, 2017.

Rodriguez, Juan Carlos. 2015. "Industry Win on Bat Listing Shows Glimpse of FWS' Future." *Law 360*. http://www .law360.com/articles/638222/industry-win-on-bat-listing-shows-glimpse-of-fws-future. Accessed August 13, 2016.

Russo, Christina. 2014. "Can Elephants Survive a Legal Ivory Trade? Debate Is Shifting against It." *National Geographic*. http://news.nationalgeographic.com/news/2014/08/ 140829-elephants-trophy-hunting-poaching-ivory-ban-cities/. Accessed July 8, 2016.

Sage Grouse Initiative. 2015. "Grazing and Sagebrush Treatments: A 25-Year Case Study in Utah." *Science to Solutions Series Number 10. Sage Grouse Initiative*, p. 4.

Salvo, Mark. 2014. "In the Red: How Proposed Conservation Plans Fail to Protect Greater Sage-Grouse." *Defenders of Wildlife Report*. https://www.defenders.org/sites/default/ files/publications/in-the-red-how-proposed-conservation-plans-fail-to-protect-greater-sage-grouse.pdf. Accessed March 22, 2017.

Sanger, David E. 2001, June 12. "Bush Will Continue to Oppose Kyoto Pact on Global Warming." *New York Times*. http://www.nytimes.com/2001/06/12/world/bush-will-continue-to-oppose-kyoto-pact-on-global-warming .html?pagewanted=all. Accessed August 29, 2016.

Scheffers, Brett R., Meester, Luc De, Bridge, Tom C. L., Hoffman, Ary A., Pandolfi, John M., Corlett, Richard, T., Butchart, Stuart H. M., Pearce-Kelly, Paul, Kovacs, Kit M., Dudgeon, David, Pacifici, Michela, Rondinini, Carlo, Foden, Wendy B., Martin, Tara G., Mora, Camilo, Bickford, David, and Watson, James E. M. 2016. "The Broad Footprint of Climate Change from Genes to Biomes to People." *Science* 543: 719–730. http://science .sciencemag.org/content/354/6313/aaf7671. Accessed September 16, 2017.

Schwartz, John. 2016. "Exxon Mobil Accuses the Rockefellers of a Climate Conspiracy." *New York Times*. https://www.nytimes.com/2016/11/21/science/exxon-mobil-rockefellers-climate-change.html. Accessed February 1, 2017.

Seasholes, Brian. 2007, September 1. "Bad for Species, Bad for People: What's Wrong with the Endangered Species Act and How to Fix It." *National Center for Policy Analysis, Policy Report* 303. http://www.ncpa.org/pdfs/st303.pdf. Accessed July 30, 2016.

Seasholes, Brian. 2015, July 9. "The Importance of Property Rights for Endangered Species Conservation." *Reason Foundation*. Testimony U.S. House of Representatives Judiciary Committee Subcommittee on the Constitution and Civil Justice, 1–15. http://reason.org/files/brian_seasholes_testimony_endangered_species_act.pdf. Accessed March 21, 2017.

Shapiro, Isaac, and Irons, John. 2011, April 12. "Regulation, Employment, and the Economy: Fears of Job Loss Are Overblown." *EPI Briefing Paper #305*. http://www.epi.org/files/2011/BriefingPaper305.pdf. Accessed August 27, 2016.

Shire, Gavin. 2015, August 13. "State Endangered Species Conservation Efforts Receive $37.2 Million to Boost through Service Grants." *U.S. Fish and Wildlife Service*. https://www.fws.gov/mountain-prairie/pressrel/2015/08132015_StateEndangeredSpeciesEffortsReceiveGrants.php. Accessed July 31, 2016.

Simmons, Randy T. April 2002. "Property Rights and the Endangered Species Act." *Institute for Research on the Economics of Taxation*, Washington, DC. http://iret.org/pub/SCRE-9.PDF. Accessed July 29, 2016.

Slagle, Kristina, Bruskotter, Jeremy T., Singh, Ajay S., and Schmidt, Robert H. 2017. "Attitudes toward Predator

Control in the United States: 1995 and 2014." *Journal of Mammalogy* 98: 7–16. https://academic.oup.com/jmammal/article/98/1/7/2977228/Attitudes-toward-predator-control-in-the-Unite. Accessed February 28, 2017.

Slezak, Michael. 2016, June 6. "The Great Barrier Reef: A Catastrophe Laid Bare." *The Guardian.* https://www.theguardian.com/environment/2016/jun/07/the-great-barrier-reef-a-catastrophe-laid-bare. Accessed September 5, 2016.

Stanford, Kristin. 2013. "A Slithering Success Story." *U.S. Fish and Wildlife Service Endangered Species.* https://www.fws.gov/Endangered/news/episodes/bu-04–2013/story1/index.html. Accessed August 26, 2016.

Staudt, Amanda, Inkley, Doug, Rubenstein, Aliya, Walton, Eli, and Williams, Jack. 2013. "Swimming Upstream: Freshwater Fish in a Warming World." *National Wildlife Federation.* https://www.nwf.org/~/media/PDFs/Global-Warming/Reports/NWF-Swimming%20Upstream-082813-B.ashx. Accessed September 12, 2016.

Stern, Paul C., Perkins, John H., Sparks, Richard E., and Knox, Robert A. 2016. "The Challenge of Climate-Change Neoskepticism." *Science* 353: 653–654.

Stone, Suzanne A., Breck, Stewart W., Timberlake, Jesse, Haswell, Peter M., Najera, Fernando, Bean, Brian S., and Thornhill, Daniel J. 2017. "Adaptive Use of Nonlethal Strategies for Minimizing Wolf-Sheep Conflict in Idaho." *Journal of Mammalogy* 98: 33–44. https://academic.oup.com/jmammal/article/98/1/33/2977254/Adaptive-use-of-nonlethal-strategies-for#58920908. Accessed February 28, 2017.

Streater, Scott. 2017, February 17. "Will Trump Revamp Complex Plan to Save Endangered Sage Grouse?." *Science.*

http://www.sciencemag.org/news/2017/02/will-trump-revamp-complex-plan-save-endangered-sage-grouse. Accessed September 24, 2017.

Suckling, Kieran, Greenwald, Noah, and Curry, Tierra. 2012. "On Time, on Target: How the Endangered Species Act Is Saving America's Wildlife." *Center for Biological Diversity.* http://www.esasuccess.org/pdfs/110_REPORT.pdf. Accessed March 21, 2016.

Taylor, Martin F. J., Suckling, Kieran F., and Rachlinski, Jeffrey J. 2005. "The Effectiveness of the Endangered Species Act: A Quantitative Analysis." *BioScience* 55: 360–367. http://scholarship.law.cornell.edu/cgi/viewcontent.cgi?article=1730&context=facpub. Accessed March 21, 2017.

Taylor, Phil. 2016, April 20. "Leaked BLM Sage Grouse Draft Memo Sparks Fear." *E & E News.* http://www.eenews.net/stories/1060035957. Accessed May 3, 2016.

Treves, Adrian, Krofel, Miha, and McMannus, Jeannine. 2016. "Predator Control Should Not Be a Shot in the Dark." *Frontiers in Ecology and Environment* 14: 380–388. http://www.esa.org/esablog/research/predator-control-should-not-be-a-shot-in-the-dark/. Accessed September 22, 2016.

Union of Concerned Scientists (UCS). 2011. "Is Global Warming Linked to Severe Weather?" http://www.ucsusa.org/global_warming/science_and_impacts/impacts/global-warming-rain-snow-tornadoes.html#.Wb1C7neZNBw. Accessed September 16, 2017.

Union of Concerned Scientists (UCS). 2015. "Progress and Problems: Government Scientists Report on Scientific Integrity at Four Agencies." *Center for Science and Democracy.* Cambridge, MA. http://www.ucsusa.org/sites/default/files/attach/2015/09/ucs-progress-and-problems-2015.pdf. Accessed October 5, 2016.

Urban, Mark C. 2015. "Accelerating Extinction Risk from Climate Change." *Science* 348: 571–573. http://science .sciencemag.org/content/348/6234/571.short. Accessed August 27, 2016.

USDA. 2016. "2014 Farm Bill Fact Sheet." *USDA Farm Service Agency.* https://www.fsa.usda.gov/Internet/FSA_ File/2014_farm_bill_customers.pdf. Accessed September 22, 2016.

USGS. 2016. "White-Nose Syndrome (WNS)." *National Wildlife Health Center.* http://www.nwhc.usgs.gov/disease_ information/white-nose_syndrome/. Accessed September 5, 2016.

Van Gils, Jan A., Lisovski, Simeon, Lok, Tamar, Meissner, Wiodzimierz, Ozarowska, Agnieszka, de Fouw, Jimmy, Rakhimberdiev, Eldar, Soloviev, Mikhall Y., Piersma, Theunis, and Klaassen, Marcel. 2016. "Body Shrinkage Due to Arctic Warming Reduces Red Knot Fitness in Tropical Wintering Range." *Science* 352: 819–821.

Verheggen, Bart, Strengers, Bart, Cook, John, van Dorland, Rob, Vringer, Kees, Peters, Jeroen, Visser, Hans, and Meuer, Leo. 2014. "Scientists' Views about Attribution of Global Warming." *Environmental Science & Technology* 48: 8963–8971.

Vignieri, Sacha. 2014. "Vanishing Fauna." *Science* 345: 392–395.

Vincent, Carol Hardy, Hanson, Laura A., and Argueta, Carla N. 2017. "Federal Land Ownership: Overview and Data." *Congressional Research Service.* https://www.fas.org/ sgp/crs/misc/R42346.pdf. Accessed March 21, 2017.

Vucetich, John A. 2016, September 19. "Selected Topics Pertaining to the Conservation and Recovery of Wolves in the United States." *Oversight Hearing: The Status of the Federal Government's Management of Wolves.* http:// naturalresources.house.gov/uploadedfiles/testimony_ vucetich.pdf. Accessed January 27, 2017.

Wake, David B., and Vredenburg, Vance T. 2008. "Are We in the Midst of the Sixth Mass Extinction? A View from the World of Amphibians." *Proceedings of the National Academy of Sciences* USA 105: 11466–11473. http://www.pnas .org/content/105/Supplement_1/11466.full. Accessed March 20, 2017.

Waldman, Scott. 2017, July 20. "Surprising Scientists, 2017, Could Be Among Hottest on Record." *Scientific American.* https://www.scientificamerican.com/article/surprising- scientists-2017-could-be-among-hottest-on-record/. Accessed September 13, 2017.

Wang, Amy B. 2016, October 3. "Bees Were Just Added to the Endangered-Species List for the First Time." *Washington Post.* https://www.washingtonpost.com/news/ speaking-of-science/wp/2016/10/03/u-s-bees-were-just- added-to-the-endangered-species-list-for-the-first-time/. Accessed October 7, 2016.

Watts, Nick et al. 2017. "The Lancet Countdown: Track Progresso in Health and Climate Change." *The Lancet* 389: 1151–1164. http://www.thelancet.com/journals/lancet/ article/PIIS0140-6736(16)32124-9/fulltext. Accessed March 20, 2017.

Western Energy Alliance. 2015, September 22. "Western Energy Alliance Applauds Secretary Jewell's Sage Grouse Not-Warranted Decision." https://www .westernenergyalliance.org/press-room/western-energy- alliance-applauds-secretary-jewell's-sage-grouse-not- warranted-decision. Accessed September 13, 2016.

Western Energy Alliance. 2016. "Environmental Groups Keep Suing Despite Vast ESA Settlement." https://www .westernenergyalliance.org/knowledge-center/legal/sue-and- settle. Accessed September 7, 2016.

Wielgus, Robert B, and Peebles, Kaylie A. 2014, December 3. "Effects of Wolf Mortality on Livestock Depredations."

PLOS One. http://dx.doi.org/10.1371/journal.pone.011
3505. Accessed March 22, 2017.

Wilson, Edward O. 1992. *The Diversity of Life*. New York:
W.W. Norton.

Winter, Michael. 2014, September 23. "Judge Restores
Protections to Wolves in Wyoming." *USA Today*. http://
www.usatoday.com/story/news/nation/2014/09/23/judge-
restores-wolf-protections-wyoming/16120133/. Accessed
August 25, 2016.

Wittemyer, George, Northrup, Joseph M., Blanc, Julian,
Douglas-Hamilton, Iain, Omondi, Patrick, and Burnham,
Kenneth P. 2014. "Illegal Killing for Ivory Drives Global
Decline in African Elephants." *Proceedings National
Academy of Science* 111: 13117–13121. http://www.pnas
.org/content/111/36/13117.full.pdf. Accessed March 20,
2017.

Yardley, William. 2015, October 28. "Control of Federal
Lands Emerges as an Issue in the GOP Presidential Race."
Los Angeles Times. http://www.latimes.com/nation/la-na-
sej-public-lands-debate-20151028-story.html. Accessed
June 20, 2016.

Introduction

Issues concerning biodiversity and endangered species are complex and take many forms ranging from climate change to ecotourism. Persons concerned about these issues have written essays for this chapter. Camille Parmesan, a scientist and member of the Intergovernmental Panel on Climate Change (IPCC), provides a hopeful message about the response of an endangered butterfly to climate change. Tom Lovejoy, a conservation ecologist who has conducted studies in the Amazon for decades, wrote of his experiences and concern about biodiversity in the Amazon. Suzanne Stone was present when the first wolves were released into the Idaho wilderness. She writes of this profound experience and her research on nonlethal means of deterring wolves from livestock. Brock Evans has been an environmental activist for decades. Despite setbacks, Brock has never lost his enthusiasm for saving ancient forests and endangered species. Mark Rockwell loves to fish. In retirement he became actively involved in saving the wild salmon and is a proponent of dam removal on the lower Snake River. Dave Stalling, a hunter, values the biological importance of wild predators. Michael Lehnert, a retired major general in the Marines, tells of how he became involved with endangered species

During California's drought there was insufficient water for young salmon (smolts) to swim to the ocean. They were loaded into floating nets and transported by tanker truck and barge from the Coleman National Fish Hatchery to the San Pablo Bay. (AP Photo/Rich Pedroncelli)

while in the military. His philosophy is "a country worth de-fending is a country worth preserving." Douglas Trent is an example of how an ecotourism business can make a significant contribution to conservation. Sarah Cohen is a marine biolo-gist who, while conducting scientific research, has witnessed the decline of sea stars and other marine organisms off the Pa-cific coast.

Conservation in a Time of Rapid Climate Change
Camille Parmesan

Human-driven climate change is fundamentally different from all of the other ways in which humans are stressing spe-cies and driving many of them toward endangerment and even extinction. Why? Given that Earth has gone through many periods of massive climatic shifts, why should we worry now? First, climate change is fundamentally different from, say, habitat destruction, in that greenhouse gases don't stay local. The rise of greenhouse gases creates a truly global problem that only global action can tackle. Second, massive historical climate shifts on geological time scales have cer-tainly occurred, but they have also caused mass extinction of life. The difference this time is that humans are driving the current climatic shift and bear the brunt of responsibility for what happens, not only to wild life but also to humans them-selves, since effects on human diseases are already apparent (Parmesan and Attrill 2016).

Why can't species evolve (genetically adapt) to climate change? They can, but in a limited way. Species with short generation times, like insects, are even evolving in response to local climate shifts. Unfortunately, these changes are small and unlikely to protect species from extinction. Existing "hot-adapted" genetic forms are becoming more common in popu-lations of many species, but truly new forms are not emerging. We are not seeing new genes that would allow species to exist in climates outside their previous ranges of tolerance. In other words, species can play around with the genetic variation they already have, but evolving to withstand even more extreme climates is a process that is likely too slow to keep pace with rapid, human-driven climate change (Parmesan 2006).

If we go back >4 million years, to a time when Earth was much warmer than today, we see that many species went extinct in the transition from this "hot" Earth to the more recent "cool" Earth. Species that live now are generally adapted to the current, relatively cool, Earth. Human-driven global warming is taking us into a future Earth that is warmer than it has been for millions of years—to an Earth that will lie outside the evolutionary experience of modern plants and animals. It would be no surprise if many wild species were to go extinct.

Does this mean we give up on endangered species? Are modern conservation efforts doomed to failure under the long-term, inexorably increasing pressure from rising global temperatures? The answer is emphatically "no!"

First, we *can* still limit future climate change (though it gets harder every year that no action is taken). Second, many traditional conservation measures will help reduce climate stress on endangered species. These include making it easier for individuals to travel between different natural and protected areas and reducing pressures from invasive species. New, more controversial measures, such as helping species move to new regions as climate space shifts across the land and oceans, are already being implemented. Hope comes, ironically, from the very species that was an early warning indicator of the impact of recent climate change—Edith's checkerspot butterfly (Parmesan 1996).

The Quino checkerspot (*Euphydryas editha quino*) is a federally listed endangered subspecies of Edith's checkerspot that lives in southwestern California and northern Baja, Mexico. Quino's case highlights both the immediate threats from climate change and a surprising resilience. Quino checkerspot populations along the southernmost range (in Mexico) face the lowest degree of threat from development, but many have already gone extinct, associated with continuing warming and drying trends. By contrast, Quino habitat that might have been available farther north has been destroyed by development in the Los Angeles-San Diego corridor. The fate of Quino seemed sealed and extinction seemed inevitable.

To the delight of many, this little butterfly surprised even the experts by managing to colonize upward, into the mountains east of San Diego, in spite of a seeming lack of host plant for the caterpillars to feed on. It did so by shifting to a novel host plant—a species of Chinese houses (*Collinsia*) that it had never used before (Parmesan et al. 2015). Edith's checkerspot may have other means of adapting to climate change. A female can alter the temperatures at which her eggs develop by as much as 32 F according to the height at which she lays her egg clutch on the host plant. Such variation in egg placement can make her eggs either cooler or hotter than the surrounding air temperature. Existing genetic variation among populations in the height of egg clutches suggests that natural selection caused by climate change could cause this trait to evolve, and thereby mitigate the temperature changes that eggs experience (Bennett et al. 2015).

The case of Quino checkerspot is thought-provoking. Climate change has not been an important cause of its decline up to the present. Although its biology clearly marks it as climate-vulnerable, it has shown an unexpected behavioral flexibility that has allowed it to track a shifting climate space up into the mountains (Parmesan et al. 2015). But the highest populations are already close to the tops of the mountains—and so, like the pika and the polar bear, Quino may soon have "nowhere to go."

The positive message is that Quino's flexibility has given conservation biologists time to develop new approaches. Quino is currently surviving best in habitats where no populations had been recorded prior to 1980. The U.S. Fish and Wildlife Service took a series of novel, proactive steps to designate several

areas at high elevation as "critical habitat" for the Quino butterfly, even though outside the known historical range. While
this action won't prevent extinction in the long term, it does
help Quino in the short term and gives us time to develop new
options as climate continues to shift (Parmesan et al. 2015).

Helping endangered species buy time, as the FWS did
for the Quino butterfly, is crucial to minimizing species' extinctions. While the international community continues to
work toward effective reductions of greenhouse gas emissions,
the pace of policy action is slower than the pace of climate
change, and time itself becomes a precious commodity for
wild species.

References

Bennett, Nichole L., Severns, Paul M., Parmesan, Camille,
and Singer, Michael C. 2015. "Geographic Mosaics of
Phenology, Host Preference, Adult Size and Microhabitat
Choice Predict Butterfly Resilience to Climate Warming."
Oikos 124(1): 41–53.

Parmesan, Camille. 1996. "Climate and Species Range." *Nature*
382: 765–766.

Parmesan, Camille. 2006. "Ecological and Evolutionary
Responses to Recent Climate Change." *Annual Reviews of
Ecology, Evolution and Systematics* 37: 637–669.

Parmesan, Camille, and Attrill, Martin. 2016. "Impacts and
Effects of Ocean Warming on Human Health (Disease)."
In *Explaining Ocean Warming: Causes, Scale, Effects and
Consequences*, edited by D. Laffoley and J. M Baxter,
439–450. IUCN Full Report, Gland, Switzerland.

Parmesan, Camille, Williams-Anderson, Alison, Mikheyev,
Alexander S., Moskwik, Matthew, and Singer, Michael C.
2015. "Climate Change Success Story? The Endangered
Quino Checkerspot Butterfly." *Journal of Insect Conservation*
19(2): 185–204. doi: 10.1111/oik.01490.

Camille Parmesan studies the impacts of global warming on wild plants and animals and helps to develop approaches to conserving biodiversity in the face of rapid climate change. She has won numerous awards from scientific societies and conservation organizations. She is a professor at Plymouth University (United Kingdom) and at the University of Texas at Austin.

Endangered Amazon
Tom Lovejoy

Nobody knows how many species occur in the Amazon but it is the largest terrestrial repository of biodiversity on Earth. It is also vast in extent: despite the optical illusion of the Mercator projection, which makes everything farther from the equator look bigger than it is, the Amazon is equivalent in area to the contiguous 48 U.S. states.

When I first set foot in the Amazon in 1965, it had but a single highway which connected Brasilia, the then quite recent capital of Brazil, to Belem, the Amazon's main port. It was the largest tropical forest wilderness in the world shared by eight countries and French Guiana with only three million people: nothing short of a biologist's wildest dream.

In the geological past the Amazon flowed into the Pacific in the vicinity of Guayaquil, Ecuador, but when the rise of the Andes blocked that route, the Amazon River system began to develop into what it is today. The Amazon contains 20 percent of all the river water in the world in a vast basin draining to the east but also draining from ancient geological highlands ("shields") to the north and the south. It contains more species of fish (around 3,000) than any river in the world.

Until the mid-1970s, the uncontested view anywhere in the world was that vegetation was simply the consequence of climate and had no influence on the climate whatsoever. Elegant studies by Brazilian scientist Eneas Salati shattered that dogma forever. He examined isotope ratios of oxygen in rainwater from the Atlantic west to the Peruvian border and demonstrated unequivocally that half of the rainfall was generated within the basin itself.

Moisture from the tropical Atlantic enters the Amazon in a westward moving air mass, drops as rain that is in large part returned to the westward moving air through evaporation off the complex surfaces of the forest or via transpiration through the leaves. This then becomes rain farther to the west in a process that repeats itself five or six times as the air crosses the basin until it hits the high wall of the Andes. It then dumps the moisture as the air rises and thus creates the mighty Amazon River system.

Over tens of millions of years this hydrological cycle has nurtured the great forest and the development of its biodiversity, well over a thousand species of birds, and a diversity of monkeys and other mammals, reptiles, and amphibians including the colorful arrow poison frogs, countless insects, and a profusion of trees and other plants species.

Indigenous people have flourished in these forests discovering valuable things like cacao, rubber, quinine, curare and more. Building on this indigenous knowledge, modern science can open the doors to much more, using the forest biodiversity as essentially a gigantic library for the life sciences. For example, transformational studies of the venom of the Bushmaster (a tropical viper) led to ACE inhibitors that benefit hundreds of millions annually by controlling hypertension. Modern medicine has taken the fish poison curare and uses it as a muscle relaxant for major abdominal surgery.

In the ensuing years since I arrived in the Amazon, development has had a major impact. Countless roads have been built with spontaneous colonization following. Deforestation has occurred at a great scale driven mostly by short-term gains from timber, cattle, and more recently soy and palm oil. Illegal alluvial gold mining wreaks havoc with river systems and adjacent forest. Deforestation hovers around 20 percent in the Brazilian Amazon, is already substantial in the Bolivian Amazon, and is growing in almost all of the other Amazon countries.

The Amazon is close to a tipping point at which the hydrological cycle will begin to degrade and fail to generate sufficient rainfall to maintain a tropical rain forest. Nobody knows precisely where the tipping point is but various things including record-breaking droughts suggest it is close at hand. I believe it is around 20 percent. Nobody—if they stop to truly consider it—sees any point in discovering where the tipping point is by actually tipping it.

So we have arrived at a point where it is clear the Amazon must be managed as the system that it is, and that cannot be achieved one battle at a time. What is needed is both integrated planning and management. While that may seem a huge challenge for a region that has always been second priority (like a backyard) to the countries of the Amazon, the benefits for doing so are great.

Many years ago, Brazil initiated the Amazon Cooperation Treaty (ACTO) in recognition of the need for coordinated action. While it has largely suffered from inattention, it has considerable potential. While it is time to begin looking at ways the treaty could help advance system management, there are less cosmic approaches that could begin to create building blocks toward that larger integrated goal.

The Amazon River system and its fisheries would be a good starting point. Elements should include an Amazon fishery treaty in which all Amazon nations have an important stake. It would also be essential to refine Amazon energy plans so they integrate with rather than impede nutrient and water flows and fish migrations.

That action could be an important step toward integrated management and safeguarding and managing the Amazon as a system. It is a great help that 50 percent of the Amazon today is under some form of protection: roughly half of that includes demarcated indigenous areas and the remainder consists of various forms of protected areas. There is interesting and promising thinking around sustainable infrastructure, "transportation without deforestation," sustainable cities and the like.

The amount of change in the Amazon in the past half century dwarfs all previously wrought by people. Fortunately, modern technology and knowledge make a salutary outcome possible—a great tropical forest region teeming with life forms known and yet to be discovered: an Amazon no longer endangered?

Tom Lovejoy, tropical and conservation biologist, has worked in the Amazon since 1965 where he conducted the first major long-term study of birds and brought international attention to the world's rainforests. He directed the World Wildlife Fund-US (1973–1987) and has been associated with Smithsonian Institute since 1987 and was recently elected IUCN-US president. He founded the popular TV series Nature *and is a professor of environmental science and policy at George Mason University and a senior fellow at the United Nations Foundation.*

The Wolves Return
Suzanne Asha Stone

It was a bitterly cold winter morning in January 1995 when the convoy departed down the Forest Service road near Salmon, Idaho. The wolves arrived the night before inside a commercial moving van and spent the night under armed federal guard in an airplane hangar on the outskirts of town. Local threats of violence had everyone on edge. The building was well positioned behind a chain-linked fence with barbed wire on top. Vehicles approaching the facility were monitored, but we didn't hang around outside in the open. We were quiet, listening for any unusual sound. Silent, motionless, the wolves cringed back if a human approached too closely. All except one. He was a large male wolf with almond shaped, green-gold eyes and thick golden and gray fur. "Chat Chaaht"[1] was painted on the radio collar around his neck. The name means "older brother" in the Nez Perce language and was chosen by the Nez Perce tribal school students. Instead of cringing at my presence, he stepped forward cautiously and returned my curious glance with a penetrating gaze of his own. I don't know what I expected, but I was instantly awestruck by the intensity of his gaze. His eyes were bright and knowing. It felt like he was looking through and beyond me. I was humbled by how much spirit and raw intelligence I saw in those eyes. I spoke to him softly, trying to reassure him—and myself—that he was going to be free soon. The other three wolves listened and watched intently but didn't stir. Sleep didn't come easy for any of us that night.

We heard the bad news early that morning. A federal judge in Wyoming had approved the administrative stay request of the American Farm Bureau, which meant the wolves could not be moved from their kennels or from the facility. Tensions were growing in town as more signs appeared in local businesses. One sign read, "Kill all the Goddam [sic] wolves and the people that brought them here." Another less angry one read, "Get your Long hair, Subaru Driving, Sandal Wearing, Wolf Hugging A*s out of here." I wondered who would wear sandals in such a cold place. On the TV, I saw a video of the truck and trailer carrying the Yellowstone-bound wolves as they entered the north gate and were greeted by cheering crowds. At least those wolves made it safely to their destination.

The next morning the judge lifted his order and we wasted no time organizing a caravan of heavy-duty trucks to carry the wolves into the backcountry to the Frank Church–River of

---

[1]Chat Chaaht, a wolf that defied death many times, became the oldest known wolf recorded in Idaho and father to many generations of pups. He died a natural death at age 14, still the alpha male of the Wildhorse Pack.

No Return Wilderness, the largest forested wilderness area in the continental United States.

The first wolf—her radio collar vividly decorated with the name "Moonstar Shadow" by the students in Idaho's Blaine County—was soon bounding her way through the snow. The next wolf, Chat Chaaht, ran about 15 yards before stopping to make his mark on his new world. Then I heard my name called out by the lead biologists on the team. "Suzanne, this one is yours," he said. Her name was spelled out in a colorful design on her radio collar: Akiata. She was a young, black wolf with green eyes and was very reluctant to leave the safety of her travel kennel. After a few fleeting moments, she bolted and gracefully sprinted through the snow without once looking back.

After the release, we finally had a moment for reflection. Wolves were back in Idaho after being absent for decades. The forests would soon echo with their ancient, soulful song. It was a very profound and emotional moment. We cried, hugged each other, and opened champagne giving toasts to the wolves. And it was just the beginning.

The wolves thrived until their endangered species status was removed in 2008. Complaints of predation on livestock led to knee-jerk decisions to kill wolves that threatened livestock operations even in remote public national forests and wilderness areas. The federal wolf managers based in Helena, Montana, claimed that it was cheaper to kill wolves than to protect livestock. Soon it became apparent that it was anything but cheap to kill wolves. The federal government, through its USDA Wildlife Services (formerly Animal Damage Control), spent hundreds of thousands of dollars using helicopters, airplanes, and high-tech equipment to kill wolves and other carnivores every year, and still the livestock losses mounted up. It became an endless cycle of conflict and loss of wolves and livestock.

Then, in 2007, a newly formed wolf pack, the Phantom Hill pack, began killing sheep along central Idaho's "sheep superhighway" in the Wood River watershed of the Sawtooth

National Forest during the summer grazing season. Normally, members of the pack or the entire depredating family of wolves would be killed in response. However, something extraordinary happened instead. A sheep ranch manager and a wolf advocate decided to work together to try nonlethal deterrents to protect the sheep from wolves and to help other ranchers in the area do the same. County commissioners and federal agencies supported the idea, and the collaborative effort was named the Wood River Wolf Project.

During the first seven years of the Wood River Wolf Project, trained field technicians strategically applied nonlethal predator deterrents and animal husbandry practices by adjusting for habitat conditions, locations of known wolf packs, and the frequency or type of nonlethal methods used. These nonlethal methods included increasing human presence, the number of livestock dogs, and monitoring the movements of radio-collared wolves. Other techniques were designed to frighten the wolves: fladry and turbo-fladry (lines of rope with strips of colored fabric), spotlighting, air-horns, blank handguns, flashing lights, and radio-activated guard boxes. Over the course of this pilot study, biologists collected data on sheep depredations by wolves in an area where sheep were protected using only nonlethal measures and compared them to data from an adjacent unprotected area where sheep grazed without the added nonlethal protection. Of the 10,000 to 22,000 sheep that grazed across nearly 1,000 square miles of the protected, study area only 30 sheep were killed over the first seven years of the project. Results showed sheep depredation losses to wolves were 3.5 times higher in the adjacent nonprotected area than in the area using nonlethal control methods. While packs of wolves were killed in adjacent areas, no wolves were killed in the protected demonstration area over the course of the project.

The Wood River Wolf Project became the first peer-reviewed study of its kind to demonstrate the effectiveness of nonlethal deterrents to protect both livestock and wolves across a large rugged forested landscape (Stone et al. 2017).

Reference

Stone, Suzanne A., Breck, Stewart W., Timberlake, Jesse, Haswell, Peter M., Najera, Fernando, Bean, Brian S., and Thornhill, Daniel J. 2017. "Adaptive Use of Nonlethal Strategies for Minimizing Wolf–Sheep Conflict in Idaho." *Journal of Mammalogy* 98(1): 33–44. doi: 10.1093/jmammal/gyw188.

Suzanne Asha Stone is Wood River Wolf Project cofounder and Defenders of Wildlife regional field representative in Idaho.

Saving the Ancient Forests
Brock Evans

There is a long and passionate history of attempts to protect the splendid and iconic ancient forests of the northwest.

The first try was to save the magnificent redwoods in California in 1916.

Then came Olympic National Park in Washington, 1938.

By then, a drastic policy change had begun inside the U.S. Forest Service, regarding its own vast holdings of ancient forests. They were to be liquidated and logging accelerated.

We—who loved the ancient forests and wished to save them from the chainsaw—went to "war": one wherein we would petition Congress directly, give these places a name, draw boundaries on a map, and thus, protect the forest, place by place.

Despite heavy and sustained opposition from economic interests, much new protective legislation was enacted in 1960 to 1980. It was a time of fiery hearings and debates, lobbying, and public education. The still-standing ancient forests of the Salmo valleys in Washington; Minam valleys in Oregon; Redwoods National Park in California, and the new parks in Alaska are there today thanks to all those who came before and saved these places!

After the last victory in 1984, three more wilderness laws protecting yet more ancient forest—the "political warfare" came to an end. Why? Because the politicians told us so: "Look, we're weary of these constant wilderness battles . . . and all the controversies . . . we can't do much of it anymore."

And there was still much more to do. We had saved much, but the chainsaws still snarled among the ancient giants. There emerged a whole new *wave of scientific research and deeper understandings* of these battered forest ecosystems: as biological havens for endangered species, reservoirs of priceless genetic material, and the cleanest, best salmon habitat anywhere.

So we determined a new kind of campaign to save what was left while we still had time.

But how?

We convened a special conference in Portland, Oregon, in September 1988.

This was no ordinary gathering; we could term it a "council of war" because the whole subject had to be: how can we carry out a major campaign to better protect the remaining northwest forests while some were left?

It was an intense three days. The only people invited to debate for that final push were the doers, the warriors, and the veterans.

Our first decision was to *unite*: to join all together and become *one* "forest alliance."

The second task was to adopt a better name, which would also be our "message" to the public.

The word "ancient" popped into my head and I blurted it out. Colleagues' reaction was instantaneous—"that's it!" Thus, at that moment we became the *Ancient* Forest Alliance—a most accurate and powerful descriptive word, which has stood the test of time for 30 years.

The third decision was the most critical: what remedies would we seek to halt the logging, and who would be our champions?

The first part was easy: it had to be a *whole new statute*, protecting everything defined as ancient forest.

"Champions" was much harder. Always before we had relied on northwest politicians, our standard procedure. But many felt it was time to change: to "go national"—to the whole Congress itself.

Here, the debate was most intense. One side argued that past strategies, while successful, were riddled with compromises, losses as well as gains. That's because powerful northwest politicians strongly favored more logging, not less.

This "side" said, "We must make our case at the national level, take it to the whole American people. . . . Make it a national campaign, like we did in the Grand Canyon and Redwoods Park issues. If we had relied only on local politicians on those issues, we would have lost; only the Legislature of the Whole People (Congress) saved them. That is how we can save our treasure—the unparalleled Northwest forests."

The other side argued that a "'national' strategy could not work here . . . because our forests, even though 'National,' affect local economies, so Northwest politicians must be pacified with compromises, or they would block all legislation."

Finally, a show of hands: most voted to "go national, try to win the whole American people; this is our Last Best Chance."

I wrote a note to myself then: "I look around at the comrades: all veterans now—but here, not in Washington. And I wonder: am I the only one here, who knows just how beautiful and how terrible the next few years will be, as we venture forth?"

Onward now. After 19 drafts and redrafts we had a single bill, gave it a name—the "Ancient Forest Protection Act."

A champion stepped forward: Jim Jontz, Democrat from northern Indiana. He not only introduced the bill, he helped us gather many cosponsors.

Next, we had to challenge the Forest Service falsehood that there was much forest left. Audubon Society created an "Adopt a Forest" program, sending local members into each forest to map exactly what was still there. These new facts were most convincing as the campaign moved forward.

It had become obvious that rare birds like the spotted owl and the marbled murrelet, whose crucial habitats were ONLY in the ancient forests, were in trouble. And it was equally obvious that logging was destroying this habitat. If a species were "put on the endangered list," the logging would have to cease in all threatened habitats.

A new lawsuit was filed ordering a reluctant government to list certain species as "endangered" under the terms of the Endangered Species Act (ESA), which required the FWS to take all steps necessary to protect, *and* recover, that species. The northern spotted owl was listed in 1990, drastically changing national forest logging programs.

Then a far-reaching lawsuit caused an injunction (May 1991) to halt all logging in 60,000 acres of key spotted owl ancient forest habitat (*Seattle Audubon v. Forest Service*) This order effectively shut down most ancient forest logging in the northwest and sent a shock wave through the industry and its political supporters.

Another turning point of the revived campaign came after the 1992 election.

The candidates had taken opposite stands: Bush for more logging; Clinton, to bring the parties together. Clinton won big.

President Clinton and his cabinet held a hearing in Portland, Oregon, in April 1993. It was a major—seminal—event in the long and difficult history of the "Ancient Forest Wars."

Afterwards, Clinton directed the Forest Service to come up with a *new* forest management scheme for all northwest national forests—one which would at last mark *finis* to the liquidation strategy, and which would fully recognize the many unique values of ancient "old growth" forests, *and* to devise ways and means of conserving them.

In 1994, the Forest Service announced its new Northwest Forest Plan.

By no means perfect, it was nonetheless a major victory for conservation activists who had struggled for change for so long. The new plan created new reserves with each one allowing certain amounts of logging; but each one also restricting greatly what had been normal logging before and reduced timber sales in all northwest forests.

Does that mean it's all over?

No! Strife still goes on, although at a much lower level. Now, every logging proposal is contested, and the conservation side usually wins. The entire nation values its ancient forests as never before.

Brock Evans, a Seattle lawyer, left that job in 1967 to become the northwest representative of the Sierra Club. His main issue then and in later years in Washington, DC, was to protect as much ancient forest as possible. Now retired in La Grande, Oregon, he serves as president of the Endangered Species Coalition and president of the Hells Canyon Preservation Council.

Dams, Rivers, and Fish—A Continuing Conundrum
Mark Rockwell

Water has always been a precious and life-sustaining necessity, both for health and for economic benefit. Rivers and streams are the source for much of the water used, and as the population grew, developing these sources for social benefit was the focus of intense public planning and effort. Dams were built on major rivers to provide more consistent water availability, and diversion of this water helped agriculture grow and allowed cities to expand. There is no doubt that water infrastructure helped the American culture and economy thrive and develop.

Beginning in the early part of the 20th century, materials and technological advances allowed massive dams to be built, blocking many of the major rivers with multiple barriers, particularly in the west: the Columbia, Willamette, Snake, Rogue, Klamath, Sacramento, and San Joaquin Rivers. As Americans dammed their rivers and streams, fish were negatively impacted, especially anadromous fish—fish that are born in fresh water in inland streams, migrate to the ocean to grow and mature, and then return to fresh water to spawn and perpetuate the species. Salmon are the most well known of these anadromous fish.

The single largest river system in the western United States is the Columbia/Snake system, stretching from the Pacific Ocean near Portland, Oregon, and into northern Washington and Idaho. In the past, 10 to 16 million salmon of all five Pacific species used this river system to begin and finish their life cycle. (Current counts of Chinook salmon average below 10,000 annually.) The Snake River connects with the Columbia and extends hundreds of miles into eastern and central Idaho. The Snake "system" is the largest spawning and rearing habitat for salmon in America.

Today there are 60 major dams, with 14 on the main stem of the Columbia River and 20 on the Snake. With over the 100 years of dam building on these rivers, the largest populations of salmon on Earth have either gone extinct or have been placed on the endangered species list because they faced extinction. The remaining fish in the system only exist today because of ESA protection, which mandates the federal government to do whatever is necessary to prevent extinction. This has caused great conflict between water users and state and federal agencies (Harrison 2016).

On the Snake River, a congressional deal was struck in the 1960s, allowing four new dams to be built for river barge traffic access to Lewiston, Idaho. This was the "last nail in the coffin" of the Columbia/Snake River salmon. Populations of salmon "crashed" following dam construction, and all species of salmon in the Snake River either went extinct or were listed as threatened or endangered. Since then billions of dollars have been spent trying to stop extinction.

Hatcheries were built in an attempt to off-set the impacts of the dams, but unexpected outcomes have now shown that hatcheries are not the long-term answer to survival. Hatchery fish that are spawned and reared in a man-made environment live a protected early life without the normal in-river challenges. This results in lost genetic viability making them less able to avoid predation and disease. Hatchery fish lack the genetic strength to be as viable as wild fish and have poor survival. Additionally, there is in-stream mixing of hatchery and wild fish, which jeopardizes the long-term viability of the genetic strength of salmon. What is now known is that hatchery fish are another stressor to the survival of wild populations, and the long-term survival of salmon is at risk when hatchery fish mix with wild populations.

Self-sustaining wild salmon populations are essential for recovery. Federal, state, and local organizations have spent tens of millions working to improve spawning habitat in Idaho with the goal to have better spawning and rearing habitat in the wild. There are ladders on the dams on both the Columbia and Snake Rivers that allow adult fish returning from the ocean to get past the dams. Historically, these have worked fairly well, but in recent years (2015 in particular) many up-river spawning fish died from increasing water temperatures driven by climate change. Additionally, because there are so many dams on the rivers, the out-migrating young fish (smolts) have to pass through many lakes and over many dams to reach the ocean. Barely 1–2 percent of fish born in the rocky streams of Idaho ever make it to the Pacific Ocean. The majority do not survive in the ocean, so less than 1 percent return to spawn.

Over the past 20 years, the federal fish agency (NOAA Fisheries) has been writing biological opinions (Bi-Op) under the ESA on how to recover salmon in the Columbia/Snake system. Five have been written since 2003 and none have been accepted by the federal district court as adequate for recovery. In the May 2016, a federal judge mandated Snake River dam removal be considered as an alternative for recovery. This new rewrite is due no later than March 2018 (Earthjustice 2016).

Dams clearly have come with a huge environmental cost—extinction of salmon and other anadromous fish species. If we are to save those that remain and recover many specific runs of fish, dam removal must be considered. Fish face many natural challenges to survival from ocean conditions, predators, or disease, and there is little people can do to reduce these impacts. However, we have a moral, biological, and economic responsibility to protect what is left for the sake of the fish, cultural benefits, and to preserve biodiversity. Salmon and other fish bring marine chemicals and biomass critical to health of the riparian and forest systems they spawn in. Inland habitats suffer when salmon disappear and these nutrients aren't delivered.

We as Americans should take great pride in the ESA, for it has saved countless numbers of fish, wildlife, insects, and plants that are vital to our heritage and our culture, as well as life itself. The salmon and other anadromous fish still alive in western rivers depend on the ESA to give them time for conditions to improve. I'm hopeful that better decisions will be made, including dam removal where appropriate, and we will once again see robust, self-sustaining salmon populations in rivers and streams in the western United States. My children and grandchildren have the right to see and experience what nature can do, and great migrations of salmon is one of those wonders.

References

Earthjustice. 2016. "U.S. District Court Sides with Wild Salmon and Communities; Feds' Columbia/Snake River Salmon Plan Found Illegal." http://earthjustice.org/news/press/2016/u-s-district-court-sides-with-wild-salmon-and-communities-feds-columbiasnake-river-salmon-plan-again-found. Accessed March 30, 2017.

Harrison, John. 2016. "Endangered Species Act and Columbia River Salmon and Steelhead." Northwest Power and Conservation Council. https://www.nwcouncil.org/history/EndangeredSpeciesAct. Accessed March 30, 2017.

Mark Rockwell is a retired doctor who served as the Pacific coast representative of the Endangered Species Coalition for 10 years specializing on fishery and water issues. He is especially interested in saving Pacific salmon from extinction. He was a negotiating party in the Klamath River restoration process that finalized four dams be removed from the river to save salmon.

Respecting Fellow Predators
Dave Stalling

Everything we hunters love about elk—their speed, wariness, agility, intelligence—was shaped and honed through thousands of years of coevolution with wolves, bears, mountain lions, and coyotes. Predators helped make elk what they are, and predators help keep elk what they are. In the wilds, everything is intimately connected; the health of the whole depends on every part. When I merge into the wilds to hunt, I feel part of the whole—not merely a visitor to the wilds, but a participant; a predator.

I love wild elk meat but also see myself as a vegetarian of sorts—living off the wild grasses, sedges, and forbs that grow near my home in western Montana. Most of these plants are not palatable to humans, so I let elk convert them to protein for me. Perhaps someday I will travel through the digestive system of a grizzly and fertilize the vegetation that elk eat: Seems only fair considering all the elk I've killed and eaten. We're all connected.

Unfortunately, many hunters don't see it this way. They show disdain and disrespect for our fellow predators. They see them as "competitors" killing and eating what they arrogantly and selfishly think is "theirs" instead of trying to understand the vital, ecological role they play in shaping and maintaining what they claim to love. Nowhere is this more apparent than in the ongoing war on wolves.

Idaho Fish and Game recently hired a paid bounty hunter to eliminate two wolf packs in a wilderness. Idaho hunters have organized wolf-killing competitions and co-ops to pay trappers to kill wolves. The state legislature and governor declared wolves a "disaster emergency" and allocated $2 million to killing wolves. More recently, Idaho Fish and Game conducted secretive aerial shootings of wolves from helicopters without public knowledge or input; they spent $30,000 to kill 23 wolves. Idaho Fish and Game is doing this and more in an ongoing effort to appease hunters to protect livestock and maintain artificially high and unhealthy numbers of elk for hunters to shoot.

Elk populations are increasing in most of the west. State wildlife departments are expanding elk hunting to reduce elk populations, while simultaneously killing wolves under the guise of protecting and boosting elk numbers. Where elk populations do appear on the decline, there are plenty of factors to consider in addition to wolves: Changes in habitat; a natural reduction in numbers where, prior to the return of wolves, populations were artificially high; lack of mature bulls and low bull-to-cow ratios in herds (often resulting from early season hunting and too much hunting pressure on bull elk), which influence the timing of the rut and breeding behavior to consequently influence the timing of spring calving and increase vulnerability of elk calves to predation; influence of other predators including mountain lions, black bears, and grizzlies; unanticipated impacts of various hunting regulations and hunting pressure; and changes in behavior and habitat use by elk in the presence of wolves.

Where I hunt, the growing presence of wolves has changed the behavior and habits of elk. Elk bunch up more for safety and move around more to evade and avoid wolves. They are a lot more wary. I have adapted and adjusted to these changes and have no problem finding elk. This is part of the beauty and value of hunting within wilderness—to adjust, adapt, and be part of the landscape; to be, as my friend David Petersen put it, part of the "bedrock workings of nature" (Petersen 1996).

We render the wilds a diminished abstract when we alter it to suit our own needs and desires and, in the process, make it less healthy and whole. There are those who espouse the virtues of backcountry hunting and yet seem apathetic or supportive toward the destruction of backcountry integrity. Those who understand the wilds know how critically important predators are to the health of the land. To remain silent about the non-scientific, politically based killing of wolves in the wildest of places is to be complacent toward the degradation of what we claim to cherish.

One of the cornerstones of our North American Model of Wildlife Conservation is that wildlife be managed based on good science. That good science shows the return of wolves to much of the western United States has resulted in significant, long-term benefits to wildlife and the habitat that sustains them—including the species we love to hunt.

Predators are rarely managed based on science or for the benefit of predators and healthy ecosystems. They're rarely managed in accordance of what most Americans accept. Hunters and anglers who buy licenses and pay excise taxes on hunting and fishing gear (along with governor-appointed commissioners) have lopsided power and influence over how wildlife is managed. Thus, wildlife management often leans more toward animal husbandry—producing more to catch and shoot, sometimes to the detriment of other wildlife. Predators get a bad deal.

A recent report about the flaws of the North American model summed it up this way: "The scientists also express concern that the interests of recreational hunters sometimes conflict with conservation principles. For example, they say, wildlife management conducted in the interest of hunters can lead to an overabundance of animals that people like to hunt, such as deer, and the extermination of predators that also provide a vital balance to the ecosystem" (Cucetich et al. 2011).

More than half a century ago, Aldo Leopold wrote: "I personally believed, at least in 1914 when predator control began, that there could not be too much horned game, and that the extirpation of predators was a reasonable price to pay for better big game hunting. Some of us have learned since the tragic error of such a view, and acknowledged our mistake" (Leopold 1944).

We still haven't caught up to Leopold.

References

Cucetich, John, Bump, Joseph, Nelson, Michael, and Paquet, Paul. 2011, Summer. "Flaws of the North American Model of Wildlife Conservation." *The Wildlife Professional.* The Wildlife Society.

Leopold, Aldo. 1944. "Review of the Wolves of North America by Stanley P. Young and Edward A. Goldman." *Journal of Forestry* 42(12): 928–929.

Petersen, David. 1996. *A Hunters Heart: Honest Essays on Bloodsport.* New York: Henry Holt.

Dave Stalling is a writer, photographer, and wildlife advocate living in Missoula, Montana.

Unlikely Partners
Michael Lehnert

I joined the Marine Corps to become a marine, not an environmentalist. To me, saving the planet meant protecting our nation and our citizens from those who would do us harm. It took several decades to realize that more than despots with evil intentions could destroy our way of life. When I left Michigan in 1973 to join the Marine Corps, I'd never seen a living bald eagle. I was an avid fisherman but couldn't eat the fish in Saginaw Bay—the nearest large body of water where I grew up—because of pollution. Ironically, I joined the Corps the same year that the ESA was signed into law. Those who didn't live during those times would find it difficult to appreciate the damage done to our environment and the assault on the biodiversity of this nation.

In 2000, I'd been improbably advanced to brigadier general and given responsibility for all environmental programs in the Marine Corps. The environmental groups and Department of Defense didn't enjoy a warm relationship. Both sides generally talked past each other. Environmental groups accused the military (with some accuracy) of not doing enough to protect the land under their stewardship, while the military responded that military readiness aboard the installations took priority over more general calls to "save the planet." However, once past the finger pointing, lawsuits, injunctions, and posturing, there seemed to be a broader purpose that could be built upon. Both the environmentalists and the Department of Defense had a strong love for this country and a desire to see it preserved.

The Marine Corps reached out to the major environmental groups to mend fences, and we started that effort with a road trip to Marine Corps Base Camp Lejeune, North Carolina, the largest amphibious training base on the East Coast. It was as unlikely a group of individuals as had ever been found on the base. A dozen very senior environmentalists from the Nature Conservancy, the Endangered Species Coalition, and Sierra Club tramped through the Carolina Pines to discover if the Corps really had an environmental ethos.

Their leader was a man named Brock Evans. Brock had been a gadfly to the Department of Defense for years holding them to the standards established by law, particularly the ESA. He had also spent several years as an enlisted marine—a machine gunner. Brock was rightfully suspicious of a "dog and pony" show but willing to give the Marine Corps a chance.

Moving through the swamps of Lejeune, we passed a group of marines in the pines. We were to learn later they were searching for a radio lost the evening before—a very bad thing for a young marine. Brock barked, "Stop the car. I want to talk to them." The marines looked at us with suspicion. We didn't fit any profile they had encountered. Brock, in his best prosecutorial manner asked, "What would happen if you disturbed the nesting site of a red cockaded woodpecker. Would you even know what a nesting site looks like?" A marine answered, "Well sir, each pine that is a nesting site is clearly marked and generally taped off so we know we aren't supposed to go into them." Not satisfied, Brock asked, "What would happen if you disturbed one of these sites?" The marine, clearly wanting to get back to his mission, responded in colorful language that if he disturbed a nesting site he would lose the most precious part of his anatomy. The senior marine clarified that was an overstatement but it would go badly for anyone violating base environmental regulations. We left them looking for their lost radio. I hope they found it.

As we reentered the vehicles, Brock turned to me and said, "I've seen enough. If the word has reached these junior marines then I believe that you really are serious about the environment."

This was the beginning of a new relationship with environmental groups. By 2005, I commanded seven Marine Corps bases west of the Mississippi and a land area roughly the size of Rhode Island. Our relationship with environmentalists had grown even stronger. They were welcome on our installations. Data and open communications became our greatest ally. We shared both. We focused on habitat preservation. We learned that many species were particularly vulnerable at certain times, generally during the breeding season, but at other times areas once thought lost for military use could be successfully shared by both marines and the endangered and threatened species that lived there. We watched populations of endangered and threatened species increase and knew we were making real progress.

Today, the Department of Defense manages approximately 28 million acres of public land with 492 endangered species, managed at a cost of about $840 million, living on these installations (Boice 2013). Some environmental groups have expressed concern that the National Defense Authorization Act of 2004 precludes critical habitat designation on any military installation arguing that this legislation allows the military to ignore the ESA. Not so. Installations are required to have an Integrated Natural Resources Management Plan (INRMP). These plans are generally more detailed than anything created in the private sector. Plans must be fully funded, and the Department of the Interior must rule that the plan is sufficient to conserve a listed species (National Defense Authorization Act 2004). The military is a steward of the lands placed in their trust by the American people. Our military has a legal and moral obligation to ensure that the lands placed in their care are properly managed, and the ESA is the law of the land. It changed America for the better. Its application must be grounded in science, not politics.

Both environmental and national defense interests have a symbiotic relationship. Both the military and environmentalist share a deep love for this nation. Any partnership needs to be built upon verifiable data, honesty, open communications, and the recognition that while we won't agree on everything, there is enough common ground for active and positive partnership. All that is required is imagination and leadership. If you believe that a country worth defending is a country worth preserving, all things are possible.

References

Boice, Peter. 2013, May. "Threatened and Endangered Species on DOD Lands." Department of Defense. http://www.dod naturalresources.net/files/TE__s_fact_sheet_5–24–13.pdf. Accessed April 19, 2017.

National Defense Authorization Act. 2004. "Section 318: Military Readiness and Conservation of Protected Species." Department of Defense. https://www.gpo.gov/fdsys/pkg/ PLAW-108publ136/pdf/PLAW-108publ136.pdf. Accessed April 17, 2017.

Major General Michael Lehnert is recently retired as the commanding general of Marine Corps Installations West.

Macaws and Jaguars: Ecotourism—Reality or a Dream?
Douglas Trent

When Mexican architect Hector Ceballos first coined the word "ecotourism" in 1983, it was envisioned as a community-based solution to both poverty and habitat conservation. Today, many countries around the world have slightly different definitions, but most include that tourism benefits both local communities and nature preserves. Since that time, however, ecotourism has been used to name any outdoor activity, from extreme sports to cruise ships, and very few community-based ecotourism projects have been sustainable, have managed to stay in business, benefit the local communities, and preserve the nature that tourists pay to experience. One major NGO speaker at an early ecotourism conference stated that "the absolute bottom line in any ecotourism project has to be conservation," and most people I have asked, agree, but this is part of the problem with projects that fail.

Ecotourism, or any tourism venture, is a business. The bottom line is profit, not conservation. When an ecotourism venture is financially successful, however, it does provide a financial incentive to preserve the nature that clients go to see. Here is one example that has worked.

To be transparent, I am a nature tour operator, based in Brazil, who got involved in tourism to be able to raise profits to help move people out of poverty and preserve nature. In the mid-1980s, I befriended a family of Pantaneiros, the cowboys of Brazil's Pantanal wetlands. They had trees full of hyacinth macaws (*Anodorhynchus hyacinthinus*), the largest member of the parrot family and an endangered species, and a wish-list bird for many nature tourists. I would stop there with my groups to purchase drinks from the small stand on the side of the road and to give my clients a chance to spend time with the macaws. As I knew the family better, I started to bring them kerosene, batteries, and groceries as they lived five hours from the closest store. After a few years, Lerinho Arruda de Falcão, the head of the family, showed me a jaguar fang and explained that it came from the last jaguar he had killed. We then made a deal: the family would stop hunting jaguars if I would get them into the ecotourism business.

My strategy to help and conserve nature in Brazil has been to charge enough for my tours to have extra funds to support conservation projects. In addition, some of my former clients have become engaged and contributed money to help develop and sustain projects. One in particular, Joanne Devlin, who was the co-owner of a pavement company in California with a conscience, agreed to pay to preserve as much land as she covered with asphalt. She gave the project funds to pay US$80 per hectare for 1,000 hectares of jaguar habitat, creating the Jaguar Ecological Reserve. I was the only professional nature tour operator in Brazil at this time and had many clients from around the world, so I could prepay "room nights," a tourism term referring to one night in a hotel room. This gave Lerinho the funds necessary to build a lodge. Once the lodge was available, I could get volunteers to come and teach English. Once the guides in training spoke English, I took them on tour so they could learn the birds and other species, understand the basics of ecology, the financial side of the business, and so on. In 2005, I arranged international media coverage (BBC, *New York Times*) and informed them that from then on they would need to continue on their own, the real test of a community project worthiness.

Over the next 10 years, businesses grew. The original guides trained another eight locals to be guides, while other local Pantaneiros opened their own ecotourism businesses, safari truck rental companies, and other related activities. Today, some 50 families are sustained by the project, and there is a strong economic reason to protect jaguars, giant river otters, hyacinth macaws, and other endangered species.

Ecotourism, however, is not a stand-alone solution to protecting endangered species. What our long-term species project has revealed is that there was an increase in hyacinth macaws in Brazil once the airlines of the world all stopped transporting live birds. In the region where much of the illegal traffic in hyacinth macaws had taken place, the poachers were captured and given long jail sentences. Breeders said it was impossible to breed this species in captivity. Once the wild stock became inaccessible, however, it became possible. Supposedly, the first captive bred hyacinth macaw was bred and born in a garbage can!

The International Union for the Conservation of Nature (IUCN) (2016) states that throughout the 1980s the hyacinth macaw suffered major declines as an estimated 10,000 birds were illegally captured for the pet trade, and widespread habitat destruction and hunting caused a further reduction in numbers. The majority of the population is now located in the Pantanal, where since 1990 the species has shown signs of a recovery and expanded its range (Pinho and Nogueira 2003), probably in response to conservation projects.

Jaguars also may be making a comeback in the Pantanal, with some credit to ecotourism, and because no one seems to want to be seen in a jaguar skin coat. Small ranches continue to kill jaguars that take cattle, but the economic threat of the skin trade for fashion was the biggest threat. For both jaguars and hyacinth macaws, ecotourism was part of the solution, but not the entire solution.

References

IUCN. 2016. *The IUCN Red List of Threatened Species. Version 2016–3*. http://www.iucnredlist.org/details/22685516/0. Accessed April 4, 2017.

Pinho, Joao Batista, and Nogueira, Flavia M. B. 2003. "Hyacinth Macaw (*Anodorhynchus hyacinthinus*) Reproduction in the Northern Pantanal Mato Grosso, Brazil." *Ornithologia Neotropical* 14: 29–38.

Douglas Trent, an American ecologist, has lived in Brazil for most of 37 years where he has been guiding bird and general nature tours in South America. He holds a degree in Ecology from the University of Kansas and is a founder of the rainforest conservation movement. He currently is the executive director of ClimaFund Brasil, a project working to prevent forest fires in parks and surrounding areas. He is the founder of the Focus Conservation Fund, a tax-exempt nonprofit organization in the United States, and SCDC do Brasil—Sustainable Community Development & Communication as well as the Brazilian non-profit Instituto Sustentar.

Marine Extinction
C. Sarah Cohen

Contemporary marine extinctions used to be a bit of an eso-teric topic, a game to see if one could think of a known single marine invertebrate extinction, or a reason why extinctions are so much rarer at sea than on land. On the other hand, in geo-logical time, mass extinctions are well known, with five famous events that dramatically changed the Earth's biodiversity due to volcanism, meteorites, or other forces. These events led to a dramatic reshaping of flora and fauna over millennia with the latest one the rise of the mammals following the demise of the large reptiles. Now, scientists are discussing the advent of a sixth mass extinction due to human-caused changes in the en-vironment. Attempts to address this looming mass extinction are varied and reflect the evolving attitude of scientists and the public toward conservation (Mace 2014).

Early in 2017, a last-ditch effort to save vaquitas, a critically endangered porpoise, gained approval. The remaining 30 animals will be captured and placed in holding pens for semi-captive breeding and protection from illegal harvesting. This charismatic species, the smallest known marine mammal, is truly on the edge of extinction, and while it is found only in the Gulf of California, there has been an active global campaign to save the species. Forces leading vaquitas to this precipice are complex and not so easily addressed, and captive breeding may only save them temporarily, because there are always risks from taking an animal into captivity. Illegal harvesting, poverty, and market globalization make the gill-netting that catches and kills vaquitas as bycatch a lucrative industry. While ecotourism has provided alternative income for some coastal human populations in need of alternatives to destructive fisheries, the vaquita is also elusive, shy, and rarely seen, even by experienced searchers. Still, scientists and environmentalists are hopeful that the vaquita may be saved by the desperate breeding attempts and organized global lobbying (McKie 2017).

Given the numbers of marine species that are difficult to see, or are even as yet unknown to science, is captive breeding an effective strategy to address the problem of marine extinctions? As a targeted plan for the vaquita, and possibly more broadly to highlight the effects of illegal harvesting, this dramatic plan may be highly successful. Other endangered marine species are receiving similarly high-profile attention with individually mandated recovery plans for various salmonid species, marine mammals, and a few invertebrates including abalone, and recently some coral species (NOAA 2015). While it is too soon to know the fate of most of these species, their recovery raises the general issue true for marine as well as terrestrial species, how can we save the species, if we don't save the habitats and ecosystems?

If the sixth global mass extinction is underway, as may be seen in diverse habitats around the globe, a more concerted approach is needed. Significant events such as the widespread bleaching and potential death of the majority of the Great Barrier Reef this past year are widely attributed to increasing ocean temperatures as well as other stressors. And, in a temperate ecosystem, the largest marine epidemic documented to date has occurred in the past few years in northeast Pacific coastal waters. Over 20 species of sea stars in an ongoing temporal and spatial mosaic of populations have died off from Alaska to southern California. While a particular densovirus of unknown origin seems implicated in the sea star epidemic, there is widespread agreement that environmental stress related to climate change may have an important role in the disease's impact. Still, broad-scale population die offs of marine species have been documented for decades, if not more, without suspicion of a broader phenomenon related to global environmental factors, so why the concern now? The extreme scale and rate of species' declines, coupled with documented environmental changes that are known to alter population viability, are reasons for alternative interpretation and urgent concern.

The Great Barrier Reef, the largest living structure on Earth, has lost two-thirds of its corals to bleaching in the past two years from higher than normal ocean temperatures. Is captive breeding for each of the greater than 400 species of coral, and the innumerable species of coral reef-dependent inhabitants, products of more than 500,000 years of evolution, a viable method to preserve this complex ecosystem? Clearly, that approach is nonsensical. Yet, the environmental stressors that are leading so many species and marine ecosystems toward extinction are challenging to address at the international scales that are required. Data on the rate and outcomes of climate change are coming increasingly into focus because it is happening before our eyes, in our lifetimes. In marine environments, the mix of stressors, lower oxygen and pH, higher temperatures, changes in precipitation and salinity, and greater storms and nearshore storm impacts, along with increased disease prevalence and intensity, are combining to challenge the resilience of many marine ecosystems from seagrass beds to food webs missing their top predators.

Still, the legal mandate for the species, and the necessity for appropriate habitat, does drive a broader view of conservation and recovery plans. But, is it broad enough? Particularly in the case of major predators, it can be hard to make appropriate plans (e.g., wolf reintroductions in rural areas). Marine environments may actually have an addressable advantage, as noted by scientists highlighting species declines that are frequently caused by overharvesting. Some apex species are apparently recovering following protection from harvest and habitat destruction such as elephant seals and sea otters, suggesting that it is not too late to act to preserve marine ecosystems.

Marine species do bring challenges, however. Lack of knowledge has made it difficult to know which stressors are the most significant in leading to decreases or hampering recovery. In the case of the sudden decline of approximately 20 sea stars, it becomes clear that we know remarkably little about sea star immunity and genomics that might lend clues to the causes of the epidemic.

Two major challenges to persistence of marine species are the direct and indirect effects of overharvesting and destruction of species high in the food web and changes in environmental conditions that sustain species. How marine species will be impacted by the changes and how able they are to adapt is an area of active investigation, but much less is documented in comparison to terrestrial species. The future can look dire, and there is the distinct possibility of a sixth mass extinction. On the other hand, acid rain was a freshwater and terrestrial human-made environmental threat that was successfully addressed via policy change. As new threats to the health of marine species and ecosystems emerge, we are fortunate to have more advanced technologies to understand and address the challenges and a galvanized will and enthusiasm to match our emerging interests.

References

Mace, Georgina M. 2014. "Whose Conservation?" *Science* 345: 1558–1560. http://science.sciencemag.org/content/345/6204/1558.full. Accessed May 7, 2017.

McKie, Robin. 2017. "Last-Ditch Attempt to Save the Endangered Vaquita Porpoise." *The Guardian.* https://www.theguardian.com/environment/2017/apr/29/bid-to-save-vaquita-porpoise-from-extinction-trained-dolphins. Accessed May 7, 2017.

NOAA. 2015. "Species in the Spotlight: Survive to Thrive, Recovering Threatened and Endangered Species, FY 2013–2014 Report to Congress." http://www.nmfs.noaa.gov/stories/2015/05/docs/noaa_recoveringspecies_report_web.pdf. Accessed May 7, 2017.

Dr. C. Sarah Cohen is an evolutionary ecologist at San Francisco State University, specializing in marine and estuarine habitats and species, from sea stars and sea squirts to sea grasses and ciliates by the sea shore.

Introduction

There are dozens of national and international environmental organizations and individuals working to save endangered species critical for maintenance of biodiversity. They range from a conservative and more traditional group like the Audubon Society to more radical groups like Greenpeace. There are ones that focus on endangered species and the Endangered Species Act (ESA) and others are more involved with habitat preservation and climate change. The people and environmental organizations featured here are a small number of the total. They are profiled because they have good reputations and proven track records working toward the protection of imperiled species. References to other organizations can be found in the Resources section of the book and on the Internet. Watch out, however, for organizations that label themselves as conservation groups and are profit-driven industries that exploit animals for money.

Sir David Attenborough, a conservationist known for his films and books about the natural world, holds a baby salt water crocodile. The American crocodile, found in southern Florida, the Caribbean, Central America, and northern South America, is endangered from habitat loss, illegal hunting, and poaching. (Daniel Berehulak/Getty Images)

People

David Attenborough (1926–): Naturalist

Through beautifully photographed wildlife documentaries, David Attenborough has become better known than almost any other producer of nature films. Generations have learned to love nature through his films and, in the process, learned biology. The films are based on science, and viewers learn about ecology, evolution, and animal behavior. More recently, Attenborough has become a vocal figure in efforts to educate the public about climate change through the BBC's series *Saving Planet Earth*.

David Attenborough was born in London in 1926 and raised on the campus of the University College, Leicester, where his father was principal. He developed a fascination with the natural world and assembled a collection of bird eggs and fossils by the age of seven. He studied natural science at the University of Cambridge and served in the Royal Navy in Wales after completing his studies. He returned to London in 1949 to work as an editor for a publishing company and began a training program at the BBC. After his training, he began a career at the BBC in 1952.

Attenborough was disturbed that the BBC had little or no programming devoted to the natural sciences. Shows that featured animals were filmed at zoos out of the animal's natural habitat. In 1954, Attenborough developed a series titled *Zoo Quest* that filmed animals both in captivity and in the wild. It was so successful that the BBC established its Natural History Unit in 1967. Today, the unit is recognized as a leader in the production of natural history films.

Attenborough left the BBC in the early 1960s to study social anthropology at the London School of Economics. He returned to the BBC in 1965 to direct programming for both the BBC and BBC Two. His love of nature drew him away from the BBC again in 1972 to write and produce TV series as a freelancer. The 96 episodes of the 1976 series *Life on Earth* made Attenborough a household name. He and his crew traveled around the world to every continent to film plants and animals in the wild with cutting-edge technology. The series examined the role of evolution in nature of every biological group.

Since *Life on Earth* Attenborough has been the writer and presenter on over 40 films and has written 84 books, many in conjunction with a series. Series are often years in the making, because much effort, planning, and expense goes into the production of each documentary. Once a topic is decided, researchers of the BBC Natural History Unit, most with biological degrees and backgrounds, obtain the most interesting and relevant scientific information through reading journals, scientific papers, and books. They contact behavioral scientists at universities and attend scientific conferences to find unique and new information that would make an interesting and educational program. Before filming, producers travel to interview scientists and inspect the areas around the globe where filming will occur. Some of the budget is spent developing new technologies before a team of several camera operators is sent out to film. Sometimes it takes several weeks or even months to obtain the desired films of the subjects. The last step is Sir David (he was knighted by Queen Elizabeth in 1985) doing the narrative in his enthusiastic folksy manner.

Animal behavior is featured in many of Attenborough's films. The *Trials of Life* was a study in animal behavior in 12 episodes ranging from predation to courtship. Much of the success of the series was the contribution of animal behavior researchers who acted as consultants on the films. Filming often took place on the researchers' study sites. *Life of Birds* (1998) and *Life of Mammals* (2002–2003), and the accompanying books, provide a comprehensive look at the evolution of birds and mammals, and *Life in the Freezer* (1993) explored the natural history of Antarctica.

Attenborough has continued filmmaking thorough a 60-year career, and at 90 he is still active. His latest series, *Planet Earth II*, was shown in the United Kingdom beginning on November 6, 2016. The six-part series was filmed over three years in 40 countries in the latest UHD and HRD formats using drones and lightweight cameras. David Attenborough is the recipient of many awards and 31 honorary degrees.

The following list consists of Sir David's natural history films that he wrote and narrated from the most recent to the earliest ones.

Planet Earth II (2016)

Great Barrier Reef (2016)

The Hunt (2015)

Natural Curiosities 2 (2014)

Natural Curiosities 1 (2013)

On the Brink (2013)

Rise of Animals: Triumph of the Vertebrates (2013)

Attenborough: 60 Years in the Wild (2012)

Madagascar (2011)

Frozen Planet (2011)

Death of the Oceans (2010)

Charles Darwin and the Tree of Life (2009)

Life (2009)

Life in Cold Blood (2008)

Planet Earth (2006)

The Truth about Climate Change (2006)

Life in the Undergrowth (2005)

Life of Mammals (2002–2003)

State of the Planet (2000)

Life of Birds (1998)

Private Life of Plants (1990)

Trials of Life (1990)

The First Eden (1987)

The Living Planet (1984)

Life on Earth (1979)

Rachel Carson (1907–1964): Catalyst of an Environmental Movement

Rachel Louise Carson gave voice to an environmental movement and challenged a post–World War II society about the ethics of human domination of nature. She was born on May 27, 1907, in rural Springdale, Pennsylvania. Her degree in biology was awarded from the Pennsylvania College for Women (now Chatham College), and she did postgraduate work at the Marine Biological Laboratory in Woods Hole, Massachusetts. In 1932, she received a master's degree in zoology from Johns Hopkins University. Carson worked at the U.S. Bureau of Fisheries during the Depression and became a scientist and editor and then editor-in-chief of all publications for the U.S. Fish and Wildlife Service. In 1951, she published *The Sea around Us*, which was on the *New York Times* bestsellers list for 81 weeks. She ended her government career in 1952 to write full time.

When Carson wrote her classic book *Silent Spring* in 1962, concerns about damage to the natural world were just beginning to surface. She articulated these concerns in a series of essays in the *New Yorker* and then in her book. Carson challenged the establishment for the practice of the widespread use of chemicals, especially the pesticide DDT, dichloro-diphenyl-trichloroethane, and other insecticides known as organochlorines.

Discovered in 1939 by a Swiss chemist, Paul Müller, DDT was used successfully during World War II by the military to control typhus, malaria, and insect parasites such as lice. After the war, DDT was promoted as a wonder chemical and sprayed widely to control agricultural pests in broadcast sprays from airplanes and used globally to kill mosquitoes for malaria control. Users of DDT soon learned that pesticides sprayed over large areas killed a large fraction of the insect population to leave behind survivors with a resistance to the effects of the chemical and the demise of predatory insects. Insect immunity occurred in only a matter of a few years to render DDT less effective for the control of insect populations.

In *Silent Spring*, Rachel Carson warned about the harm of pesticides to the environment and possibly to human health. She explained how pesticides were accumulating in the food chain to cause damage to the environment and to threaten populations of predatory birds. In contrast to other pesticides that broke down quickly, DDT persisted in the environment and concentrated in the tissues of insects and other animals. At each step of the food chain, concentrations of DDT in the tissues increased until top predators consumed high amounts of it in their prey. This response was seen in predatory birds, especially fish-eating eagles and falcons. The DDT had accumulated in the fish these birds ate. The accumulated pesticide did not kill the birds but affected their reproduction to produce thin eggshells. The thin eggshells often broke before the chick was ready to leave the egg causing the chick to die.

Although the pesticide and agricultural industries attacked and ridiculed Carson, she eventually was proven correct on many of her predictions in *Silent Spring*. DDT was initially effective in malaria eradication programs, but insect resistance made it ineffective as early as 1951. The U.S. Department of Agriculture, before establishment of the Environmental Protection Agency (EPA), began regulating DDT in the late 1950s and 1960s because of mounting evidence of the pesticide's declining benefits and a concern about its toxicological effects on human health. In 1972, the EPA stopped its use for agriculture in the United States. The global malaria campaign was abandoned in 1969, mainly because DDT was no longer effective. In 1996, the Stockholm Convention under the UN program enacted global bans or restrictions on a group of persistent organic pollutants, including DDT. Carson was awarded the President Medal of Freedom Award in 1980.

The Rachel Carson Council was founded in 1965 to continue her work. The council focuses on three areas: climate and energy, sustainable food, and healthy communities free from exposure to nuclear testing, pesticides, toxic chemicals and hazardous wastes.

Eugenie Clark and Sylvia Earle: Marine Biologists Protecting Oceans

Eugenie Clark (1922–2015)

Known as the "shark lady," Eugenie Clark spent most of her life studying sharks and other fish. She was also an avid supporter of marine conservation. She wrote popular publications and made public appearances to dispel assumptions about shark behavior and intelligence in an effort to prevent the killing of sharks and encourage the preservation of marine environments.

Eugenie Clark was born in New York City on May 4, 1922. As a youngster, she liked to view the sharks in the New York Aquarium at Battery Park. She pursued her dream to be an ocean explorer and earned a BA in zoology from Hunter College in 1942 and a master's and then a PhD in 1950 from New York University. She entered the male-dominated field of marine biology and became a role model and mentor to a new generation of women marine biologists, who later became passionate marine conservationists.

Clark worked at the Marine Biological Laboratory in Woods Hole, Massachusetts, and was a member of the staff of the American Museum of Natural History, New York City, from 1948 to 1966. In 1955, Clark founded the Cape Haze Marine Laboratory in Sarasota, Florida, later renamed Marine Mote Laboratory. Its initial focus on sharks was later expanded to include wild fisheries, coral reef restoration, marine biomedical research, and other conservation issues. In 1968, she joined the faculty of the University of Maryland, where she taught marine biology until her retirement in 1992. She stayed connected with the Mote Laboratory as a trustee. Although she was a serious researcher, her greatest legacy may be her ability to connect to the general public and talk about the importance of protecting the oceans and conservation of species.

Clark conducted 72 submersible dives as deep as 12,000 feet and led over 200 field research expeditions to the Red Sea and Gulf of Aqaba, Caribbean, Mexico, Japan, Palau, Papua New Guinea, the Solomon Islands, Thailand, Indonesia, and Borneo to study sand fishes, whale sharks, deep sea sharks, and spotted oceanic triggerfish. She wrote three books (*Lady with a Spear*, 1953; *The Lady and the Sharks*, 1969; and *Adventures of a Shark Scientist*, 2000) and more than 175 articles, including research publications in leading peer-reviewed journals such as *Science* and a dozen popular stories in *National Geographic* magazine.

Sylvia Earle (1935–)

Sylvia Earle is an outspoken ocean conservationist dedicated to raising public awareness about the damage to the ocean from pollution, acidification, and environmental degradation. She is an oceanographer, explorer, author, and lecturer as well as a field research scientist, government official, and director for corporate and nonprofit organizations. She has been a National Geographic Society explorer-in-residence since 1998. Formerly chief scientist of the National Oceanic and Atmospheric Administration (NOAA), Earle is the founder of Deep Ocean Exploration and Research, Inc., Mission Blue, Sea Alliance, and chair of the Advisory Councils of the Harte Research Institute and the Ocean in Google Earth.

Sylvia Alice Earle was born in Gibbstown, New Jersey, and raised on a small farm in Camden, New Jersey. When she was 13, her family moved to Florida on the Gulf of Mexico where she became interested in marine biology. She received a BS degree in botany from Florida State University in 1955, a MS from Duke in 1956, and a PhD from Duke University in 1966. She was a research fellow at Harvard University and then a resident director of research at Cape Haze Laboratory in Florida. In 1970, she led the first all-female crew in a Tektite II experiment sponsored by the Navy. Sylvia and four other women scientists dove 50 feet below the ocean surface to live in a small structure underwater doing research for two weeks.

Sylvia Earle has led numerous undersea expeditions over her career to the Galapagos Islands, China, and the Bahamas. In the 1970s, she began an association with the National Geographic Society to produce books and films on the Earth's oceans. In 1976, she became a curator and a research biologist at the California Academy of Sciences, and in 1979 she became curator of phycology (study of algae) there. Between 1990 and 1992, she was the chief scientist at NOAA, the first woman to serve in that position.

To fulfill her commitment to saving the ocean, Dr. Earle established Mission Blue as an initiative of the Sylvia Earle Alliance (SEA) with the mission to ignite public support for the protection of special places that are vital to the health of the ocean. Mission Blue consists of a coalition of over 100 respected ocean conservation groups and like-minded organizations with the goal to establish a global network of marine-protected areas large enough to save and restore the oceans. Mission Blue seeks to identify and protect certain vulnerable areas of marine life around the globe to increase ocean protected areas from less than 4 percent today to 20 percent by the year 2020. At present, Mission Blue has identified over 50 "hope" spots, including the Central Arctic Ocean, the Bahama Reefs, the Gulf of California, and the Micronesian Islands.

Sylvia Earle has authored more than 200 scientific, technical, and popular publications; lectured in more than 80 countries; and appeared in hundreds of radio and television productions. The following is a list of recent books:

Blue Hope: Exploring and Caring for Earth's Magnificent Oceans, 2014

The World Is Blue: How Our Fate and the Oceans Are One, 2010 (with Bill McKibben)

Jumping into Science: Coral Reefs, 2009

Ocean: An Illustrated Atlas, 2008 (with Linda K. Glover)

The Oceans, 2001 (with Ellen J. Prager as first author)

National Geographic Atlas of the Ocean: The Deep Frontier, 2001

Hello Fish! Visiting the Coral Reef, 1999

Dive: My Adventures in the Deep Frontier, 1999

Sea Change: A Message of the Oceans, 1996

Jane Goodall, Dian Fossey, and Birute Galdikas: Champions of Primate Conservation

Three women scientists became leading advocates of conservation for endangered apes: chimpanzees (*Pan troglodytes*), mountain gorillas (*Gorilla gorilla beringei beringei*) and the Borneo orangutans (*Pongo pygmaeus*). They all shared an interest in animals from an early age and were mentored by the well-known anthropologist Louis Leakey. All three women started out as researchers but when they realized the species they studied were critically in danger of extinction, they turned their efforts to conservation and established conservation organizations to save the species.

Jane Goodall (1934–)

Jane Goodall is a British primatologist known for her long-term study of chimpanzee social behavior and her devotion to conservation. In 1977, she founded the Jane Goodall Institute for Wildlife Research, Education, and Conservation. The institute works to protect chimpanzees and other primates in the wild through education and community-centered support. An important goal of the institute is to reduce wildlife trafficking by providing sanctuaries and enforcing laws.

The Jane Goodall Institute is involved in many community-based programs in nine countries. This community-centered conservation approach involves the local community as stakeholders in their natural resources and conservation of local wildlife. The institute promotes sustainable livelihoods and increased access of education for girls and women. In 1994, Jane and a group of Tanzanian students started the program "Roots and Shoots" to work on local and global service projects. This global environmental program for young people of all ages consists of 150,000 members in over 130 countries.

Jane Goodall was working as a secretary to anthropologist Louis Leakey when he sponsored her to study chimpanzees in Tanzania, Africa. He thought, rightly so as it turned out, that she had the temperament to endure long hours of isolation studying the primates. As a result of her patience, Jane habituated chimpanzees to her presence and obtained new information about their behavior, including the use of tools. She established the Gombe Reserve in 1960 where research is still ongoing today and received her PhD in ethology (animal behavior) from Cambridge University in the United Kingdom in 1965. In that same year, a National Geographic television documentary gave Jane's research international recognition. As a celebrity, she has become a major spokesperson for endangered species with numerous speaking engagements and as an author of over 80 books. Her first book in 1971 titled *In the Shadow of Man* has become a classic.

Dian Fossey (1932–1985)

Dian Fossey was an American zoologist who spent 18 years studying the mountain gorillas. Three years after Dian met Louis Leakey, and at her urging, he hired her to study the mountain gorillas in the Democratic Republic of Congo. Conflict in the country forced her to leave, and in September 1967 she established a small research station in neighboring Rwanda, the Karisoke Research Center. There were about 240 mountain gorillas when Fossey began her studies. The population of mountain gorillas today, although still endangered, has risen to about 880 animals, a testimony to the success of her work and legacy.

Through imitation of gorilla behavior, Fossey was able to habituate some families of gorillas to her presence. She spent thousands of hours of observation and discovered the peacefulness of the species and learned about the tight social structure. Gorillas had the reputation of being ferocious, scary animals. Fossey saw very little aggressive behavior and was able to dispel the myth.

Fossey developed such strong feelings for the gorillas that she began to spend a majority of her time engaged in their protection. Instead of working with the local people, however, she became a vigilante and engaged in conflict with the people who lived in the villages nearby. She systematically destroyed the snares they set for antelope and organized anti-poaching patrols. Her obsession with protecting the gorillas probably led to her murder in her cabin at Karisoke in 1985.

The Dian Fossey Gorilla Fund International, established by Fossey in 1978, continues to study, conserve, and protect gorillas in their natural habitats in Africa. In 1985, the Fund expanded to include protection of the eastern lowland gorillas and other species in the gorillas' habitats, including golden monkeys, amphibians, many plants, and common bird species.

The Fossey Fund works with Rwanda park rangers and local communities to protect the gorillas 365 days of the year. Revenue from tourists who pay about $1,000 each for permits to trek to view the gorillas supports the rangers and provides opportunities for employments for local guides, who lead the tours to view habituated gorilla groups in their natural habitat in the Virunga volcanos area in Rwanda.

Fossey wrote a best-selling book about her experiences with the gorillas in 1983, *Gorillas in the Mist*, which was made into a film starring Sigourney Weaver.

Birute Galdikas (1946–)

Birute Galdikas is a Canadian anthropologist, primatologist, author, and professor at Simon Fraser University in British

Columbia, Canada. She received her PhD in anthropology at UCLA in 1978. In 1971, she traveled to Indonesian Borneo where she established "Camp Leakey" to begin her study of orangutans. Despite difficulty in observing these elusive apes, Galdikas was able to document their social structure as solitary in adult males. Females, however, because of their long birth interval of eight years, keep young with them for extended periods and teach them how to survive in the rainforest.

Similar to Jane Goodall and Dian Fossey, Galdikas soon began to become an active conservationist and founded the Orangutan Foundation International in 1986 to fund research and sponsor tours. Today, activities of the foundation include community projects and rain forest protection. Birute Galdikas lobbied the Indonesian government to set aside parks to curb illegal logging and orangutan trading, and in 1998 the Indonesian government to set aside 76,000 hectares (about 150,000 acres) as an orangutan reserve. Development of palm-oil plantations, however, continues to destroy orangutan habitat in Borneo at an alarming rate.

After arrival in Borneo, Galdikas soon began to take care of young orangutans that had been orphaned by poaching or habitat destruction at Camp Leakey and at her home. The intent was to rehabilitate the young animals and return them to the wild. This conservation effort eventually took most of Galdikas's time. The project was highly controversial. There was serious doubt about how well the captive orangutans would fare in the wild and the danger of spreading disease and competition for food in wild populations. Currently, the Orangutan Foundation and similar organizations in Borneo claim some successes in rehabilitation and reintroduction of young orangutans to the wild.

Dr. Galdikas has written four books. Her biography about her life in Borneo was published in 1996, *Reflections of Eden* (Harcourt Brace & Company).

The Cousteaus: Three Generations of
Marine Conservation

Jacques-Yves Cousteau (1910–1997)

A passionate marine explorer and conservationist, Jacques Cousteau was instrumental in educating the public about the wonders of the ocean. He inspired generations with his quest on his expedition ship, *Calypso*, to study and protect the planet's marine environments.

Jacques Cousteau, born in Saint-André-de-Cubzac, France, on June 11, 1910, is best known for his acclaimed television series *The Undersea World of Jacques Cousteau*. Millions of homes around the world tuned in from 1966 to 1976 to view the exotic undersea explorations of Cousteau and his crew aboard the *Calypso*. Cousteau also made Oscar-winning films, *The Silent World* and *World without Sun*. The films introduced millions of people to the biodiversity of the oceans. Cousteau wrote, in collaboration with his coauthors, more than 50 books that were published in more than a dozen languages. These included *The Cousteau Almanac* (1981), *Jacques Cousteau's Calypso* (1983), *Jacques Cousteau's Amazon Journey* (1984), *and Jacques Cousteau Whales* (1988).

Cousteau saw the pollution that was fouling the oceans, and in the 1960s campaigned to stop the French from underwater dumping of nuclear wastes. He was especially concerned about the killing of whales and intervened personally with heads of state to help generate the necessary numbers for the International Whaling Commission (IWC) to pass a moratorium on commercial whaling in 1986.

The Cousteau Society was founded in 1973 by Jacques Cousteau to help people understand the fragile world of life in the ocean. There are more than 50,000 members today in this nonprofit, environmental group. Projects include investigation of the impacts of noise in the ocean, the oceans as the heart of climate change, defending sharks and rays to restore the balance of the ocean's ecosystems, planting trees on East Island Maururu, and a commitment to preserving the critically endangered vaquita (*Phocoena sinus*), a Gulf of Mexico porpoise and probably the most endangered marine mammal in the world. The Cousteau Society continues its international pressure for a permanent moratorium on commercial whaling.

Jean-Michel Cousteau (1938–)

The oldest son of Jacques Cousteau, Jean-Michel Cousteau has been involved in many different activities to bring the plight of the oceans to public attention. As with other members of the family, he has produced a number of films with topics relating to the ocean. He showed his film *Northwestern Hawaiian Islands* to President George W. Bush and Mrs. Bush to encourage the formation of a preserve. Shortly thereafter Bush created the large marine sanctuary, the Northwestern Hawaiian Islands Marine National Monument, to protect the region and its inhabitants. Cousteau is now working on cleaning the Mississippi River from pollution. Pollution dumped into the river has caused a dead zone in the Gulf of Mexico the size of Massachusetts, where no marine life thrives at all.

Jean-Michel founded the Ocean Futures Society in 1999 to carry on his work. It is a nonprofit marine conservation and education organization that communicates in the media the importance of wise environmental policies governing the sea. As Ocean Future's spokesman, Jean-Michel serves as an impassioned diplomat for the environment.

Philippe Cousteau (1940–1979)

The youngest son of Jacques Cousteau was a documentary filmmaker who specialized in environmental issues. He was an underwater photographer and filmed his father's underwater films. Until his death in 1979, he coproduced numerous documentaries with his father, including *Voyage to the Edge of the World* (1976) and his own PBS series, *Oasis in Space* (1977), concerning environmental issues. He died in an airplane accident at age 38.

Alexandra Cousteau (1976–)

Alexandra Cousteau was born in California to Philippe Cousteau and his American wife, Jan Alexandra. She is a National Geographic Emerging Explorer, filmmaker, and water advocate who promotes water conservation and is concerned about droughts, storms, floods, and degraded water quality. She works to make conservation relevant to people's lives and is currently working on a book that will redefine what it means to live on a planet with interdependent water ecosystems around the world.

Alexandra Cousteau established Blue Legacy International in 2008 to tell the story of the importance of water to the world. Its purpose is to educate and inspire people to take meaningful action on critical water issues and to help shape society's dialogue to include water as one of the defining issues of the century and a critical component of climate change.

Philippe Cousteau Jr. (1979–)

Philippe Cousteau Jr., grandson of Jacques and brother of Alexandra, is an Emmy-nominated TV host, author, and speaker who has established himself as a leader of the environmental movement inspired by his family. With his wife, Ashlan, he produced and hosted the highly rated cable show, *Nuclear Sharks*, for Discovery Channel. He is host and producer of *Awesome Planet*.

In 2000, Philippe Cousteau Jr. founded EarthEcho with his sister Alexandra in honor of their father Philippe. The nonprofit, environmental organization is dedicated to inspiring youth to understand environmental challenges and to act for a sustainable planet. EarthEcho each year sponsors the World Water Monitoring Challenge program to build public awareness and involvement in protecting water resources. Citizens conduct basic monitoring of local watersheds. Approximately, 4.5 million participants in 142 countries monitor 70,927 bodies of water.

Aldo Leopold (1887–1948): The Father of Wildlife Conservation

Aldo Leopold founded the field of wildlife management and ecology and the Wilderness Society. His classic book, *A Sand County Almanac* (1949), is one of the more influential books about the environment ever published. In the book, written in the final year of his life, Leopold summarized the lessons he learned as a conservation scientist, teacher, and farmer. He understood that conservation meant a state of harmony between humans and the land.

Leopold wrote in the *Sand County Almanac* about experiences that formed his thinking about nature. One formative experience occurred when he was a young man in New Mexico in 1924. Accepting the current thinking that wolves should be killed on sight and fewer wolves meant more deer to hunt, Leopold shot an older female wolf. After he watched her die he questioned his actions. He later saw the extirpation of wolves followed by overpopulation of deer that ate every edible bush, tree, and seedling to the ground. He realized that healthy environments require the diversity of all living things, including wolves.

Aldo Leopold's proposal of a "land ethic" was perhaps his greatest contribution to conservation. Ahead of his time, he thought that humans have a moral responsibility to take care of the natural world, instead of abusing the land because it is regarded as a commodity. As a scientist and ecologist, Leopold viewed land (now called an ecosystem) as a system of interdependent parts, the soil-plant-animal food chain, best regarded as a community. Society tends to dismiss the role of the land and to view it only in economic terms. Instead of conquering the land, humans must be part of it. Leopold thought that if humans were to see land as a community to which they belong, they may begin to use it with love and respect. Only ignorant people would say of an animal or plant, "What good is it?"

Aldo Leopold was born in 1887 in Burlington, Iowa, in a home overlooking the Mississippi River. He spent his childhood in the bottomlands where he developed an interest in the natural world. In 1909, he graduated from the Yale School of Forestry and pursued a career in the newly established U.S. Forest Service (1909–1928). He first worked in Arizona and New Mexico territories as one of the first professional foresters in the area. In 1924, Leopold transferred to Madison, Wisconsin, and in 1935 he left the Forest Service when he accepted a new position in game management at the University of Wisconsin. His book *Game Management* (1933), probably the first of its type, defined the skills and techniques for managing and restoring wildlife populations. This was a new science that intertwined forestry, agriculture, ecology, biology, education, and communication. He also became director of the Audubon Society and founded the Wilderness Society.

While working for the Forest Service, in response to the extensive logging he saw, Leopold convinced his bosses in Washington, D.C., to set aside land in its natural state as a wilderness. In 1924, three-quarters of a million acres was set aside in New Mexico and designated as the Gila Wilderness. Forty years later, more wilderness areas were established and the Gila was made official when Congress passed the Wilderness Act in 1964.

In 1935, the Leopold family bought a worn out old farm near Madison, the Wisconsin River farm, and began to restore it. This farm became the setting for many of the essays in *A Sand County Almanac*. Now a National Historic Landmark, the Aldo Leopold Shack and Farm is approximately 264 acres. The property fronts the Wisconsin River and is mostly a floodplain with sandy loam soil. Aldo Leopold reflected on his interactions with the land and how it had enriched his life. He died of a heart attack in 1948 after fighting a grass fire on the neighbor's farm. He was only 61 years old.

The Sand County Foundation is Aldo Leopold's legacy. Established by Aldo Leopold's children, the foundation manages the original Leopold farm. Because farmers, ranchers, and foresters who own and manage private land are important to maintaining a healthy environment, the Sand County Foundation seeks to inspire private landowners to manage the natural resources in their care so future generations can have clean and abundant water and wildlife. Whether on private or public land, new ideas are needed to expand landowner incentives, reduce conflict, and speed the recovery of endangered animals and plants. The foundation sponsors projects to make America's endangered species policy more effective at restoring wildlife through the use of conservation banking and other effective types of habitat offset markets. They encourage the efficient use of federal fund and quicker decision-making based on the best science available.

John Muir and David Brower: Wilderness Warriors
John Muir (1838–1914)

John Muir is known for his poetic essays and books about nature and the environment. He was also one of the earliest advocates and the most eloquent spokesperson of national parks. In *Our National Parks*, in 1901, he wrote: "Climb the mountains and get their good tidings. Nature's peace will flow into you as sunshine flows into trees. The winds will blow their own freshness into you, and the storms their energy, while cares will drop off like autumn leaves." Of all the national parks, Muir is most closely associated with Yosemite, a place he loved and protected. In his 1912 book *Yosemite*, he wrote: "Everybody needs beauty as well as bread, places to play in and pray in, where nature may heal and give strength to body and soul alike."

Born in Dunbar, Scotland, John Muir grew up in the wilderness frontier of Wisconsin after his family immigrated to the United States when he was 11 years old. He studied science, philosophy, and literature at the University of Wisconsin where he was influenced by the writings of Henry David Thoreau and Ralph Waldo Emerson. After he spent a summer in the wilderness hiking down the Wisconsin River, Muir decided he wanted to study botany and explore the natural world. After traveling to South America, Muir arrived in California at the age of 30 in 1868. He visited Yosemite and was so impressed he returned the following year and worked as a shepherd. In a short while he began to work in a sawmill near todays Lower Yosemite Falls trail. While in Yosemite, he studied the flora and fauna and later published a book of his experiences in 1911: *My First Summer in the Sierras.*

Muir began publishing his ecology-oriented articles in the early 1870s, and his first printed essay in the *New York Tribune* in 1871 postulated on his theory that glaciers formed Yosemite Valley, an idea ahead of its time. Throughout the 1870s, Muir's newspaper publications grew. He was a prolific writer and was particularly concerned about the preservation of natural landscapes. He was unafraid of controversy, and in 1876 he published an article about how California's woodlands were being recklessly depleted by logging.

During the 1880s, Muir focused his attention more and more on issues of conservation. He was alarmed at the extensive damage livestock caused to the delicate High Sierra ecosystems in areas surrounding the state-administered Yosemite valley and Mariposa Grove. These areas had been given to the state of California via the Yosemite Grant of 1864. In 1889, he took the editor of *Century Magazine* to the Yosemite area to show him the damage sheep were doing to the land. Muir then published an essay in the magazine that helped generate a bill in the U.S. Congress to create a new federally administered park. Yosemite officially became a national park in 1890, 18 years after the first national park in Yellowstone. A camping trip with President Theodore Roosevelt in 1903 persuaded Roosevelt to return Yosemite valley and the Mariposa Grove to federal protection as part of Yosemite National Park.

Yosemite National Park today includes 748,000 acres with 94.5 percent designated wilderness. Approximately 90 mammals, 150 birds, 12 amphibians, 22 reptiles, and 6 native species of fish reside in the park. Of these, the Sierra Nevada bighorn sheep (*Ovis canadensis sierrae*) and yellow-legged frog (*Rana muscosa*) are federally endangered, and the valley elderberry longhorn beetle (*Desmocerus californicus dimorphus*), California red-legged frog (*Rana draytonii*) and Yosemite toad (*Anaxyrus canorus*) are on the federal threatened list.

Muir was involved in the preservation of several other areas. The vandalism and the carrying away of logs to make items for tourists disturbed Muir when he visited the Petrified Forest in northern Arizona in 1905. In December 1906, at Muir's suggestion, President Teddy Roosevelt created the Petrified Forest National Monument. In 1908, also at Muir's prodding, Roosevelt created Grand Canyon National Monument. Congress later enlarged the monument and created what we know today as Grand Canyon National Park. Muir also pushed for designation of Sequoia National Park in California at about the same time.

Muir's last epic environmental fight lasted from 1908 to 1913. He and the Sierra Club, which he helped establish, fought hard against the proposed construction of a dam in a beautiful glaciated valley in Yosemite National Park called Hetch Hetchy (a name derived from the Miwok tribe of Native Americans to describe a seed). The dam was being built to provide a reservoir of water for the city of San Francisco. The appropriation of a section of a national park for the exclusive use of a city was an unprecedented act, and Muir railed against his opponents, calling them "devotees of raging commercialism." Congress, however, passed the Raker Act allowing the building of the dam, and President Woodrow Wilson signed it in December 1913. The dam was built and water flooded the

Hetch Hetchy valley, thus providing a clean water supply to the city of San Francisco but destroying the valley. Since then citizens inspired by John Muir have stopped proposals to dam national parks and proposed to restore Hetch Hetchy valley from time to time.

David Brower (1912–2000)

David Brower was a passionate environmentalists and conservationists who was considered one of the most influential environmental leaders in the 20th century. He was also an activist and a trailblazer who strived to continue the legacy of John Muir. As the first executive director of the Sierra Club (1952–1969), he transformed the quiet organization of backpackers and hikers into a powerful environmental advocacy group and increased the membership from about 2,000 to 77,000 members.

David Brower grew up in Berkeley, California. As a young man, he explored the Sierra Nevada mountains and Yosemite National Park where he became a world-class climber. He attended the University of California at Berkeley to study entomology but dropped out after two years because of financial problems. He worked in Yosemite for several years, and in 1941 he became editor of the University of California Press and was voted on the board of the Sierra Club. He served in the Tenth Mountain Division in World War II earning a Bronze Star.

As executive director of the Sierra Club, Brower fought many environmental battles. He also moved the organization into the publishing field to create the magnificent photo (coffee table) books that spotlighted the beauty and the dangers faced by America's wilderness. Brower was instrumental in gaining passage of the Wilderness Act of 1964 to protect millions of acres of public lands in pristine condition. He fought to establish 10 new national parks and seashores, including Kings Canyon, the North Cascades, Redwood National Park, and the Point Reyes and Cape Cod national seashores.

Brower led the Sierra Club in fights to stop construction of dams in national monuments and national parks. He successfully led the fight to prevent a dam from being built that would flood Dinosaur National Monument in the Upper Colorado River. When the Bureau of Reclamation offered to move their planned dam to Glen Canyon, the Sierra Club reluctantly agreed not to fight this location. Brower regretted that decision and was instrumental in the Sierra's Club decision to support decommissioning the Glen Canyon Dam and restoration of the Colorado River. In 1996, he joined the board of the Glenn Canyon Institute and worked with the organization until his death to drain Lake Powell Reservoir and restore the Glen Canyon.

Brower led the fight over another dam at another national treasure, the Grand Canyon. It might seem shocking today that the Bureau of Reclamation could ever propose flooding part of this natural wonder. At that time, however, Earth Day was three years off, American environmental awareness was still building, and the Bureau of Reclamation claimed a mandate to build the dam. Under Brower's aggressive leadership, the Sierra Club spent time and money to block the dam, including taking out full page ads in the *New York Times* and *Washington Post*. This action caused suspension of the Club's tax-exempt status. The dam, however, was never built, and Congress enlarged the Grand Canyon National Park in 1975.

Disagreements over the level of activism pressured Brower to leave the Sierra Club in 1969 and form Friends of the Earth, where he served as chairman for over 10 years. At the same time he established the League of Conservation Voters (LCV), a grassroots, political action group that supports candidates who advocate an environmental agenda. The LCV provides factual information about environmental voting records in the U.S. Congress via their National Environmental Scorecard published each year and target candidates who consistently side against the environment on their "dirty dozen" list, irrespective of party affiliation, for defeat in national and state-level elections.

E. O. Wilson (1929–): Champion of Biodiversity and Endangered Species

Edward O. Wilson, professor emeritus at Harvard University, is widely accepted as one of the greatest researchers, theorists and authors of our time. For over 30 years, Dr. Wilson has been a leading voice to alert policy makers and the public to the threats of biodiversity loss and species extinction. He believes that humans are creating a sixth mass extinction, "we are also eliminating species at a very rapid rate. If we continue to utilize and use up the remaining wild environments, as we are doing now, we will lose or push to the point of extinction as many as half of the world's species by the end of this century."

Professor Wilson is an accomplished scientist known in the scientific world as an evolutionary biologist who studies the communication and social organization of ants. He is considered the leading expert on ant ecology and behavior and has published over 400 scientific papers and numerous books on the subject. In 1971, he published a major synthesis of the existing knowledge of the behavior of ants, social bees, social wasps, and termites in *The Insect Societies*. In 1990, he published the definitive work and Pulitzer Prize–winning book, *The Ants*, with Dr. Bert Hölldobler, another Harvard professor, and in 2008 the two teamed up again to write *The Superorganism: The Beauty, Elegance, and Strangeness of Insect Societies*.

E. O. Wilson was born in Birmingham, Alabama, and grew up looking at "bugs" in the countryside around Mobile. He earned his BS and MS degrees at the University of Alabama and a PhD from Harvard University in 1955. As a junior fellow at Harvard's Society of Fellows from 1953 to 1956, he journeyed to many parts of the South Pacific to research ants, and in 1956 he joined the Harvard faculty. His work and his conception of species richness on islands led him to the theory of island biogeography, which he developed with the late Robert H. MacArthur of Princeton University, and publication of the 1967 book *The Theory of Island Biogeography*. The theory greatly influenced the discipline of ecology and became a cornerstone of conservation biology.

E. O. Wilson published his controversial book, *Sociobiology: The New Synthesis* in 1975. It gained him acclaim, recognition, and criticism. Sociobiology is the study of the biological basis of social behavior that evolves through natural selection. The sociobiological theory that evolutionary principles control animal social behavior changed the study of animal behavior. The book was controversial because Wilson proposed that the biological principles on which animal societies are based also apply to humans.

By the late 1970s, Wilson was actively involved in global conservation and the promotion of biodiversity research. Much of his influence was through the publication of several books on biodiversity and its influence on humans and the environment. In 1984 he published *Biophilia*, which explored the evolutionary basis of human's attraction to the natural environment. In 1988 Wilson edited *BioDiversity*, a book based on the proceedings of the first U.S. national conference on biodiversity, leading to the creation of the field of biodiversity studies. In 1992 Wilson published *The Diversity of Life*, which synthesized the principles and most important practical issues of biodiversity. His 2002 work *The Future of Life* has also become influential.

Wilson's latest manifesto for preserving the Earth is in his new book, *Half Earth: Our Planet's Fight for Life*. He argues that the problems created by humanity are global and progressive and the loss of biodiversity is too large to be solved piecemeal. He proposes, therefore, a radical solution to equal the magnitude of the problem. If we commit half the surface of the Earth to nature, there is hope to save the life-forms that compose it. Preserving half the planet's habitat could potentially save 80 percent of species from extinction. The Half-Earth plan does not mean dividing the planet in hemispheric halves. Instead, it stipulates setting aside the largest reserves possible. According to the World Database on Protected Areas, a little less than 15 percent of Earth's land area and 2.8 percent of the ocean have been preserved. Wilson considers this area much too small to halt the acceleration of species extinction.

E. O. Wilson with colleagues and friends launched the Biodiversity Foundation in 2005 as a nonprofit organization that uses education, technology, and business strategies to further the preservation of the world's biodiversity. On June 30, 2014, the foundation issued a new high school biology textbook, *E. O. Wilson's Life on Earth*, as an iBooks textbook consisting of 41 chapters in 7 separate units.

Organizations

Center for Biological Diversity

The Center for Biological Diversity (CBD) is an activist environmental group that works through science and the law to save imperiled species. They actively seek listings for endangered and threatened species under the ESA using biological data, legal expertise, and the "citizen suit" provision of the ESA. The CBD has grown from a regional organization in New Mexico and the southwestern United States to protection of species throughout the Pacific and Atlantic Oceans and international regions such as the North and South Poles.

The CBD began as a grassroots movement in New Mexico in 1990 when three men in their early twenties, Kieran Suckling, Peter Galvin, and Todd Schulke, were surveying owls for the U.S. Forest Service. They discovered the nest of a rare Mexican spotted owl (*Strix occidentalis lucida*) in an old-growth tree that was slated to be cut in a massive timber sale. Although the Forest Service had established rules that 100-acre areas around known owl nests were "no touch" zones, the federal agency planned to continue with the timber sale. The three activists joined forces with Robin Silver, a Phoenix emergency room physician, and others to advocate for an ESA petition to protect the Mexican spotted owl. Their campaign to protect the owl and other species helped to curtail the large-scale logging on public lands in the southwestern United States and to protect 4.6 million acres of forest as critical habitat for the Mexican spotted owl.

A major activity of the CBD is their strategy of lawsuits against the federal government using the ESA. According to a *New York Times* report published in March 2010, the CBD filed 700 lawsuits that were successful 93 percent of the time. Those suits forced the government to list 350 endangered species and designate 120 million acres of critical habitat for their recovery. An important case was the *Center for Biological Diversity v. Kempthorn*, because it highlighted the issue of species endangerment from climate change by pressuring the Interior Department to list the polar bear as a threatened species from global warming. Additional law suits have been filed seeking protection of other species from climate change including the Pacific walrus (*Odobenus rosmarus*) and the mountain-dwelling pika (*Ochotona princeps*).

In other actions, the CBD negotiated a historic settlement with the U.S. Fish and Wildlife Service in July 2011, to make decisions about 757 imperiled plant and animal species that the center thought deserved protection. Many of these species had languished on the FWS Candidate List for years. In 2012, the CBD submitted another petition seeking ESA protection for 53 of the rarest and most sensitive U.S. amphibians and reptile species. The CBD also championed designation of critical habitat for imperiled species, including 120 million acres of protected habitat for the polar bear, the largest critical habitat designation in ESA history. The CBD is ever vigilant to protect the ESA from aggressive attempts by conservative lawmakers to gut the law by supplying supportive science and statistical analysis to policy makers.

Oceans are also an important consideration for the CBD. The center defends marine species and habitats from overfishing and offshore drilling. The Ocean Programs helped halt harmful fishing practices such as set-gill and long line fisheries that drown sea otters, harbor porpoises, sea lions, and seabirds caught in the nets. In 2013, the center won protection for three Florida plant species threatened by rising sea levels. Rising seas increase dangerous storm surges and erode habitats.

The center has launched a series of different media campaigns. They use public service announcements and ads in New York's Times Square on subjects from extinction to unsustainable human population to pesticides. They have a large, diverse group of videos available ranging from vanishing ice in the Arctic to the declining populations of monarch butterflies. Free e-cards are available for Endangered Species Day in May. The CBD also uses social media. On Earth Week, 2016, they launched a campaign to celebrate and protect public lands. The campaign placed the health of public lands, climate, water, and wildlife first before industrialization and land uses that harm species such as off-road vehicle use, livestock grazing, industrial logging, and uranium and fossil fuel extraction.

The CBD uses humor to get their message out. They distributed "Endangered Species Condoms" to raise awareness about overpopulation and unsustainable consumption. Endangered species ringtones of roars, songs, and howls of more than 100 species are available. The center's senior counsel, who coordinates legal and policy work, was outside the 2016 Republican National Convention in a polar bear suit to raise awareness of climate change and the plight of the bears. The CBD presents their annual "Rubber Dodo Award" to a person or organization the membership considers has done the most to destroy wild places, species, and biological diversity. Previous winners include Utah Congressman Bob Bishop (2016), Monsanto (2015), the U.S. Department of Agriculture's Wildlife Services (2014), oil industrialists the Koch brothers (2013), climate change denier James Inhofe (2012), the U.S. Chamber of

Commerce (2011), former CEO of BP Tom Hayward (2010), and former Alaska governor Sarah Palin (2008).

The CBD's main office is in Tucson, Arizona. It has other offices in Alaska, Arizona, California, Florida, Hawaii, Mexico, Minnesota, New York, Oregon, Vermont, Washington, and Washington, D.C.

Conservation International

Conservation International (CI) is one of many international organizations working to preserve biodiversity. They are a non-profit organization with headquarters in Arlington, Virginia, and offices globally. With the support of more than 1,000 employees and 2,000 partners, CI works on thousands of projects in 30 countries. Their mission is to empower human communities to care for nature. They do not focus on one sector or issue and are interested in long-term solutions built on a foundation of science, partnerships, and field work. In addition to protection of places, CI works with governments to ensure policies to promote sustainability.

CI works on a broad spectrum of projects related to climate change, deforestation, global stability, fresh water, and oceans. They have projects in the Amazon, Indonesia, sub-Saharan Africa, the Mekong region in Southeast Asia, and on many of the tropical and semitropical islands and shorelines of the Pacific Ocean. Their work includes field projects, financial assistance, partnering with businesses and governments, and scientific research.

CI strives to prevent climate change by reducing greenhouse gas emissions. They also help communities to adapt to the effects of the changes that are already happening. CI partners with the Blue Carbon Initiative, a coordinated, global program to mitigate climate change through conservation and restoration of mangroves, salt marshes, and seagrasses in coastal environments on every continent except Antarctica. Besides storing large quantities of carbon, mangroves, tidal marshes, and seagrasses are critical for coastal water quality, healthy fisheries, and coastal protection against floods and storms.

Deforestation and forest degradation are occurring at an alarming rate with the loss of nearly half of the world's forests. For nearly 30 years, CI has worked to ensure that forests are protected and used sustainably with the goal of zero net deforestation in Amazonia by 2020. CI strives to make forests more valuable when they are standing than when they are cut. In the Reduced Emissions from Deforestation and Degradation (REDD) program, the sustainable management of forests is part of the solution to climate change. There are also economic incentives. In the Amazonian state of Amapá in Brazil, CI works on a fund to cofinance a biodiversity corridor. In Ecuador, CI offers families and indigenous communities direct economic incentives to conserve their native forests. The Global Conservation Fund (GCF), made possible by substantial grants from U.S. donors, helps to design and support sustainable financing for a steady flow of funds to protected threatened areas.

CI has an extensive network of ocean programs around the world. Through its Seascapes program, governments, businesses, communities, and other stakeholders work together to conserve the diversity and abundance of marine life and promote human well-being. CI is protecting the oceans from overfishing, pollution, and illegal fishing in the Eastern Tropical Pacific region along the coasts of Costa Rica, Panama, Colombia, and Ecuador. CI has directly supported the creation of 573 million acres of protected areas in Indonesia to sustain the health of the about 95 percent of Indonesia's beautiful coral reefs that are threatened.

Conservation International has identified 25 biodiversity "hotspots." These areas are both biologically rich and deeply threatened. They contain more than 1,500 endemic species and have lost more 70 percent of the original habitat.

CI has many suggestions about what an individual can do to help protect the planet: reduce energy consumption, drink sustainable coffee, waste less food, compost food scraps, reject illegal wildlife products, travel sustainably, and support ecotourism.

Defenders of Wildlife

Defenders of Wildlife has a long history of efforts to protect and restore imperiled species throughout North America. A nonprofit, the U.S. conservation organization focuses on wildlife and habitat conservation to safeguard biodiversity in the belief that no species can be protected without simultaneously protecting the habitat on which it relies. In conjunction with biologists, regional experts, local conservation groups, and grassroots activists Defenders aggressively advocates for the protection of endangered and threatened species and imperiled ecosystems.

Defenders of Wildlife is a strong advocate and protector of the ESA. The ESA is the strongest and most important federal law protecting species and everything possible must be done to promote its implementation and to prevent it from being weakened by congressional action. Although Defender's work covers almost all aspects of the ESA, its focus is mostly on recovery planning, habitat conservation, permitting, listing, and conservation tools to prevent listing in the first place.

Defenders works hard to obtain endangered and threatened listings for species and supports the use of incentives to conserve species that are "candidates" for listing under the ESA. When the government fails to do its job under the ESA, Defenders goes to court to act as legal counsel on behalf of North America's wildlife. Through these efforts Defenders has had many successes during the almost 70 years of its existence. Their legal teams work throughout the country at all levels of the federal court system and are based in Washington, D.C., and Denver, Colorado.

Defenders of Wildlife is a persistent protector of imperiled species. For example, Defenders and colleagues have been fighting for over 20 years for federal protection of wolverines, *Gulo gulo* (relatives of otters, weasels, and mink), in the lower 48 states where climate change threatens their future, because the animals require deep, persistent snow to cover their dens to survive the winters. Defenders filed a petition with the FWS in 2000 requesting protection of the wolverine under the ESA. After legal action in 2005 and 2008, the FWS determined that the wolverine warranted protection but was precluded from further action because of higher priorities. In 2013, the FWS finally proposed to protect the wolverine as threatened under the ESA. However, a review by the regional director concluded that wolverines were not threatened by climate change and their population numbers were actually increasing. This conclusion was contrary to scientific evidence that declining wolverine populations numbered no more than about 250 to 300 individuals, and the FWS had no new evidence to support their claims. The denial of protection under the ESA of the wolverine-led Defenders and other conservation groups to challenge this decision and file a federal lawsuit against the FWS to overturn the decision.

In April 2016, the U.S. District Court found for the conservation groups and ordered the FWS to make a new final listing determination to list the wolverine under the ESA. The judge further ruled that the FWS ignored the best available science by dismissing the threat to wolverines and suggested political interference in the FWS decision. The court's decision was a major victory for conservationists who spent 20 years fighting to obtain the listing. In addition, listing the wolverine would show that animals at risk of extinction because of climate change deserve protection that comes with the federal listing.

Defenders of Wildlife works to protect and strengthen the National Wildlife Refuge System, which is the only system in the United States devoted to wildlife conservation and habitat preservation for hundreds of species. Defenders is concerned about the lack of funding and other problems facing the refuges. The Arctic National Wildlife Refuge (ANWR) has been the center of a long-term controversy about whether to open its shores to oil exploration and extraction. Defenders has fought against this action because ANWR is the largest national refuge of pristine habitat and home to polar bears, caribou, musk oxen, and hundreds of migratory birds. Defenders was also involved in protesting a road that would slice through the Izembek National Wildlife Refuge at the tip of the Alaskan Peninsula. The Alaskan congressional delegation proposed the road through this ecologically diverse area of wetlands and mountains and home to diverse wildlife. The Department of Interior denied the request and a federal study upheld the decision.

Defenders believes that climate change is one of the leading threats to wildlife and a huge problem that needs to be addressed on multiple fronts. They support renewable energy to combat climate change. To avoid destruction of important wildlife habitat from construction of renewable energy project on public lands, Defenders worked with the BLM to create the Desert Renewable Energy Conservation Plan. The state of California and the Department of Interior identified 3.8 million acres of land to receive permanent protection from development of renewable energy projects.

Defenders of Wildlife is a strong advocate of wolves and has been a leader in the reintroduction, recovery, and fight to prevent delisting of the gray wolf. Defenders worked with ranchers to pave the way for the reintroductions of wolves in the Western Rockies in 1995 and 1996. For 23 years (1987–2010), Defenders compensated ranchers at fair market value for verified livestock losses caused by wolves in Montana, Idaho, Wyoming, and parts of southern Alberta. Altogether livestock producers received $1.4 million for verified losses until the program ended because compensation failed to sway livestock owners into supporting wolves. Today, Defenders supports and promotes nonlethal control of wolves.

Defenders is involved in projects to save imperiled species all over the United States. In the southeast, the focus is on landscapes in the Greater Everglades, the Florida Panhandle, the Carolina coast, and the southern Appalachians. One primary species for this area is the critically endangered red wolf. Defenders is redoubling efforts to bring the red wolf back from the brink of extinction and to hold the FWS accountable for its recovery. Defenders is collaborating with agency officials to ensure that new plans for national forests and rivers and streams in Appalachia preserve vital habitat for declining and threatened species.

Earth Day

Earth Day on April 22, 1970, is considered the beginning of the modern environmental movement. Inspired by the antiwar movement, the first Earth Day gave voice to a fledging awareness that the planet was becoming unhealthy. Many Americans were oblivious to environmental concerns and accepted dirty rivers and lakes, belching smoke and polluted air, and transportation by huge gas guzzling cars. Some Americans, however, were becoming concerned about the decline of the bald eagle, fires on the highly polluted Cuyahoga River in Ohio, and air pollution in LA and other major cities. It was Earth Day, also called the "National Teach-In on the Crisis of the Environment," that tapped into growing concerns and stimulated a grassroots movement on college campuses and elsewhere leading to major environmental legislation in the decade to follow, including the ESA.

Gaylord Nelson (1916–2005), U.S. senator from Wisconsin, after witnessing the ravages of the 1969 oil spill in Santa Barbara, formulated the idea to have a special day dedicated to the Earth. To make the event bipartisan, Senator Nelson persuaded Pete McCloskey, a conservation-minded Republican representative from California, to serve as cochair. Senator Nelson also appointed environmental activist Denis Hayes, a Stanford graduate, as the first coordinator. At a conference in Seattle in September 1969, Senator Nelson announced that in the spring of 1970 there would be a nationwide, grassroots demonstration on behalf of the environment, and he invited everyone to participate. The project captured media attention, and the wire services carried the story from coast to coast. Denis Hays sent 12,000 letters to universities and high schools and received about 10,000 letters back. Earth Day on April 22 was highly successful with 2,000 colleges and universities, 10,000 high schools, and about 20 million participants gathering in U.S. parks, streets, and auditoriums to learn about and rally for environmental regulation and protection.

Earth Day generated the catalyst necessary to focus members of the U.S. Congress on the environment and passage of environmental legislation. Just three months following Earth Day, President Richard Nixon, recognizing the necessity for marine protection, established the National Oceanic and Atmospheric Administration (NOAA). On October 3, 1970, the Environmental Protection Agency was formed. Soon thereafter Congress passed the Clean Air Act (1970), Clean Water Act (1972), Federal Pesticide Control Act (1972), Marine Mammal Protection Act (1972), and the ESA (1973), all signed by Republican president Richard Nixon.

Earth Day as a global movement now spreads environmental awareness to all corners of the planet. Denis Hayes led the effort to mobilize 200 million people in 141 countries for Earth Day in 1990, the 20th anniversary of the first Earth Day. The day helped generate recycling efforts worldwide and paved the way for the 1992 United National Earth summit in Rio de Janeiro. In 2000, on the 30th Earth Day, concerned citizens came together in person and online to demand clean energy. Earth Day 2000 reached a record 184 countries with 5,000 environmental groups participating. Earth Day campus events in 2009 included youth voter registration projects on college campuses and a call for action on climate change. In 2010, the Washington, D.C.-based Earth Day Network led 225,000 people in a rally at the National Mall for Earth Day's 40th anniversary with the goal to reestablish the day as a launching pad for environmental engagement in the United States. In 2017,

Earth Day supporters joined the March for Science in global marches. In 2020, Earth Day will celebrate its 50th anniversary. As the day approaches plans are made for a global collaboration to broaden the environmental movement worldwide to protect the Earth for future generations.

The Earth Day Network is involved in environmental activism, community engagement, civic involvement, and the green movement. Its varied activities involve voter registration, sustainable development, the planting of millions of trees, green schools, education programs, promotion of women as environmental and economic leaders, green funding of schools, ocean cleanup, and climate change.

Earthjustice

"The earth needs a good lawyer" is the motto of Earthjustice. This large, nonprofit, environmental organization uses legal measures to protect wildlife and their habitats. To these lawyers, the ESA only works when enforced, an action they are committed to doing. These environmental lawyers strive to ensure that the ESA is enforced and allowed to reach its full potential in protection of species in danger of extinction.

Earthjustice was formed as the Sierra Club's Legal Defense Fund in 1971 after a five-year fight to save Mineral King, a beautiful valley in the Sierra Nevada mountains of California, from development of a large ski resort complex by Walt Disney. The case went to the Supreme Court, which ruled in favor of Disney and the U.S. Forest Service. The court ruled that the Sierra Club had no standing to sue. A minority opinion, however, suggested that Mineral King lawyers could obtain standing if they demonstrated how private citizens would have been harmed by the development. The lawyers returned to court and argued harm to their members and private citizens and won the suit. Today, Mineral King is part of the Sequoia and Kings Canyon National Parks. The lawsuit set a precedent securing standing for private citizens to sue for the environment. This precedent became a major legal tool for environmentalists who wanted to mount a legal challenge on behalf of endangered species.

In 1997, the Sierra Club Legal Defense Fund changed its name to Earthjustice to reflect its broader role in representation of diverse organizations besides the Sierra Club. Supported by foundations and individual donors, Earthjustice represents cases for hundreds of clients ranging from municipalities and sporting associations to tribal and environmental groups. They are able to represent these groups because their work is based on supporting the environment, rather than ability to pay.

Earthjustice is involved in many recent cases to protect endangered species and their habitats. On August 18, 2016, Earthjustice filled an injunction under the ESA to prevent the U.S. Army Corp of Engineers from dredging Port Everglades in Fort Lauderdale, Florida. The Corp previously had dredged the port of Miami to result in widespread destruction to endangered coral and the habitat. In another case, Earthjustice challenged the Navy's use of mid-range sonar off the coasts of southern California and Hawaii. Scientific studies documented a connection between high-intensity, mid-frequency sounds and harm to marine mammals ranging from stranding and deaths to cessation of feeding and habitat avoidance and abandonment. The Navy agreed to a settlement to reduce their activities, including a prohibition from using mid-frequency sonar in whale habitats.

Earthjustice works to protect endangered fish species. In May 2016, the lawyers won a victory after a 20-year fight to protect and restore salmon to the Columbia and Snake Rivers. The judge invalidated the government's inadequate plan for the Columbia basin and ordered the government to give serious consideration to removing the four dams on the lower Snake River that are responsible for devastating salmon populations. In another case, Earthjustice represented Oceana, an environmental organization, in a suit against the National Marine Fishery Services to end overfishing of dusky sharks

(*Carcharhinus obscurus*) in U.S. waters. Populations of the shark have fallen by about 85 percent as a result of overfishing and incidental captures of fish. An agreement was reached in May 2016, for the Fisheries Services to develop new rules to address shark conservation. Earthjustice and Oceana continue to work to ensure strong and effective rules in rebuilding the dusky shark population to a healthy level.

Earthjustice advocates for strong forest protection and preservation of roadless areas. In 2012, Earthjustice led a campaign to protect more than 50 million acres of wild, roadless lands saved by a Clinton-era roadless rule. Earthjustice defended the lands from a torrent of legal challenges and attempts to dismantle the protections. Their landmark victories preserved the wildlife and plant species in a vast amount of land for future generations to enjoy.

Earthjustice often represents conservation groups who sue the U.S. Fish and Wildlife Service (FWS) for denying ESA protection to imperiled species. For instance, Earthjustice filed a lawsuit against the FWS for reversing its decision to list the wolverine as threatened under the ESA. In April 2016, the judge ruled for the conservationists and ordered the FWS to reconsider the wolverine for ESA listing. (In the lower 48 states, there are believed to be only about 300 wolverines left.)

In another example, two flowering plants, the Graham's (*Penstemon grahamii*) and White river beardtongue (*Penstemon scariosus albifluvis*), are found only in a limited habitat of oil shale in Utah and Colorado. Threatened by oil and gas development, the two species had been waiting for listing under the ESA since 1973 and 1985 respectively. In 2014, the FWS reversed course and withheld protection based on the claim that threats to the species were ameliorated by a last-minute, voluntary "conservation agreement" between the FWS, the Bureau of Land Management, and several state and county agencies with active roles in energy development. On

October 25, 2016, a federal court ruled in favor of the ESA listing because the FWS agreement did not use the best available science required by the ESA. In the Arctic, Earthjustice is working to keep the fragile Arctic Ocean free from drilling for oil and gas. They challenged the FWS for allowing oil company activities in walrus foraging areas and incidental "take" of walrus.

Earthjustice has been actively involved in issues pertaining to protection and recovery of wolves. The lawyers gained a recent court settlement that directed the FWS to complete a recovery plan for the Mexican gray wolf with the goal to build a sustainable wild population across its range in the southwestern United States. With only 97 wolves in the wild, it is one of the most endangered mammals in North America. Earthjustice is also battling efforts in Congress to abolish, via "riders" to spending bills, endangered species protection for gray wolves in Wyoming and in the upper Midwest states.

Endangered Species Coalition

The Endangered Species Coalition's (ESC) mission is to protect endangered species and the ESA. It is an umbrella organization consisting of a national network of hundreds of environmental, scientific, outdoor, business, religious, and community organizations dedicated to the protection of endangered species and their habitats.

The ESC was founded in 1982 by a consortium of individuals from national environmental groups who wanted to form an organization to protect and ensure effective implementation of the ESA. The ESC, therefore, is a grassroots movement that involves people in issues relating to biodiversity and species extinctions through outreach and education. The ESC is also committed to working with member groups to support policy decisions, educational information, and decisions about which species deserve ESA listing using the best scientific information available. A Scientific Advisory Committee comprised of distinguished and experienced professionals is available for consultation and participates in selection of species for the yearly Top 10 report.

The ESC has released a Top 10 report for the past nine years to the public and policy makers to educate them about pressing conservation issues and the state of the nation's endangered species. The yearly Top 10 report features different topics ranging from climate change ("It's Getting Hot Out There," 2010) to connectivity ("No Room to Roam," 2015). The reports focus on 10, primarily U.S., endangered species that are linked with one another by a common theme. This annual report has proven especially successful at framing issues in the media, and it frequently attracts attention from state and federal lawmakers. ESC partner organizations use the report to highlight the work they do on specific species across the country. These reports also act as a springboard for an ESC campaign, such as the "Vanishing Species Campaign" in 2014. This campaign highlighted species that may go extinct and was titled "Vanishing: Ten American Species Our Children May Never See." The goal of the Vanishing campaign was to educate, inspire, and engage the next generation of students, their families, and their communities about the importance of fighting to protect the ESA and America's biodiversity.

The ESC sponsors Endangered Species Day each year on the third Friday of May. First proclaimed by the U.S. Congress in 2006, Endangered Species Day has celebrated the nation's wild places and wildlife and highlighted the plight of at-risk and endangered species. The day provides an opportunity, especially for young people, to learn about protecting endangered species and the progress made to protect wildlife since passage of the ESA in 1973. Initiated by the ESC, the celebration has grown to partner with the U.S. Fish and Wildlife Service, NOAA and the National Wildlife Federation. Also participating are the National Park Service and U.S. Forest Service. Numerous conservation, education, community, and youth organizations support Endangered Species Day, including the Girl Scouts, the Association of Zoos and Aquariums, the North American Association for Environmental Education, Sierra Club, the National Association of Biology Teachers, the National Science Teachers Association, Center for Biological Diversity, Jane Goodall Institute, National Audubon Society, and Defenders of Wildlife.

Endangered Species Day is observed nationally at zoos, parks, gardens, wildlife refuges, museums, schools, universities, libraries, and community centers. The day has also begun to be observed internationally in Australia, England, Canada, Costa Rica, Ireland, Peru, and others. Specific international issues that endanger wildlife and must be addressed include wildlife trafficking, poaching, and habitat destruction.

The Saving Endangered Species Coalition Youth Art Contest is one of the more popular elements of Endangered Species Day. Each year students from K-12 submit their artwork highlighting endangered and threatened species. The winner is selected by a panel of judges consisting of artists, photographers, and conservationists who select a winner from many submissions. The grand prize-winner and one guardian receive a round-trip flight to Washington, D.C., and accommodations chosen by the ESC to attend a rewards ceremony. The grand prize-winner will also receive an art lesson from a professional wildlife artist (in person or via Skype) and $50 worth of art supplies. Each of the grade-level winners receives a plaque and art supplies.

Wildlife Voices is an initiative of the ESC to feature a cross section of individuals and organizations that cherish wildlife and are concerned about their declining populations. These people are scientists, farmers, ranchers, from the military, religious, business owners and fishermen. Their diverse voices support safeguarding wildlife, and they value open spaces and diversity. They do their best to live their lives to preserve the natural heritage of this country to pass on to their children and grandchildren. The *Wildlife Voices* provides an opportunity for these Americans to tell why they are passionate about maintaining wildlife and the economic benefits that come from them.

Greenpeace

Greenpeace is an activist environmental organization that can be confrontational at times with peaceful protests, nonviolent confrontations, and communication to expose governments and corporations that abuse environmental laws. Greenpeace accepts no donations from corporations or governments and is supported by individuals and grants from foundations. The organization claims 2.8 million supporters and operates in 55 countries. There are about 250,000 members in the United States.

In 1971, a group of scientists, volunteers, and journalists sailed a small boat into an area in northern Alaska to protest U.S. nuclear testing. Shortly thereafter the group decided to organize officially and call themselves "Greenpeace." Today Greenpeace uses a fleet of ships to sail into remote areas of the world to take action against environmental destruction. The first ship in the fleet is the *Rainbow Warrior*, named from a North American Cree Indian legend. The *Arctic Sunrise* is a keel-less boat used to navigate icy seas to document the effects of climate change in the Arctic and to monitor marine pollution from oil. The third and newest ship, the *Esperanza*, has been used in the southern oceans to stop Japanese attempts to pursue its "scientific" whaling.

Greenpeace pursues several goals to change attitudes and to protect and conserve the environment. These goals include addressing climate change, defending oceans, protecting the world's ancient forests, providing safer alternatives to toxic chemicals, rejecting genetically engineered organisms, protecting biodiversity, and encouraging responsible farming. Greenpeace uses research, lobbying, and quiet diplomacy to pursue its goals, as well as their better known high-profile, nonviolent conflict to raise the level and quality of public debate.

Greenpeace volunteers and staff are engaged in a high-energy campaign to stop global warming. They actively expose polluters, lobbyists, and politicians who deny climate change and block environmental regulations. A 100 percent renewable energy future is part of Greenpeace's vision. Oil, coal, and gas must remain in the ground. In view of the number of oil spills and other disasters as well as global warming, Greenpeace promotes a ban on all new drilling as the only way to avoid another oil disaster.

Zero deforestation by 2020 is an important goal of Greenpeace to protect and save what remains of the existing 20 percent of the world's forests. To achieve the goal, industries must change their destructive practices and inspire consumers to demand sustainable products. For instance, Greenpeace has worked hard to push for sustainable palm oil production, because the palm oil industry is a leading cause of deforestation and peatland destruction in Indonesia and Malaysia. Indonesia has lost 31 million hectares of forest, an area the size of Germany, since 1990 to impact endangered orangutan populations among other animals. With pressure from Greenpeace supporters, corporate giants like Nestlé and Unilever are changing to sustainable palm oil sources to help protect Indonesia's rainforests and peatlands.

Greenpeace actively protects the oceans and encourages sustainable fishing and the formation of marine sanctuaries. Greenpeace was involved in the establishment of the world's largest ocean sanctuary (roughly the size of three states of Texas) in the Ross Sea off the coast of Antarctica in October 2016. This was shortly after President Barack Obama made history by establishing the National Marine Monument in the Pacific Ocean near Hawaii and the first National Marine Monument in the Atlantic Ocean. Although these sanctuaries are an important step to preservation of the vital biodiversity of the oceans, there is much more to be done to accomplish the goal of protecting 30 percent of the ocean by 2030. President

Trump, however, has signed an executive order to reevaluate these areas for new oil leases.

Greenpeace works on scores of international projects in different countries ranging from stopping coal mining and dam construction to uncovering and protesting logging. For example, after a two-year investigation Greenpeace uncovered that 3,200 acres of pristine natural forest in the Sichuan Giant Panda Sanctuaries had been illegally clear cut. Greenpeace demanded that the Chinese government issue new regulations to protect the pandas. Working with local people, Greenpeace protested a decision by the Indian government to commission new coal mines in ancient forests of the Mahan region. Greenpeace argued that the filthy process of mining coal would destroy acres of forest and displace thousands who lived in the area. The Indian government viewed Greenpeace's actions as too aggressive and sent in state auditors to inspect the books. Banks froze Greenpeace funds, and travel of Greenpeace employees and volunteers was restricted. The courts cleared travel and overturned the bank block, and the Indian government agreed to cancel the new coal mine. Despite this victory, there are other areas of the forest that still lack protection.

Some environmental groups and governments view Greenpeace as too radical because of its practice of extreme protests. On the other hand, Greenpeace is preferred by others because it is one of the only environmental organizations to engage in active protests. As part of its protests Greenpeace has blocked Japanese whaling ships and chained members to oil rigs to prevent drilling in the Arctic. In August 2015, Greenpeace activists hung from a bridge in Portland, Oregon, to block a Shell Oil ship from heading to the Arctic to drill. Police removed the protesters and the ship proceeded on its way (Shell Oil withdrew from the Arctic after realizing the hazards of trying to explore and drill for oil in the harsh environment.) During a protest against the Russian state-owned oil company, Gazprom, in September 2013, the ship *Arctic Sunrise* was boarded by Russian armed troops and 30 activists and journalists were detained and threatened with long jail sentences. The Russians eventually released the protestors and dropped charges. A permanent court of arbitration found that the Netherlands is entitled to compensation with interest for material damages to the *Arctic Sunrise*.

National Audubon Society

The National Audubon Society is a nonprofit, environmental organization known for its dedication to the conservation of birds. The organization consists of 41 Audubon centers and nearly 500 local chapters that engage in grassroots conservation actions ranging from protection of vital bird habitat to engagement in plans and actions to educate lawmakers, agencies, and the public to shape and support conservation policies.

The organization originated at end of the 19th century from concern about the decline of shorebirds from the plume trade. Two Boston society women, Harriet Hemenway and Minna Hall, began to host afternoon teas to convince women to stop wearing hats with bird feathers. These meetings culminated in the founding of the Massachusetts Audubon Society in 1896. They named the organization in honor of John James Audubon (1785–1851), who as a naturalist painted, cataloged, and described the birds of North America in his famous book *Birds of America* published in sections between 1827 and 1838. Other states soon began to form their own Audubon societies, and in 1905 the National Association of Audubon Societies was incorporated in New York. In 1940 it became the National Audubon Society.

The National Audubon Society was an important factor in the passage of one of the strongest laws protecting North American birds, the Migratory Bird Treaty Act (MBTA), signed into law by President Woodrow Wilson in 1918. This act makes it illegal for anyone to take, possess, import, export, sell, purchase, or barter any migratory bird without a federal permit. Shortly after passage of the MBTA, the Audubon Society began the first of is large-scale, scientifically based conservation efforts when it established its first system of water bird sanctuaries in seven states along the eastern coast of the United States. Today, the Audubon Society is pushing to strengthen the MBTA to address 21st-century threats that kill birds including, oil pits, power lines, communication towers, wind turbines, natural gas flares, and other deadly hazards that kill millions of birds each year.

The Audubon Society is known for its incorporation of "citizen scientists" into the collection of data. The annual Christmas Bird Count has taken place every year for over a century. On Christmas day 1900 the tradition was born when 27 bird counters set out to document the birds in locations that ranged from Toronto, Ontario, to Pacific Grove, California. Today Audubon researchers, conservation biologists, wildlife agencies, and other interested individuals use the data to study the long-term health and status of bird populations across North America. Combined with the Breeding Bird Survey, a picture of how the continent's bird populations have changed in time and space over the past hundred years can be developed. The Coastal Bird Survey, established in response to the BP oil spill and used to survey oiled birds, provides data for addressing conservation needs of coastal water birds that breed, winter, and migrate along the Gulf Coast.

Since its inception, the Audubon society has expanded and grown into a multipurpose conservation organization. No longer only a group for bird watchers, their 2016–2020 Strategic Plan includes protection of coastal habitats, promotion of policy changes on climate change at the local, state, and federal levels, protection of birds on private property through collaboration with landowners, collaboration with local partners to craft water policy to restore habitats on rivers, wetlands and deltas, and coordination with local partners to create bird-friendly spaces. Audubon is involved in recovery efforts for the California condor (*Gymnogyps californianus*) and brown pelican (*Pelecanus occidentalis*), continuation of restoration of the Everglades and Long Island Sound, and green energy development.

Coastal stewardship is a priority for the Audubon Society. Their Coast's Initiative focuses on the 16 most threatened bird species that rely on coastal habitats for breeding, stopover, and wintering along North American coasts. The goal is to stabilize and enhance the populations of these species while simultaneously benefiting at least 375 other species that rely on similar habitats. The Audubon Society has also joined other conservation groups in fighting for permanent protection of the coastal plain of the ANWR. ANWR is one of the most intact ecosystems in America and home to over 200 species of birds, 42 species of fish, and 45 mammal species. This pristine area has been under threat to oil and gas drilling almost since its establishment as a refuge by President Dwight Eisenhower in 1960. The risk to the wildlife from advocates of oil drilling will continue to occur until the area is given permanent wilderness protection. As an alternative to oil extraction for energy, Audubon promotes solutions to the country's energy problems through raising fuel-efficiency standards, energy conservation, and responsible development of renewable-energy sources.

The Audubon Society has made a strong commitment to support efforts to curb greenhouse gases to curtail climate change. In 2014, Audubon scientists published a seven-year, groundbreaking study, *Audubon Birds and Climate Change Report*, that revealed dozens of avian species across the country could be heading for extinction by 2080. Based on hundreds of thousands of citizen-science observations and sophisticated climate models, the reports illustrate that the future of birds in a warming world is not good. Of 588 species studied, 314 are likely to be in serious trouble. The report provides range maps that show the climate conditions a bird needs to survive in three future times, 2020, 2050 and 2080. These "climate" ranges indicate where the bird species may find suitable climate conditions for each time period. Audubon scientists will continue to identify priorities for conservation and the places that are critical for birds as the climate changes.

The National Audubon Society is known for its field guides to birds. Its *Field Guide to North American Birds* receives high ratings and is used by many birders and naturalists who enjoy birding. Audubon now publishes guides to mammals, butterflies, wild flowers, fishes, trees, reptiles and amphibians, insects and spiders. The Audubon bird guide app offers a mobile field guide to identify 821 species of birds.

Natural Resource Defense Council

Science is the foundation of the Natural Resource Defense Council's (NRDC) work to understand and solve environmental problems. A group of law students and attorneys founded the NRDC in 1970 as a New York-based, nonprofit organization that uses law and science to protect wildlife and wild places. The NRDC has the support of over two million members and the expertise of 500 scientists.

More than 60 scientists work at the NRDC, and every program has one or more staff scientist. The NRDC Science Center supports scientific research and collaborates with scientists at universities and research labs and other institutions. Staffed by experts in environmental science, public health, and science communication, the NRDC advances science-based environmental policies in government, courts, and communities. The Science Center manages independent peer review of NRDC's publications to ensure scientific accuracy of all material.

The NRDC is committed to protecting wildlife and the ESA. They successfully led the fight to add animals and plants to the Endangered Species List and are engaged in stopping threats and securing long-term protections of imperiled wildlife. They defend vulnerable wildlife in court and were litigants in the decision to restore federal ESA protection to the gray wolf in the Northern Rockies in 2010. Its lawsuits have forced the U.S. Navy to limit sonar testing that harms and kills whales.

A priority of the NRDC is the protection of keystone species (species other species depend on in an ecosystem). The NRDC vigorously advocates for science-based management of wolves and grizzly bears and takes the government to court when necessary. NRDC is also working to protect iconic species from energy development. For example, oil and gas wells, wind farms, and other energy projects continue to chisel away at habitat of the greater sage grouse. The NRDC supports comprehensive recovery plans for the bird at the state and national levels.

The U.S. Department of Agriculture's Wildlife Services practice of killing and poisoning predators as a subsidy to the livestock industry is strongly opposed by the NRDC. For instance, the NRDC sued California's Mendocino County for a contract with Wildlife Services that killed 459 animals in a single year without examining the science of how wildlife and ecosystems would be affected. The NRDC also promotes alternatives. They work with ranchers, commissioners, legislators, state and federal officials, and citizens to implement nonlethal strategies to prevent conflicts between predators and livestock.

The NRDC has joined Greenpeace and other environmental groups to stop commercial whaling. They push for diplomatic sanctions and international rulings against Japan and Iceland and support a campaign to pressure U.S. companies to stop doing business with companies that benefit from killing whales. NRDC research shows that many U.S. companies buy from seafood firms that have ties to the whaling industry. The NRDC also supports bringing Japan to the United Nations International Court of Justice. In 2014, the court ruled that Japan's whaling was illegal, but in 2015 Japan was back in the ocean killing whales, and Iceland also continues to hunt and kill whales.

NRDC works to end destructive fishing practices that leave many aquatic species severely depleted and some on the brink of extinction. Scientists estimate that the world's large ocean fish, including tuna and swordfish, have declined by up to 90 percent from preindustrial levels. The NRDC, therefore, strives to end overfishing, to rebuild depleted fisheries, and promote the long-term sustainability of fisheries through catch limits based on scientific evidence. Based in part on the NRDC's scientific data, the United States became the first nation in the world to set science-based catch limits for all of its managed species.

NRDC works with government agencies, local communities, and businesses to develop practical strategies for keeping U.S. rivers and lakes healthy while providing adequate water supplies for growing populations and economies. In California, the NRDC led a broad coalition of conservation and fishing groups that won an 18-year battle to restore water and salmon to the San Joaquin River. On the East Coast, NRDC negotiated a commitment from New York City to clean up Jamaica Bay. In Alaska, the NRDC worked with a coalition of conservation groups, fishermen, and business owners to prevent construction of a large hydroelectric dam on the pristine Susitna River, home to chinook and sockeye salmon, caribou, moose, bald eagles, and bears. The NRDC has helped preserve migration routes for grizzly bears and other species, and in partnerships with ranchers, farmers, and business owners promoted ways for livestock to coexist with wolves, coyotes, and other wild predators.

The NRDC has an active climate change program that advocates cutting carbon pollution and expanding clean, renewable energy. Renewable energy development, however, must have the lowest possible environmental risks and impact on wildlife. There must be smart development of wind and solar power projects that avoid pristine landscapes and wildlife corridors. The NRDC helps direct projects away from sensitive habitat and toward lands that have already been used by agriculture, grazing, or mining. They help the Bureau of Land Management and other federal agencies in long-term planning for renewable energy development and transmission.

The NRDC helped to secure the first ever U.S. limits on carbon pollution from power plants and pushes a movement to go beyond dirty fuels. The organization calls for permanent protection of the Arctic from oil companies wanting to drill near polar bear habitat, whale-migration routes, and deep water corals. The unstable and unpredictable weather and sea ice conditions make drilling in the Arctic dangerous. An oil spill in the area would prove almost impossible to clean up. Congress has failed to strengthen any safety standards for offshore drilling since the 2010 BP Deepwater Horizon disaster in the Gulf of Mexico. The NRDC has taken energy companies to court and pushed for stronger state and national regulations and challenged permits by Shell Oil to drill in the Arctic.

Tar sands development is considered by the NRDC as a destructive activity that causes the environment unjustified costs. The organization, therefore has partnered with scientists, financial advisors, and First Nations to stop the expansion of tar sand development. They were one of the first groups to bring attention to the destructive power of tar sands oil and the extraction that causes strip-mining and destruction of the wild Boreal forest in Canada. Besides preventing habitat loss for wildlife, keeping the Boreal forest intact is important to fight climate change. The forest holds at least 22 percent of the Earth's land-based carbon. The NRDC also opposes tankers and pipelines carrying tar sand oil.

National Wildlife Federation

In 1936 at the height of the Great Depression a group of hunters, anglers, and conservationists met in Washington, D.C., at the invitation of President Franklin Roosevelt for the first American wildlife conference. They formed the General Wildlife Federation (later changed to National Wildlife Federation) with the idea of uniting anyone with a stake in wildlife behind a common goal of conservation. Jay Norwood "Ding" Darling (1876–1962), a well-known conservationist at the time, became the first president.

"Ding" Darling was born in Norwood, Michigan, and spent most of his youth in Sioux City, Iowa. He graduated from Beloit in Wisconsin and accepted a position as a journalist with the *Sioux City Journal*. His area of expertise was as a cartoonist, and by 1917 his cartoons were syndicated across the country through the New York *Herold Tribune*. Darling twice won the Pulitzer Prize for his cartoons, in 1923 and again in 1942. He used his satire to promote issues of conservation and to bring national attention to environmental concerns. Most important to Darling, an avid waterfowl hunter, were issues of wildlife exploitation and the destruction of irreplaceable waterfowl habitat. President Roosevelt appointed Darling as head of the U.S. Biological Survey (precursor to the U.S. Fish and Wildlife Service). The Duck Stamp Act of 1934 was developed and Darling himself designed the first stamp. Hunters were required to purchase a stamp before they could hunt legally. The revenue from the purchases went to support wildlife habitat.

The NWF was founded during the Great Depression when bad farming practices and drought had turned part of the midwestern United States into a dust bowl. President Roosevelt established the Civilian Conservation Corp (CCC) (1933–1942) to put Americans to work on projects that had environmental benefits. The CCC employees fought forest fires, planted trees, built trails and bridges, reseeded lands, implemented soil-erosion controls, and stocked fish. The Corp was disbanded in 1942 to redirect its funds to the war effort.

The NWF believes that wildlife belongs to the people. Today, the mission of the NWF is to unite all Americans to ensure wildlife will thrive in a rapidly changing world of global warming, loss of habitat, and the disconnection of people from nature. To accomplish their mission, the NWF works to help implement federal and state policies that will improve wildlife conservation on public, tribal, and private lands. The organization encourages Congress to pass legislation that includes adequate funding for natural resources. The NWF directs federal agencies to include climate science in their wildlife management programs.

Endangered species are a priority for the NWF. They actively advocate for them and participate in Endangered Species Day with numerous events. The NWF is concerned about invasive species and works to solve the problem by advocating for new legislation to strengthen federal policy on the importation of invasive species. Connectivity is another issue for the NWF, and they believe strongly in the establishment of wildlife corridors to solve the problem of fragmented habitats and road kills. They are working to provide pathways so that wildlife can cross into habitats safely by creating underpasses, bridges, and culvert for safe crossing.

The NWF is a founding member of the Teaming with Wildlife Coalition consisting of more than 6,300 members who support increased public funding for wildlife conservation and related education. The coalition includes state fish and wildlife agencies, wildlife biologists, hunters and anglers, bird watchers, hikers, and nature-based businesses. The goal is to help state wildlife agencies obtain the funding they need to implement their action plans. The NWF and the Teaming with Wildlife Coalition pressured Congress to invest in wildlife habitats by creating the State Wildlife Grants Program to provide federal money to all states and six territories for implementation of state action plans to prevent wildlife from becoming endangered.

In agreement with many other environmental organizations, the NWF considers climate change the greatest existing threat to American wildlife. They are working to reduce greenhouse gas emissions by promoting clean energy in the United States and internationally by reduction of deforestation. The NWF works with the states to incorporate climate change into their action plans, and they are currently assessing the vulnerability to climate change in four states: New York, Vermont, Virginia, and Washington. After the assessment, states can update their wildlife plans to better protect wildlife and habitats from the effects of climate change.

The NWF is involved in several restoration activities. They are working to return free-ranging bison to their native habitats on the 1.1 million acre Charles M. Russell National Wildlife Refuge and on tribal lands. The NWF is helping with the restoration of the red wolf in North Carolina and is part of the consortium to save the greater sage-grouse.

Education has always been a priority for the NWF. They connect with kids through the popular *Ranger Rick* magazine and numerous outdoor programs. Work with teachers and youth organizations helps to develop lessons plans, curriculum, and resources for connecting to kids. NWF offers an ongoing series of webinars, nature play spaces, and other tools to help kids connect with nature.

Sierra Club

John Muir (1838–1914) with a group of 182 volunteers founded the Sierra Club in 1882 and acted as president for 24 years until his death. Because many of the Sierra Club's charter members were scientists, scientific exploration was vigorously pursued by the organization. On May 28, 1892, in its newly obtained office in San Francisco, the Sierra Club became incorporated with three stated purposes: (1) "to explore, enjoy, and render accessible the mountain regions of the Pacific Coast; (2) to publish authentic information concerning them"; and (3) "to enlist the support and cooperation of the people and government in preserving the forests and other natural features of the Sierra Nevada."

For the next several decades, the Sierra Club mainly concentrated on sponsored wilderness and outdoor recreational activities consisting of mountain climbing, backpacking, and camping. The club also sponsored educational events, public addresses, and scientific meetings. Under the leadership of

John Muir, Yosemite's boundaries were kept intact and areas managed by the state were moved into the national park. In 1940, the Sierra Club was instrumental in the creation of Kings Canyon National Park.

By the 1950s, David Brower and others began to challenge the philosophy of the Sierra Club as they witnessed the burden wilderness travel was having on some area. At their encouragement, the statement of purpose was changed from "to explore, enjoy and render accessible" to "explore, enjoy and preserve." Individual outings grew smaller and extended beyond California to areas of conservation interest.

The Sierra Club has grown into one of the largest and more active advocate of the environment and has waged many campaigns to protect and preserve millions of acres of wild national forests, deserts, and rivers. In 1951, the club began a successful fight to protect Dinosaur National Monument from two dams, and it successfully campaigned from 1963 to 1968 to keep dams out of the Grand Canyon National Park. The club campaigned to set aside millions of acres in Alaska and to establish a wilderness review program for the Bureau of Land Management's 341 million acres. Several wilderness areas and national parks and monuments have been established with support of the Sierra Club: the North Cascades National Park and Alpine Lakes wilderness in Washington State, the Big Thicket Preserve in Texas, Big Cypress Preserve in Florida, additions to Grand Canyon and Redwood National Parks, addition of Mineral King to Sequoia National Park in California, Escalante Grand Staircase National Monument in Utah, Tongas National Forest in Alaska, and Mojave desert wilderness in southern Nevada.

The Sierra Club first published the *Sierra Club Bulletin* in 1893, which continues today as *Sierra* magazine. The publication included reports of Sierra Club sponsored excursions, guides to geography, and scientific papers on natural history. The Sierra Club is an activist organization that supports the ESA and has been involved in many environmental fights and policy decisions over the past 125 year. They have been involved in protection of millions of acres of wilderness and passage of the Clean Air Act, Clean Water Act, and ESA. Recently, the Club promotes moving away from dirty fossil fuels that cause climate disruption and toward clean energy. There are 2.4 million members and supporters of the Sierra Club with 64 local chapters.

Today, the Sierra Club continues its legacy of protecting America's beautiful wildlands. They view healthy forests more important than ever as sources of clean water, wildlife habitats, and recreation. They envision a world of 100 percent clean energy through their "Beyond Dirty Fuels Campaign," and advocate fossil fuels kept in the ground through protection of public lands and marine resources from destructive mining and drilling.

The Nature Conservancy

The Nature Conservancy (TNC) is unique among environmental organizations because its primary purpose is to buy land for preservation of biodiversity. With the mission of "conserve the lands and waters on which all life depends," the TNC has spent the past 64 years preserving habitat through the direct acquisition of private lands via land trusts, conservation easements, formation of private reserves, and incentives. The conservancy has helped protect approximately 21 million acres in the United States and more than 103 million acres globally.

For the purpose of pursuing conservation, a small group of scientists formed the Ecologists Union within the Ecological Society of America in 1946. They changed the name to Nature Conservancy in 1950 and incorporated it as a separate, nonprofit organization in the District of Columbia in 1951. The organization grew quickly with local chapters in New York State and then across the rest of the United States. Membership reached one million members in 1999.

In 1955, TNC provided a loan of $7,500 for its first land acquisition of 60 acres along the Mianus River Gorge on the New York-Connecticut border. The loan was to be repaid for use in other conservation efforts. This revolving loan fund resulted in the Land Preservation Fund that is still the organization's foremost conservation tool today.

In 1961, TNC received its first conservation easement in which the landowner retains title to an ecologically valuable property while giving the conservancy the right to enforce restrictions on certain types of harmful activities. In 1966, TNC embarked on the strategy of purchasing private lands and then selling them to the government, thus freeing up money to purchase additional land.

In recent years, TNC has launched its conservation buyers project. Private, conservation-minded individuals who are interested in acquiring and protecting ecologically valuable lands can work with TNC to acquire the land. TNC identifies and purchases the properties and then markets them to buyers who agree to place a conservation easement on the land. A conservation easement permits private land use, such as farming, ranching, and timber harvesting. The agreement may require the landowner to protect land and water resources and to refrain from developing or subdividing the land.

TNC launched its International Conservation Program in 1980 to identify natural areas and conservation organizations in Latin America. The first "debt-for-nature" swap occurred in 1988 with the purchase of $240,000 of Costa Rican debt to support conservation in the Braulio Carrillo National Park. The conservancy began its African program in 2006.

TNC has had many notable and important projects in the United States. The almost total disappearance of tall grass prairie in the midwest from being plowed under for agriculture led TNC to purchase a 32,000-acre ranch in Oklahoma's Osage Hills to establish the Tall Grass Prairie Preserve in 2000. The purchase required a huge restoration effort to reintroduce native grasses, bison, and fire into the ecosystem. In 2003, TNC and the National Park Service jointly purchased the 116,000-acre Kahuku Ranch for addition to Hawaii Volcanos National Park, increasing its size by 50 percent. After working a decade, TNC completed the last real estate transaction for protection of the 151-square mile Baca Ranch in Colorado, later made into the Great Sand Dunes National Park.

TNC works to acquire conservation easements on ranches to prevent them from being subdivided. In 1990, TNC spent $18 million to purchase the 502-square mile Gray Ranch (now called the Diamond Ranch) tucked into the southeastern corner of New Mexico near the Arizona-Mexico border. Through negotiations with the FWS, the property was slated to be made into a wildlife refuge and all the cattle removed to protect the rich diversity of more than 700 species of plants, 75 mammals, 50 plus reptiles and amphibians, and over 170 species of breeding birds. The wildlife refuge, however, was not to be. Neighboring cattle ranchers lobbied hard against the idea, and the secretary of interior did not support the deal. TNC, therefore, sold the ranch to a coalition of ranchers, the Malpai Borderlands Group, under a conservation easement that banned development but allowed cattle grazing. TNC features the Malpai Group as an example of the compatibility of ranching and conservation, however, scientists and many conservationists disagree. Cattle are exotic species that destroy riparian and arid habitats and trample and disturb the soil to lead to invasive species. They believe TNC made a mistake by buckling to pressure and not following through with the wildlife refuge to preserve the rich biodiversity of the Gray Ranch.

Science is considered central to TNC's mission. There are 600 scientists on the staff in disciplines of marine conservation, ecology, economics, U.S. federal conservation policy, global climate change, and ecological genetics. TNC scientists engage in basic research and publish their results in some of the best peer-reviewed journals. They engage in many different projects and are often engaged in the identification and assessment of habitats. For instance, in the wetlands of the

Upper Green River basin in Wyoming, the scientists are measuring conditions of wetlands and habitat for bird species. In anticipation of global warming, TNC scientists in New York study lake trout (*Salvelinus namaycush*) with the New York State Department of Environmental Conservation and private fisheries managers to catalog all known lake trout habitats in the Adirondack Park and to identify which Adirondack trout lakes are vulnerable and which show potential to serve as refuges in a warmer future. They plan to use the information to craft a long-term management strategy for cold-water fish in similar lakes.

TNC recognizes the climate change threat and is developing comprehensive, nature-based plans to minimize greenhouse gas emissions. They believe that 30 percent of climate change goals can be achieved through the power of nature through stopping deforestation, investing in soil health, and restoring coastal ecosystems. As part of the fight to curb global warming, conservationists must work with governments to spur the private sector to engage in the renewable energy movement. The benefits of natural climate solutions can be used to unlock a more diverse group of investors who are interested in business and sustainability solutions.

World Wildlife Fund

The iconic panda logo of the World Wildlife Fund (WWF) represents a huge international organization with over 6 million supporters globally, 6,000 staff, and operations in over 100 countries. The WWF was founded in 1961 in a small town in Switzerland by a consortium of scientists, business and government leaders, and two royals, Prince Bernhard of the Netherlands, and Prince Philip, Duke of Edinburgh, who was the first president. Since its founding, the WWF has grown into the largest independent conservation organization in the world. Today, the mission is to conserve the world's biodiversity, ensure that renewable natural resources are sustainable, and to promote the reduction of pollution and wasteful consumption.

In the United States, Russell E. Train was an important founder and chairman of the WWF. Before acting as WWF president and chairman of the board (1978–1990), he served as administrator of the Environmental Protection Agency (EPA) under Presidents Nixon and Ford (1973–1977). Under his guidance, WWF-U.S. grew from a small, primarily grant-making organization into a global conservation force with over 1 million members. To honor Russell Train, the WWF established the Russell E. Train Education for Nature fellowship program in 1994. The fellowship funds conservation leaders in Africa, Asia, and Latin America to pursue master's or doctoral degrees in conservation. The fellowships have been critical for recipients to accomplish their degrees to advance their careers. Each year Train Fellowships support one of these six goals: wildlife, freshwater, oceans, forests, climate, and food.

The WWF focuses on the preservation and recovery of 100 species worldwide, many critically endangered, that are important to their ecosystems because they form a key element in the food chain, help to stabilize the habitat, and demonstrate broader conservation needs. These species include monarch butterflies, elephants, polar bears, sea turtles, rhinos, lions, great apes, tigers, whales, cacti, coral, leopards, salmon, yellowfin and bluefin tuna, river dolphins, and sharks.

Despite efforts, the world's wildlife is declining at an alarming rate. In the 2016 edition of the "Living Planet" report (published every two years), the WWF summarizes a variety of research to provide a comprehensive view of the health of the planet, including biodiversity, ecosystems, and demand on natural resources. The report documents a disturbing loss of wildlife. Animal populations have declined 58 percent between 1970 and 2012. The largest loss is in freshwater systems where the decline is 81 percent. Terrestrial vertebrates have declined 38 percent, and marine populations declined 36 percent. Habitat loss and degradation is the most common threat to wildlife.

Climate change is an increasing threat, and overexploitation through poaching, unsustainable hunting and harvesting is an added danger.

The WWF is leading a global campaign to stop wildlife crime. On the strength of their worldwide network, the WWF has been able to influence and partner with governments to fight poaching. In Kenya, for instance, the WWF designed and installed two systems to identify poachers with infrared cameras mounted on stationary poles lining the border of a park. The activated camera signals mobile units atop a truck used by rangers. At the encouragement of the WWF, Thailand, a major consumer of elephant ivory, instigated a ban on their ivory trade. The WWF also announced that world tiger populations have increased for the first time in 100 years. One reason for the increase is the lowered frequency of poaching in countries like Nepal. Despite, the success, the threats are still there. Poaching and habitat loss are still serious problem in Indonesia and Malaysia.

The WWF focuses on the conservation of 35 critical regions around the planet. Some of the featured regions include the Arctic, Coral Triangle, Madagascar, Mekong River, and the Mediterranean. Priority ecosystems are deserts, forests, freshwater, marine, and mountains. Priority places by region include the Amazon, Borneo forests, the western Indian Ocean, the Southern Ocean, Congo basin, southwestern Pacific, coastal East Africa, the Mediterranean, and southwestern Australia. These regions have been scientifically identified as home to unreplaceable and threatened biodiversity where there is an opportunity to conserve the largest and most intact representative of their ecosystems.

The WWF has designated the Northern Great Plains in the United States as one of the critical regions of the world. This prairie grassland spans five states and two Canadian provinces. Energy development is placing exorbitant pressure on the area with traditional oil extraction and the growth of fracking. The WWF is forming partnerships with public agencies, tribal nations, and private landowners to create a sustainable future for the temperate grasslands. The northern Great Plains team especially works with ranchers to encourage them to conserve the native prairie grasses. The goal is to restore the prairie by increasing the amount of native habitat from 1.5 percent to 10 percent and to increase populations of native species of American bison (*Bison bison*), black-footed ferret (*Mustela nigripes*), black-tailed prairie dog (*Cynomys ludovicianus*), and pronghorn (*Antilocapra americana*).

Another critical area in the United States is the Chihuahua desert. This desert is a biologically rich and diverse ecosystem with freshwater biota that consists of some of the most unique species in the world only found in that one area. Water withdrawals as a result of population growth and agricultural activities, overgrazing, mining, and pollution threaten many of these freshwater communities. WWF is working with Mexican and American governmental agencies, landowners, and local NGOs on projects to implement water policy reforms, better water management practices, and restoration strategies.

The third critically threatened region designated by the WWF in the United States includes the rivers and streams of the American southeast from southern Virginia to Tennessee south to Alabama and Florida. The rivers and streams of the area are unusually rich in aquatic biodiversity. This freshwater ecoregion, covering nearly 10 percent of the United States, includes a wide variety of habitats and some of the most species-rich freshwater systems in the world. Humans are competing with aquatic species for the water. Aquatic habitats are modified through dams and widespread channelization. Pollution from acid rain, deforestation, roads, agriculture, urbanization, and industrialization places undue stress on native species.

Introduction

This chapter provides relevant data and documents about endangered species and the factors that affect them. The data section illustrates the cause and consequences of climate change, the decline of species from poaching, and the precipitous decline of amphibians. The tables show consequences of rising sea levels along U.S. coasts, and list species, dates, and other factors involved in the listing and recovery of endangered species in the United States. Also included are 10 areas in the world that are in decline with the most endangered species and traits of organisms most vulnerable to becoming endangered. The documents sections include excerpts from the Endangered Species Act, the written opinion of the Supreme Court in the *Tennessee Valley Authority v. Hill case*, and the executive order signed by newly elected Donald Trump to begin the process of turning back efforts of the Obama administration to curb U.S. carbon dioxide emissions responsible for climate change.

_____

A motorbike navigates through floodwater caused by a seasonal king tide. High tides intensified by sea level rise from climate change frequently flood south Florida coastal areas on sunny days. (AP Photo/Lynne Sladky)

Data

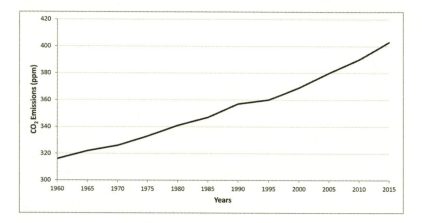

Figure 5.1   Increases in Global CO$_2$ Emissions in the Past 55 Years

Source: https://www.climate.gov/maps-data.

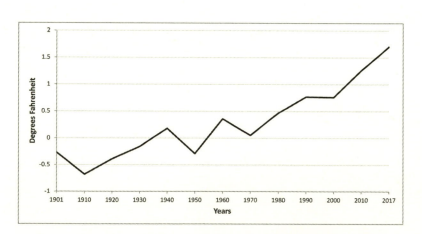

Figure 5.2   Annual Global Temperature Increases Worldwide since 1901 in Degrees Fahrenheit

Source: https://www.epa.gov/climate-indicators/climate-change-indicators-us-and-global-temperature.

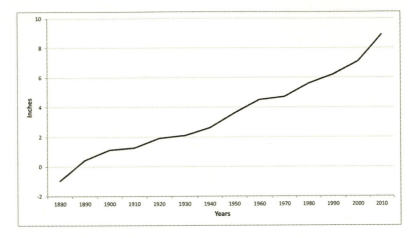

Figure 5.3 Cumulative Change in Sea Level for the World's Oceans since 1880

Source: https://www.epa.gov/climate-indicators/climate-change-indicators-sea-level.

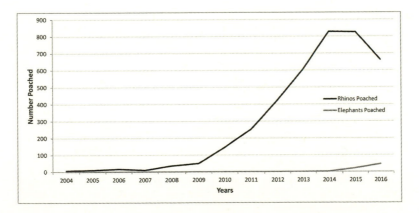

Figure 5.4 Results of Rhinoceros and Elephant Poaching in Kruger National Park, South Africa

Source: Poaching Facts, http://www.poachingfacts.com/poaching-statistics/rhino-poaching-statistics/, www.poachingfacts.com/poaching-statistics/rhino-poaching-statistics/.

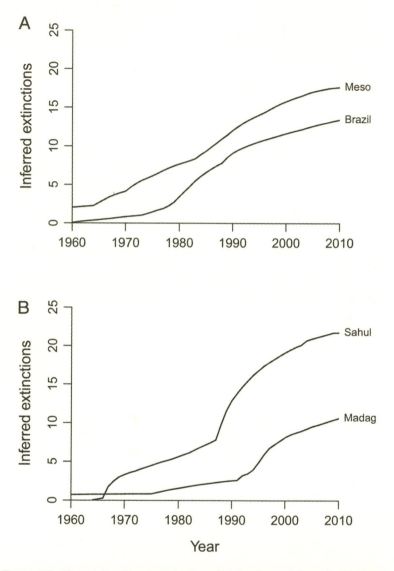

Figure 5.5   Cumulative Number of Inferred Extinctions of Frogs in (A) Meso-america and Brazil, and (B) Madagascar and Sahul Region Where Highly Concentrated in New Guinea

Note: Mesoamerica is a cultural region of Central America extending from central Mexico to Belize, Guatemala, El Salvador, Honduras, Nicaragua, and northern Costa Rica.

Source: Alroy, John. 2015. "Current Extinction Rates of Reptiles and Amphibians." *Proceedings of the National Academy of Science* 112: 13003–13008. http://www .pnas.org/content/112/42/13003.full.pdf. Used by permission.

"Sunny Day" flooding is increasing along the coasts when high tides encroach on dry land along the shore. The coastal areas from Atlantic City to Charleston, South Carolina, seem especially vulnerable to sea level rise.

Table 5.1 Average Number of Flood Days on U.S. Coasts 1950–1959 Compared with Flood Days during 2010–2015.

City	1950–1959	2010–2015
Boston	1.8	6.8
Providence, RI	1.0	2.33
Battery, NY	1.0	4.0
Atlantic City, NJ	1.8	24.5
Baltimore, MD	2.2	15.7
Annapolis, MD	4.0	46.3
Washington, DC	6.0	32.2
Wilmington, NC	0.9	49.2
Charleston, SC	2.4	26.3
Key West, FL	0	3.8
La Jolla, CA	0.5	6.3
San Francisco, CA	3.6	11.7
Seattle, WA	0.9	3.3

Source: https://www.epa.gov/climate-indicators/climate-change-indicators-coastal-flooding.

The U.S. Fish and Wildlife Service (FWS) keeps a tally of the total number of domestic and foreign species it has listed as threatened and endangered. Also included are the number of recovery plans, which lag behind the listings.

Table 5.2 Summary of Number of Listed Endangered and Threatened Species and Recovery Plans in the United States under the Endangered Species Act.

Group	Endangered	Threatened	Total	Recovery Plans
Amphibians	20	15	35	22
Annelid Worms	0	0	0	0

(continued)

Table 5.2 (*continued*)

Group	Endangered	Threatened	Total	Recovery Plans
Arachnids (Spiders)	12	0	12	12
Birds	81	21	102	87
Clams	75	14	89	71
Corals	0	6	6	0
Crustaceans	24	4	28	18
Fishes	92	73	165	105
Flatworms	0	0	0	0
Roundworms	0	0	0	0
Hyoids	0	0	0	0
Insects	74	11	85	42
Mammals	68	27	95	61
Millipedes	0	0	0	0
Reptiles	17	28	45	34
Snails	40	12	52	30
Sponges	0	0	0	0
Animal Totals	503	211	714	482
Conifers and Cycads	1	3	4	3
Ferns and Allies	36	2	38	26
Flowering Plants	735	163	898	646
Lichens	2	0	2	2
Plant Totals	774	168	942	677
Grand Total	1,277	379	1,656	1,159

Note: Foreign species are not included.

Source: ECOS. 2017. U.S. Fish and Wildlife Species. https://ecos.fws.gov/ecp0/reports/box-score-report. Accessed September 21, 2017.

The time between listing and delisting illustrates how long it takes for a species to be considered recovered and removed from endangered species list. The average time for delisting of these species is 25 years with a range of 8–48 years. (Extinct species were not included in the calculation.)

Table 5.3   Dates Domestic Species Were Declared Extinct, Listed as
Endangered and Then Delisted as Recovered under the 1973 Endangered
Species Act in the United States (Data Errors and Foreign Species Are
Omitted).

Species	Year Listed	Year Delisted	Status
Tecopa Pupfish (*Cyprinodon nevadensis calidae*)	1970	1982	Extinct
Blue Pike (*Stizostedion vitreum glaucum*)	1967	1983	Extinct
Longjaw Cisco (*Coregonus alpenae*)	1967	1983	Extinct
Santa Barbara Song Sparrow (*Melospiza m. graminea*)	1973	1983	Extinct
Sampson's Pearlymussel (*Epioblasma sampsoni*)	1976	1984	Extinct
Brown Pelican, Atlantic Coast (*Pelecanus occidentalis*)	1970	1985	Recovered
Palau Owl (*Pyrroglaux podargina*)	1970	1985	Recovered
Palau Fantail Flycatcher (*Rhipidura lepida*)	1970	1985	Recovered
Palau Ground Dove (*Gallicolumbia canifrons*)	1970	1985	Recovered
American Alligator (*Alligator mississippiensis*)	1967	1987	Recovered
Amistad Gambusia (*Gambusia amistadensis*)	1980	1987	Extinct
Dusky Seaside Sparrow (*Ammodramus m. nigrescens*)	1967	1990	Extinct
Gray Whale (*Eschrichtius robustus*)	1994	1994	Recovered
Arctic Peregrine Falcon (*Falco p. tundrius*)	1970	1994	Recovered
American Peregrine Falcon (*Falco p. anatum*)	1970	1999	Recovered
Aleutian Canada Goose (*Branta c. leucopareia*)	1967	2001	Recovered

(continued)

Table 5.3   *(continued)*

Species	Year Listed	Year Delisted	Status
Robbins' Cinquefoil (*Potentilla robbinsiana*)	1980	2002	Recovered
Columbian White-Tailed Deer (*Odocoileus v. leucurus*)	1967	2002	Recovered
Hoover's Woolly-Star (*Eriastrum hooveri*)	1990	2003	Recovered
Mariana Mallard (*Anas oustaleti*)	1977	2004	Extinct
Guam Broadbill (*Myiagra freycineti*)	1984	2004	Extinct
Tinian Monarch Flycatcher (*Monarcha takatsukasae*)	1970	2004	Recovered
Eggert's Sunflower (*Helianthus eggertii*)	1997	2005	Recovered
Bald Eagle, lower 48 states (*Haliaeetus leucocephalus*)	1967	2007	Recovered
Caribbean Monk Seal (*Monachus tropicalis*)	1979	2008	Extinct
Brown Pelican, Atlantic Coast (*Pelecanus occidentalis*)	1970	2009	Recovered
Maguire Daisy (*Erigeron maguirei*)	1985	2011	Recovered
Tn. Purple Coneflower (*Echinacea tennesseensis*)	1979	2011	Recovered
Lake Erie Water Snake (*Nerodia s. insularum*)	1999	2011	Recovered
Concho Water Snake (*Nerodia paucimaculata*)	1986	2011	Recovered
Morelet's Crocodile (*Crocodylus moreletii*)	1970	2012	Recovered
Virginia Northern Flying Squirrel (*Glaucomys s. fuscus*)	1985	2013	Recovered
Magazine Mt. Shagreen (*Inflectarius magazinensis*)	1989	2013	Recovered

Species	Year Listed	Year Delisted	Status
Steller Sea Lion—Eastern (*Eumetopias jubatus*)	1990	2013	Recovered
Island Night Lizard (*Xantusia riversiana*)	1977	2014	Recovered
Oregon Chub (*Oregonichthys crameri*)	1993	2015	Recovered
Delmarva Peninsula Fox Squirrel (*Sciurus n. cinereus*)	1967	2015	Recovered
Modoc Sucker (*Catostomus microps*)	1985	2016	Recovered
Johnston's Frankenia (*Frankenia johnstonii*)	1984	2016	Recovered
Louisiana Black Bear (*Ursus a. luteolus*)	1992	2016	Recovered
Santa Rosa Island Fox (*Urocyon l. santarosae*)	2004	2016	Recovered
Santa Cruz Island Fox (*Urocyon l. santacruzae*)	2004	2016	Recovered
San Miguel Island Fox (*Urocyon l. littoralis*)	2004	2016	Recovered
Humpback Whale (*Megaptera novaeangliae*)	1970	2016	Recovered
White-Haired Goldenrod (*Solidago albopilosa*)	1988	2016	Recovered
Northern Rocky Mts. Gray Wolf (*Canus lupus*)	1978	2017	Recovered
Greater Yellowstone Grizzly Bear (*Ursus horribilis*)	1975	2017	Recovered

Source: "ECOS Environmental Conservation Online System." U.S. Fish and Wildlife Service. https://ecos.fws.gov/ecp0/reports/delisting-report.

The species in this table illustrate the variation in types of species and the causes for their low population numbers. Even species listed as threatened and endangered still experience extremely low number that slow and threatened their recovery.

Table 5.4   A Sample of Highly Endangered Species in the United States, Their Approximate Distribution, Estimated Number, and Cause of Decline.

Species	Distribution	Number	Cause
Mammals			
Black-Footed Ferret (E) *Mustela nigripes*	Great Plains	206	Loss of prairie dog food source
Florida Bonneted Bat (E) *Eumops floridanus*	Florida	3,000–5,000	Habitat loss
Florida Panther (E) *Puma concolor coryi*	Florida	100–160	Habitat loss
Gray Bat (E) *Myotis grisescens*	SE United States	In rapid decline	White nose disease, human disturbance
Mexican Wolf (E) *Canis lupus baileyi*	Southwest	90 in wild	Illegal hunting
Hawaiian Monk Seal (E) *Monachus schauinslandi*	Hawaiian Islands	632	Food limitation, fishing nets
Red wolf (E) *Canis rufus*	North Carolina	< 100	Habitat loss, hunting
Stephen's Kangaroo Rat (E) *Dipodomys stephensi*	California	Declining	Habitat loss
Texas Ocelot (E) *Leopardus pardalis*	Texas	1,000	Overhunting
Utah Prairie Dog (T) *Cynomys parvidens*	Utah	<10,000	Poison, disease, lost habitat

Birds

Akikiki (honeycreeper) (E) *Oreomystis bairdi*	Hawaii	150–610	Habitat loss
California Condor (E) *Gymnogyps californianus*	California	106	Lead shot, illegal shooting
Florida Scrub Jay *Aphelocoma coerulescens*	Florida	4,000–6,000	Habitat loss
Greater Sage Grouse *C. urophasianus*	Western United States	50% decline	Habitat loss, fragmentation
Gunnison Sage-Grouse (T) *Centrocercus minimus*	Southwest Colorado, Utah	1,700	Habitat loss, low genetic variation
Hawaiian Goose (E) *Branta sandvicensis*	Hawaii	250–999	Habitat loss
Ivory-Billed Woodpecker *Campephilus principalis*	Arkansas, Cuba	1–49	Habitat loss
Palila (E) *Loxioides bailleui*	Hawaii	1,000–2,499	Habitat loss, goats
Piping Plover (E) *Charadrius melodus*	Atlantic Coast	8,000	Human disturbance
Puerto Rican Parrot (E) *Amazona vittata*	Puerto Rico	33–47	Habitat loss, rats
Whooping Crane (E) *Grus Americana*	Texas	~400	Habitat loss, illegal hunting

(continued)

257

Table 5.4 *(continued)*

Species	Distribution	Number	Cause
Reptiles			
Kemp's Ridley Turtle (E) *Lepidochelys kempii*	Texas coast	Unknown	Oil spills, bycatch, human disturbance
Dunes Sagebrush Lizard *Sceloporus arenicolus*	New Mexico, Texas	Decreasing	Habitat loss, oil and gas extraction
Gopher Tortoise (T) *Gopherus polyphemus*	Florida, Georgia	Steep decline	Habitat loss
Amphibians			
Berry Cave Salamander *Gyrinophilus gulolineatus*	Tennessee	Decreasing	Habitat loss
Crested toad (E) *Peltophryne lemur*	Puerto Rico	< 80	Habitat loss
Dusky Gopher Frog (E) *Lithobates sevosus*	Mississippi	2,000	Habitat loss, Chytrid fungus
Mississippi Gopher Frog *Lithobates sevosus*	Mississippi	60–100	Lost wet lands, Chytrid fungus
Ramsey Canyon Leopard Frog *Lithobates subaquavocalis*	Arizona	>400	Chytrid fungus, Habitat loss
Striped Newt (C) *Notophthalmus perstriatus*	Florida, Georgia	Rapid decline	Habitat loss, exploitation

Fish

Alabama Sturgeon (E) *Scaphirhynchus suttkusi*	Alabama	Critically Endangered	Overfishing, habitat loss
Apache Trout *Oncorhynchus gilae Oncorhynchus apache*	Arizona Native	Critically Endangered	Invasive species
Cape Fear Shiner (E) *Notropis mekistocholas*	North Carolina	1,500–3,000	Toxic chemicals, impoundments
Giant Sea Bass *Stereolepis gigas*	California, Mexico	84–539	Overfishing
Moapa Dace (E) *Moapa coriacea*	Nevada	50% decline	Habitat loss
Pallid Sturgeon (E) *Scaphirhynchus albus*	Missouri River	50–100	Impoundments
Snake River Salmon (E,T) *Oncorhynchus sp.*	Idaho, Oregon	< 20,000	Impoundments

Invertebrates

Elkhorn Coral (T) *Acropora palmate*	Florida Keys	80% decline	Climate change
Lange's Metalmark Butterfly (E) *Apodemia m. langei*	California	150	Habitat loss, herbicides

(continued)

Table 5.4 (continued)

Species	Distribution	Number	Cause
Monarch Butterfly *Danaus p. plexippus*	Midwest, South West	90% decline	Habitat loss, pesticide, herbicides
Rusty Patched Bumble-bee (E) *Bombus affinis*	Midwest	< 1% historic range	Pesticides, habitat loss
Staghorn Coral (T) *Acropora cervicornis*	Florida	97% decline	Climate change, disease
Tan Riffleshell (E) *Epioblasma f. walker*	Tennessee, Virginia	~2,000	Coal mining, coal ash
Plants			
Arizona Agave *Agave arizonica*	Arizona	< 100	Habitat loss
Texas Wild Rice (E) *Zizania texana*	Texas	140 clumps	Impoundments
Western Prairie (T) Fringed Orchid *Platanthera praeclara*	Midwest	Continuous Decline	Habitat loss

Sources: IUCN RedList. http://www.iucnredlist.org/; U.S. Fish & Wildlife, https://www.fws.gov/endangered/.

Note: E = Endangered, T = Threatened, C = Candidate, species without letter have not been listed.

Many species show multiple causes of endangerment and the main ones are given. Species with extremely low numbers, the Amur leopard and vaquita, will go extinct without major conservation efforts similar to those to save the California condor.

Table 5.5   Sample of Critically Endangered and Endangered Species Globally from IUCN Red List.

Critically Endangered	Country	Estimated Number	Cause
Addax (white antelope) *Addax nasomaculatus*	Sahara desert	30–90	Uncontrolled hunting
Amur Leopard *Panthera p. orientalis*	China/Russia	60	Habitat loss, poaching
Black Rhinoceros *Diceros bicornis*	Namibia Coastal East Africa	5,000	Poaching
Bornean Orangutan *Pongo pygmaeus*	Borneo	> 50% decline	Habitat loss, hunting
Brazilian Merganser *Mergus octosetaceus*	Brazil	~ 250	Farming and mining
Brown Spider Monkey *Ateles hybridus*	Colombia	Declined 80% in 45 years	Habitat loss, hunting
Chinese Crested tern *Thalasseus bernsteini*	China	~ 30–49	Habitat destruction
Chinese Pangolin *Manis pentadactyla*	China	Declined 90% in 20 years	Poaching
Cross River Gorilla *Gorilla g. diehli*	Congo Basin	200–300	Habitat loss, poaching
Eastern Lowland Gorilla *Gorilla beringei graueri*	Congo basin	Declined 50%	Habitat loss, poaching

(continued)

Table 5.5   (*continued*)

Critically Endangered	Country	Estimated Number	Cause
Golden-Headed Langur *Trachypithecus poliocephalus*	North Vietnam	< 70	Poaching
Hawksbill Turtle *Eretmochelys imbricata*	Oceans	Unknown	Exploitation
Javan Rhinoceros, *Rhinoceros sondaicus*	Java, Indonesia	40–60	Poaching
Malayan Tiger *Panthera tigris jacksoni*	Thailand	250–340	Poaching
Morelet's Tree Frog *Agalychnis moreletii*	Central America	Declining	Disease, Fragmentation
Mountain Gorilla *Gorilla beringei beringei*	Uganda, Rwanda	~800	Habitat loss, poaching
Northern Bald Ibis *Geronticus eremita*	Morocco, Syria	200–249	Habitat loss, hunting
Philippine Eagle *Pithecophaga jefferyi*	Philippine islands	180–500	Deforestation
Rough Moss Frog *Arthroleptella rugosa*	South Africa	1,000	Fires
Saola *Pseudoryx nghetinhensis*	Mekong, Vietnam	Rare	Poaching
Siamese Crocodile *Crocodylus siamensis*	SE Asia	500–1,000	Habitat loss
South China Tiger *Panthera tigris amoyensis*	SE China	Functionally extinct	Hunted as pest
Sumatran Elephant *Elephas m. sumatranus*	Borneo, Sumatra	2,400–2,800	Habitat loss
Sumatran Orangutan *Pongo abelii*	Borneo, Sumatra	14,613 80% decline	Habitat loss, Illegal trade

Critically Endangered	Country	Estimated Number	Cause
Sumatran Rhinoceros *Dicerorhinus sumatrensis*	Indonesia	275	Illegal hunting
Sumatran Tiger *Panthera tigris sumatrae*	Borneo, Sumatra	400–500	Poaching
Sheath-Tailed Bat *Coleura seychellensis*	Seychelles	Decline 90%	Habitat loss
Vaquita (Desert Porpoise) *Phocoena sinus*	Mexico	< 60	Drown in fish nets
Western Lowland Gorilla *Gorilla, gorilla, gorilla*	Congo basin	60% decline	Poaching, disease
Yangtze Finless Porpoise *Neophocaena asiaeorientalis*	Yangtze River	1,000–1,800	Pollution

Endangered	Country	Estimated Number	Cause
African Wild Dog *Lycaon pictus*	Coastal E. Africa	6,600	Habitat loss, illegal hunting
Amur Tiger *Panthera tigris altaica*	Russia	540	Habitat loss, poaching
Asian Elephant *Elephas maximus indicus*	Eastern Himalayas, Greater Mekong	40,000	Habitat loss, poaching
Bengal Tiger *Panthera tigris tigris*	India	2,500	Poaching
Blue Fin Tuna *Thunnus spp.*	Oceans	In rapid decline	Overfishing
Bonobo *Pan paniscus*	Congo basin	10,000–50,000	Habitat loss, poaching
Borneo Pygmy Elephant *Elephas m. borneensis*	Borneo, Sumatra	1,500	Habitat loss

(continued)

Table 5.5   *(continued)*

Endangered	Country	Estimated Number	Cause
Chimpanzee *Pan troglodytes*	Congo Basin	172,000–299,000	Habitat loss, hunting
Darwin's Fox *Lycalopex fulvipes*	Chile	659–2,499	Domestic dogs, disease, human-caused mortality
Ethiopian wolf *Canis simensis*	Ethiopia	197	Humans, disease
Fin Whale *Balaenoptera physalus*	Ocean	50,000–90,000	Hunting, habitat loss
Galapagos Penguin *Spheniscus mendiculus*	Galapagos Islands	< 2,000	Pollution, climate change
Ganges River Dolphin *Platanista g. gangetica*	Eastern Himalayas	1,200–1,800	Loss of habitat, pollution
Grevy's Zebra *Equus grevyi*	Ethiopia, Kenya	2,000	Habitat loss, illegal hunting
Green Turtle *Chelonia mydas*	Oceans		Hunting, overharvest
Hector's Dolphin *Cephalorhynchus hectori*	New Zealand coast	~7,000	Fish bycatch
Red Panda *Ailurus fulgens*	Myanmar, China	Decline 50% in three generations	Habitat loss, poaching
Silverstone's Poison Frog *Ameerega silverstonei*	Peru	Decreasing	Pet trade

Source: World Conservation Congress list of 100 most endangered species of the world compiled by 8,000 IUCN scientists as published in Cota-Larsen. 2012. "Report Lists 100 Most Endangered Species." *Annamiticus*. http://annamiticus. com/2012/09/11/report-lists-100-of-the-most-endangered-species/.

Petitions to list a species as threatened or endangered under the ESA can be made by any individual, group or organization to the FWS. The FWS has 90 days to review a petition to list a species. After 90 days, a species is classified as either "not substantial" or "substantial." A "not substantial" finding indicates the petition does not present adequate scientific or commercial information to warrant action on the petition. "Substantial" petitions present enough scientific or commercial information to justify that actions are warranted. If substantial, the FWS publishes an announcement in the Federal Register about plans to initiate a review of the status of the species to determine whether the petitions meet the criteria for listing.

After 12 months, a decision must be made on the substantial petitions whether action is warranted, warranted but precluded, or not warranted. The not warranted species are dropped, unless there is a new petition. The warranted but precluded species move to the candidate list, and the warranted species proceed to a comment period and hearings followed by a final ruling.

Table 5.6 is based on active petitions received by the FWS for the listing and delisting of species. Some petitions receive multiple actions. Only the last action on the petition and the date of the action are given in the table. The website contains information about prior actions, species distribution, person(s) and groups initiating the petition, and petition documents.

Table 5.6   Endangered Species Act Petitions Received by the Fish and Wildlife Service (FWS).

Petition Title	Date Received by FWS	Requested Action	Petition Findings
Dixie Valley Toad (*Anaxyrus williamsi*)	09/18/2017	Listing: Threatened or Endangered	No yet made
Venus Flytrap (*Dionaea muscipula*)	10/21/2016	Listing: Endangered	Not yet made

(continued)

Table 5.6   (*continued*)

Petition Title	Date Received by FWS	Requested Action	Petition Findings
Lesser Prairie Chicken (*Tympanuchus pallidicinctus*)	09/08/2016	Listing: Endangered	90 Day Substantial 11/30/2016
Sturgeon Chub and Sicklefin Chub	08/15/2016	Listing: Threatened or Endangered	Not yet made
Leopard (*Panthera pardus*) All Leopards	07/25/2016	Listing: Endangered	90 Day Substantial 11/30/2016
Oblong Rocksnail (*Leptoxis compacta*)	06/21/2016	Listing: Threatened or Endangered	Not yet made
Tricolored Bat (*Perimyotis subflavus*)	06/16/2016	Listing: Threatened	Not yet made
Florida Black Bear (*Ursus americana floridanus*)	03/17/2016	Listing: Threatened or Endangered	90 Day Not Substantial 04/19/2017
Lassics Lupine (*Lupinus constancei*)	01/15/2016	Listing: Endangered	90 Day Substantial 09/14/2016
Joshua Tree (*Yucca brevifolia*)	09/29/2015	Listing: Threatened	90 Day Substantial 09/14/2016
Western Bumble Bee (*Bombus occidentalis*)	09/15/2015	Listing: Threatened or Endangered	90 Day Substantial 03/16/2016
Yellow-Banded Bumble Bee, (*Bombus terricola*)	09/15/2016	Listing: Threatened or Endangered	90 Day Substantial 03/16/2016
California Spotted Owl (*Strix o. occidentals*)	08/25/2015	Listing: Endangered	90 Day Substantial 09/18/2015
Moose, Central United States	07/09/2015	Listing: Threatened	90 Day Substantial 06/03/2016

Petition Title	Date Received by FWS	Requested Action	Petition Findings
Blue Calamintha Bee (Osmia calaminthae)	02/05/2015	Listing: Threatened or Endangered	90 Day Substantial 09/18/2015
Tricolored Blackbird (Agelaius tricolor)	02/05/2015	Listing: Endangered	90 Day Substantial 09/18/2016
Northern Bog Lemming (Synaptomys borealis)	10/03/2014	Listing: Threatened or Endangered	90 Day Substantial 09/18/2015
Rio Grande Sucker (Catostomus plebeius)	10/03/2014	Listing: Threatened	90 Day Substantial 03/16/2016
Monarch Butterfly (Danaus p. plexippus)	08/26/2014	Listing: Threatened	90 Day Substantial 12/31/2014
Bracted Twistflower (Streptanthus bracteatus)	08/05/2014	Listing: Threatened or Endangered	12 Month Warranted but Precluded 12/24/2015
San Joaquin Valley Giant Flower-Loving Fly (Rhaphiomidas trochilus)	06/30/2014	Listing: Endangered	90 Day Substantial 04/10/2015
Relict Dace (Relictus solitarius)	06/30/2014	Listing: Endangered	90 Day Substantial 04/10/2015
Yellow-Cedar (Callitropsis nootkatensis)	06/25/2014	Listing: Threatened or Endangered	90 Day Substantial 04/10/2015
Silvery Phacelia	03/07/2014	Listing: Threatened	90 Day Substantial 07/01/2015
Tufted Puffin	02/14/2014	Listing: Threatened	90 Day Substantial 09/18/2015
9 Species Caribbean Skinks	02/11/2014	Listing: Endangered	90 Day Substantial 09/14/2016

(continued)

Table 5.6   (*continued*)

Petition Title	Date Received by FWS	Requested Action	Petition Findings
Mojave Shoulderband (*Helminthoglypta greggi*)	01/31/2014	Listing: Threatened	90 Day Substantial 04/10/2015
Tinian Monarch (*Monarcha takatsukasae*)	12/12/ 2013	Listing: Threatened or Endangered	90 Day Substantial 09/18/2015
Rio Grande Chub (*Gila pandora*)	09/30/2013	Listing: Threatened	90 Day Substantial 03/16/2016
Fisher (*Martes pennanti*)	09/24/2013	Listing: Threatened or Endangered	90 Day Substantial 01/12/016
Scott Riffle Beetle (*Optioservus phaeus*)	09/20/2013	Listing: Threatened	90 Day Substantial 01/12/2016
Narrow-Footed Diving Beetle (*Hygrotus diversipes*)	07/17/2013	Listed: Threatened or Endangered	90 Day Substantial 01/12/2016
Regal Fritillary (*Speyeria idalia*)	04/24/2013	Listing: Threatened or Endangered	90 Day Substantial 09/18/2015
Great Basin Silverspot (*Speyeria n. nokomis*)	04/24/2013	Listed: Threatened or Endangered	90 Day Substantial 01/12/2016
Virgin River Spinedace (*Lepidomeda m. mollispinis*)	11/20/2012	Listing: Threatened or Endangered	90 Day Substantial 09/18/2015
Clear Lake Hitch (*Lavinia exilicauda chi*)	09/25/2012	Listing: Threatened or	90 Day Substantial 04/10/2015
False-Foxglove (*Agalinis calycina*)	09/19/2012	Listing: Endangered	90 Day Substantial 03/16/2016
Marble Island Butterfly (*Euchloe ausonides insulanus*)	08/22/2012	Listing: Endangered	12 Month Warranted but Precluded 04/05/2016

Petition Title	Date Received by FWS	Requested Action	Petition Findings
Black Backed Woodpecker (*Picoides arcticus*)	05/08/2012	Listing: Threatened or Endangered	90 Day Substantial 04/09/2013
53 Species of Reptiles and Amphibians	04/24/2012	Listing: Threatened or Endangered	90 Day Substantial09/14/2016
Heller Cave Springtail (*Typhlogastrura helleri*)	01/11/2012	Listing: Threatened or Endangered	90 Day Substantial 11/14/2012
3 Grassland Thicket Species	01/06/2012	Listing: Threatened or Endangered	90 Day Substantial 12/04/2012
Rattlesnake, Eastern Diamondback (*Crotalus admanteus*)	12/12/2011	Listing: Threatened	90 Day Substantial 05/10/2012
2 Species of Butterfly *Euphilotes sp.*	10/06/2011	Listing: Threatened or Endangered	90 Day Substantial 08/07/2012
Penasco Least Chipmunk (*Tamias m. atristriatus*)	10/05/2011	Listing: Threatened or Endangered	90 Day Substantial 11/21/2012
Rocky Mountain Monkeyflower (*Mimulus gemmiparus*)	10/04/2011	Listing: Threatened or Endangered	90 Day Substantial 08/29/2012
Black-capped Petrel (*Pterodroma hasitata*)	09/06/2011	Listing: Threatened or Endangered	90 Day Substantial 06/21/2012
Boreal Toad (*Anaxyrus b. boreas*)	05/25/2011	Listing: Threatened or Endangered	90 Day Substantial 04/12/2012
Sierra Nevada Red Fox (*Vulpus v. necator*)	04/27/2011	Listing: Threatened or Endangered	12 Month Not Warranted 10/08/2015
Western Glacier Stonefly (*Zapada glacier*)	1/10/2011	Listing: Endangered	12 Month Warranted 10/04/2016

(continued)

Table 5.6   (*continued*)

Petition Title	Date Received by FWS	Requested Action	Petition Findings
Carolina Hemlock (*Tsuga caroliniana*)	12/13/2010	Listing: Endangered	90 Day Substantial 09/27/2011
Dessert Massasauga (*Sistrurus catenatus edwardsii*)	11/01/2010	Listing: Threatened or Endangered	90 Day Substantial 08/09/2012
Gila Mayfly (*Lachlania dencyanna*)	09/27/2010	Listing: Endangered	90 Day Substantial 07/26/2012
Saltmarsh Topminnow (*Fundulus jenkins*)	09/07/2010	Listing: Threatened or Endangered	90 Day Substantial 08/10/2011
White-tailed Ptarmigan (*Lagopus l. altipetens Lagopus l. rainierensis*)	08/26/2010	Listing: Threatened or Endangered	90 Day Substantial 06/05/2012
Bicknell's Thrush (*Catharus bicknelli*)	08/26/2010	Listing: Threatened or Endangered	90 Day Substantial 08/15/2012
2 AZ Plants (*Graptopetalum bartramii Pectis imberbis*)	07/07/2010	Listing: Threatened or Endangered	90 Day Substantial 08/08/12
Franklin's Bumble Bee (*Bombus franklini*)	06/28/2010	Listing: Endangered	90 Day Substantial 09/13/2011
40 SE Aquatic Species	04/20/2010	Listing: Threatened or Endangered	12 Month Not Warranted 10/06/2016
Arapahoe Snowfly (*Capnia arapahoe*)	04/06/2010	Listing: Endangered	12 Month Warranted but Precluded 11/21/2012

Petition Title	Date Received by FWS	Requested Action	Petition Findings
Leatherback Sea Turtle (*Dermochelys coriacea*)	02/23/2010	Revised	90 Day Substantial 08/04/2011
Sand-Verbena Moth (*Copablepharon fuscum*)	02/17/2010	Listing: Threatened or Endangered	90 Day Substantial 02/17/2011
Golden-winged Warbler (*Vermivora chrysoptera*)	02/10/2010	Listing: Threatened or Endangered	90 Day Substantial 06/02/2011
Prairie Chub (*Macrhybopsis australis*)	01/25/2010	Listing: Threatened or Endangered	90 Day Substantial 04/14/2011
Spot-Tailed Earless Lizard (*Holbrookia lacerata*)	01/21/2010	Listing: Threatened or Endangered	90 Day Substantial 05/25/2011
Texas Kangaroo Rat (*Dipodomys elator*)	01/15/2010	Listing: Threatened or Endangered	90 Day Substantial 03/08/2011
Caribou (*Rangifer t. pearyi, R. t. groenlandicus*)	09/15/2009	Listing: Threatened or Endangered	90 Day Substantial 04/05/2011
42 Snail Species *Pyegulopis sp. Tryonia sp.*	02/27/2009	Listing: Threatened or Endangered	90 Day Not Substantial 09/13/2011
Puerto Rico Harlequin Butterfly (*Atlantea tulita*)	02/25/2009	Listing: Threatened or Endangered	12 Month Warranted but Precluded 11/21/2012
Whitebark Pine (*Pinus albicaulis*)	12/09/2008	Listing: Endangered	12 Month Warranted but Precluded 11/21/2012
5 Southwest Mussels	10/15/2008	Listing: Threatened or Endangered	12 Month Warranted but Precluded 11/21/2012

(*continued*)

Table 5.6   (*continued*)

Petition Title	Date Received by FWS	Requested Action	Petition Findings
Wright's Marsh Thistle (*Cirsium wrightii*)	10/15/2008	Listing: Threatened or Endangered	12 Month Warranted but Precluded 11/21/2012
Chihuahua Scurfpea (*Pediomelum pentaphyllum*)	10/15/2008	Listing: Threatened or Endangered	90 Day Substantial 12/16/2009
Striped Newt (*Notophthalmus perstriatus*)	07/15/2008	Listing: Threatened or Endangered	12 Month Warranted but Precluded 11/21/2012
29 Species of Snails and Slugs	03/17/2008	Listing: Threatened or Endangered	12 Month Not Warranted 09/18/2012
Pacific Walrus (*Odobenus r. divergens*)	02/08/2008	Listing: Threatened	12 Month Warranted but Precluded 11/21/2012
Longfin Smelt (*Spirinchus thaleichthys*)	08/08/2007	Listing: Endangered	12 Month Warranted but Precluded 11/21/2012
206 Mountain Prairie Region Species	07/30/2007	Listing: Threatened or Endangered	90 Day Substantial 01/12/2016
475 SW Species	06/25/2007	Listing: Threatened or Endangered	90 Day Substantial 11/30/2016
Dusky Tree Vole (*Arborimus longicaudus*)	06/22/2007	Listing: Threatened or Endangered	12 Month Warranted but Precluded 11/21/2012
Gopher tortoise (*Gopherus polyphemus*)	01/18/2006	Listing: Threatened	12 Month Warranted but Precluded 11/21/2012
Hermes Copper Butterfly (*Hermelycaena hermes*)	10/26/2004	Listing: Endangered	12 Month Warranted but Precluded 11/21/2012
Berry Cave Salamander (*Gyrinophilus gulolineatus*)	01/22/2003	Listing: Endangered	12 Month Warranted but Precluded 11/21/2012

Petition Title	Date Received by FWS	Requested Action	Petition Findings
Louisiana Pine Snake (*Pituophis ruthveni*)	07/19/2000	Listing: Endangered	12 Month Warranted but Precluded 11/21/2012
Spine Flower (*Chorizanthe parryi var. fernandina*)	02/29/2000	Listing: Endangered	12 Month Warranted but Precluded 11/21/2012
Solanum conocarpum	11/21/1996	Listing: Endangered	12 Month Warranted but Precluded 10/26/2011
Swallowtail Kite (*Eurytides lysithous*)	01/10/1994	Listing: Endangered	12 Month Warranted but Precluded 12/07/2004
African Elephant Forest and Savannah	02/12/2015	Uplist to Endangered to Two Species	90 Day Substantial 03/16/2016
Cabinet Grizzly Bear (*Ursus arctos horribilis*)	12/22/2014	Uplist to Endangered	Findings Not Yet Made
Northern Spotted Owl (*Strix o. caurina*)	08/21/2012	Uplist to Endangered	90 Day Substantial 04/10/2015
Delta Smelt (*Hypomesus transpacificus*)	03/09/2006	Uplist to Endangered	12 Month Warranted but Precluded 11/21/2012
Pariette Cactus (*Sclerocactus brevispinus*)	04/18/2005	Uplist to Endangered	12 Month Warranted but Precluded 12/02/2016
Desert Tortoise (*Gopherus agassizii*)	06/20/2002	Uplist to Endangered	Not Yet Made
Cotton-Top Marmoset (*Saguinus oedipus*)	05/06/1992	Downlist to Threatened	90 Day Substantial 11/10/1993

(*continued*)

Table 5.6   (*continued*)

Petition Title	Date Received by FWS	Requested Action	Petition Findings
North Cascade Grizzly (*Ursus arctos stikeenensis*)	03/14/1990	Uplist to Endangered	12 Month Warranted but Precluded 12/26/2011
Deseret Milk-Vetch (*Astragalus deserticus*)	10/06/2015	Delist: Recovery	90 Day Substantial 03/16/2016
Yellow-Billed Cuckoo (*Coccyzus americanus*)	05/04/2017	Delist: Data Error	Not Yet Made
Preble's Meadow Jumping Mouse (*Zapus hudsonmius preble*)	03/30/2007	Delist: Data Error	Not Yet Made
Southwestern Willow Flycatcher (*Empidonax trailli extimus*)	08/25/2015	Delist: Data Error	90 Day Substantial 03/16/2016
American Burying Beetle (*Nicrophorus americanus*)	08/21/2015	Delist: Data Error, New Information	90 Day Substantial 03/16/2016
Cabinet Grizzly (*Ursus arctos horribilus*)	07/27/2015	Delist: Data Error New Information	12 Month Warranted but Precluded 07/24/1991
MN Gray Wolf (*Canus lupus*)	03/16/2010	Delist: Recovery	90 Day Not Substantial 07/01/2015
Plymouth Redbelly Turtle (*Pseudemys rubriventris bangsi*)	02/08/1997	Delist: Data Error New Information	90 Day Substantial 09/27/2011
Ute Ladies'-tresses (*Spiranthes diluvialis*)	05/10/1996	Delist: Data Error, New Information	90 Day Substantial 10/12/2004

Source: https://ecos.fws.gov/ecp/report/table/petitions-received.html.

Conservation International designated the following areas as having the most species in danger of extinction.

Table 5.7   Ten Shrinking Areas with the Most Threatened Species.

1. The Atlantic forest in Brazil, Paraguay, and Argentina has gone from 1.2 million square kilometers to less than 0.1 million square kilometers. Home to 8,000 endemic plant species and 950 birds, sugar, and coffee plantations have destroyed the forest.

2. The Cape Floral region in South Africa contains the highest concentration of plant species in the world. Of about 9,000 different plant species, 1,435 are threatened.

3. The biologically rich Cerrado region of Brazil, the largest woodland savannah in South America, has shrunk from over 2 million km^2 to less than 450,000 km^2 from the clearing of land for grazing and growing crops.

4. The coastal forests in eastern Africa are threatened by agricultural expansion that threatens two critically endangered primate species.

5. The Himalaya region of Nepal, Bhutan, Pakistan, Bangladesh, Myanmar, and China is a huge area of mountains, alpine meadows, grasslands, and subtropical broadleaf forests. Originally four times larger, the area supports dwindling populations of tigers, elephants, and vultures.

6. The Indo-Burma region is located in tropical Asia in the countries of Myanmar, Thailand, Cambodia, Vietnam, India, and China. The region contains many threatened species including 10 bird species, 25 mammal species, and 35 amphibians.

7. The Madrean, Pine-Oak Woodlands of Mexico originally extended across Mexico and parts of the southern United States. Extensive logging has diminished the area to a fifth of its original size. This hotspot is famous for the millions of monarch butterflies that migrate through the region.

8. The Mesoamerica area of Mexico, Guatemala, Belize, Honduras, El Salvador, Costa Rica, and Panama consists of subtropical and tropical ecosystems known for their rich diversity of species of plants, birds, amphibians, and mammals. This hotspot is now only about a fourth of its original size.

9. The Polynesia-Micronesia Southern Pacific Ocean includes coral atolls, coastal wetlands, tropical rainforests, and savannahs. Conservation International considers it the center of the global extinction crisis. Twenty-five birds have gone extinct in the past 200 years from overhunting and invasive species with 90 endemic bird species threatened.

10. The Philippines consists of over 7,000 islands rich in endemic plant species and birds.

Source: https://sustainabilitywriter.wordpress.com/2012/04/18/10-of-the-worlds-most-threatened-biodiversity-hotspots/.

Species vulnerable to extinction often share similar biological and ecological traits. By identifying these traits, predictions can be made about the likelihood of extinctions before population numbers fall below the point of no return. The best strategy is to preserve species while their populations are still healthy after recognizing that human activities are upsetting the balance in previously stable environments. Listed next are the traits and an explanation of the characteristics shared by species vulnerable to extinction.

Table 5.8   Traits of Vulnerable Species.

1.	Native species with small populations and distributions are more vulnerable to extinction than species with larger populations and distributions. When populations become small and isolated, species tend to inbreed. Inbreeding affects individual fitness with decreased sperm quality, smaller litter sizes, higher juvenile mortality, and increased disease. Fragmented populations and island species especially are prone to inbreeding resulting in reduced gene flow and genetic diversity. This lack of genetic diversity, therefore, hinders adaptability and can lead to extinction.
2.	Species with specialized habitats or diets can only thrive in a narrow range of environmental conditions and are more extinction prone than a generalist able to thrive in a wide variety of conditions. For instance, the endangered giant panda specializes on a diet of 95 percent bamboo. If bamboo were to disappear, the panda would quickly become extinct. The endangered black-footed ferret specializes on a diet of prairie dogs and has even evolved a streamline body to enable it to hunt in prairie dog burrows. Healthy prairie dog colonies are essential for the survival of the ferret.
3.	Long-lived species with a low reproductive rates and low mortality may show rapidly declining populations in response to losses in their numbers from poaching, lost habitat, and other human disturbances. They often do not breed until a relatively advanced age and have few young. Many large, long lived bird species, including condors, eagles, and large parrots such as macaws, have low reproductive rates and have been especially susceptible to extinction.
4.	Introduction of non-native species can seriously affect the vitality of native (endemic) species. Predation by exotic species has caused extinction of numerous native animals, especially on islands. These extinctions have occurred among flightless birds such as the dodo bird and great auk, because they lacked defensive behaviors to avoid predation. Invasive rat species introduced by humans are widespread on islands in all the tropical oceans and are major predators of turtles and bird eggs. Tropical seabirds have been especially deleteriously affected by rats.

5.   Animals of large body size are vulnerable because they usually have a
        low reproductive rate and are hunted for their body parts and by trophy
        seekers. It is not surprising, therefore, that most of the large mammals
        on Earth are listed as endangered on the IUCN Red List: whales,
        elephants, rhinoceros, large antelope, bears, tigers, and lions.
        Although wolves are important factors in the balance of ecosystems,
        they are killed by livestock owners and others who consider them
        threats.

6.   Wild plants and animals that are used for human food, pets, and
        medicine are vulnerable to overexploitation. Many fish species are in
        decline because of overfishing. Bluefin tuna, prized for their sushi, has
        suffered a disastrous decline, and they may soon be functionally extinct.
        The tuna's large body size makes them slow to mature and reproduce.
        The lack of sufficient regulation and enforcement and their monetary
        value (a single fish can sell for up to a million dollars) seems to doom
        this species. Another example is the once abundant sturgeon,
        sources of expensive caviar of the Caspian Sea, are now critically
        endangered. The bushmeat markets of West and Central Africa sell
        tons of slaughtered monkeys, forest antelope, chimpanzees, gorillas,
        and other wildlife, devastating species whose tropical forest habitats
        are being logged. Trophy hunting of endangered species by wealthy
        hunters is a threat to a growing number of animals, especially since the
        largest specimens are killed; these are the ones that should be left to
        breed. The higher the value of the animal or product, the greater the
        threat to that species.

7.   Highly social species that depend on group protection or to locate food
        are vulnerable when the social unit is disrupted. Reproduction can be
        limited to an alpha pair (wolves), and removal of an alpha animal can
        destabilize the social group and make it vulnerable to extinction. The
        passenger pigeon was a colonial nesting bird and could only survive
        among large numbers of its own species. Fragmented flocks declined
        to critically low levels, even though their total numbers may have been
        in the thousands. Many species of birds depend on courtship displays
        and will not breed unless males are able to display courtship behavior
        in the company of other males to exhibit a mate choice to females;
        cocks-of-the-rock in South America, prairie chickens and grouse of
        North America are among birds that display for the benefit of females.
        Such birds require specific conditions to breed, and habitat alterations,
        reductions in their populations or hunting pressure that keeps them
        from exposing themselves in the open can prevent their breeding.
        Elephants and manatees are among endangered species with
        many vulnerable traits, including large size, high sociality, slow
        reproduction, low natural mortality, and longevity. In addition,
        they are also slow moving and valuable in trade and as food
        sources.

(continued)

Table 5.8   (continued)

8.	Human-developed technology and weaponry have made all living creatures vulnerable. Predators, never preyed upon in their evolutionary history, are now targeted by hunters, trappers, and poisoners. Guns equipped with telescopic sights can fire at targets miles away to maim and kill even the swiftest and most intelligent animals. These devices give humans such an advantage that they render the natural protections that animals have evolved over eons completely ineffective. The course of evolution is changed from survival of the fittest to survival of animals that are tolerated by humans and those able to persist in polluted, damaged, and ecologically impoverished natural environments.

Source: Adapted from Nilsson, Greta. 1983. "What Is Threatening Species? Traits of Vulnerable Species." *Endangered Species Handbook*. Washington, DC: Animal Welfare Institute, pp. 18–22.

Documents

Excerpt from the Endangered Species Act of 1973

The ESA is known as one of the strongest environmental laws ever passed. The more important sections of the ESA are provided below.

Purpose and Policy

PURPOSES.—The purposes of this Act are to provide a means whereby the ecosystems upon which endangered species and threatened species depend may be conserved, to provide a program for the conservation of such endangered species and threatened species . . .

POLICY.—(1) It is further declared to be the policy of Congress that all Federal departments and agencies shall seek to conserve endangered species and threatened species and shall utilize their authorities in furtherance of the purposes of this Act.

(2) It is further declared to be the policy of Congress that Federal agencies shall cooperate with State and local agencies to resolve water resource issues in concert with conservation of endangered species.

Sec. 4. Determination of Endangered Species and Threatened Species

(a) GENERAL.—(1) The Secretary [of Interior] shall by regulation promulgated in accordance with subsection (b) determine whether any species is an endangered species or a threatened species because of any of the following factors:

(A) the present or threatened destruction, modification, or curtailment of its habitat or range;

(B) overutilization for commercial, recreational, scientific, or educational purposes;

(C) disease or predation;

(D) the inadequacy of existing regulatory mechanisms; or

(E) other natural or manmade factors affecting its continued existence.

(b) BASIS FOR DETERMINATIONS.—(1)(A) The Secretary shall make determinations required by subsection (a) (1) solely on the basis of the best scientific and commercial data available to him after conducting a review of the status of the species and after taking into account those efforts, if any, being made by any State or foreign nation, or any political subdivision of a State or foreign nation, to protect such species, whether by predator control, protection of habitat and food supply, or other conservation practices, within any area under its jurisdiction, or on the high seas.

(B) In carrying out this section, the Secretary shall give consideration to species which have been—

(i) designated as requiring protection from unrestricted commerce by any foreign nation, or pursuant to any international agreement; or

(ii) identified as in danger of extinction, or likely to become so within the foreseeable future, by any State agency or by any agency of a foreign nation that is responsible for the conservation of fish or wildlife or plants.

(2) The Secretary shall designate critical habitat, and make revisions thereto, under subsection (a)(3) on the basis of the best scientific data available and after taking into consideration the economic impact, the impact on national security, and any other relevant impact, of specifying any particular area as critical habitat. The Secretary may exclude any area from critical habitat if he determines that the benefits of such exclusion outweigh the benefits of specifying such area as part of the critical habitat,

unless he determines, based on the best scientific and commercial data available, that the failure to designate such area as critical habitat will result in the extinction of the species concerned.

(3)(A) To the maximum extent practicable, within 90 days after receiving the petition of an interested person under section 553(e) of title 5, United States Code, to add a species to, or to remove a species from, either of the lists published under subsection (c), the Secretary shall make a finding as to whether the petition presents substantial scientific or commercial information indicating that the petitioned action may be warranted. If such a petition is found to present such information, the Secretary shall promptly commence a review of the status of the species concerned. The Secretary shall promptly publish each finding made under this subparagraph in the Federal Register.

(c) LISTS.—(1) The Secretary of the Interior shall publish in the Federal Register a list of all species determined by him or the Secretary of Commerce to be endangered species and a list of all species determined by him or the Secretary of Commerce to be threatened species . . .

(d) PROTECTIVE REGULATIONS.—Whenever any species is listed as a threatened species pursuant to subsection (c) of this section, the Secretary shall issue such regulations as he deems necessary and advisable to provide for the conservation of such species. The Secretary may by regulation prohibit with respect to any threatened species any act prohibited under section 9(a)(1), in the case of fish or wildlife, or section 9(a)(2), in the case of plants, with respect to endangered species; except that with respect to the taking of resident species of fish or wildlife, such regulations shall apply in any State which has entered into a cooperative agreement pursuant to section 6(c) of this Act only to the extent that such regulations have also been adopted by such State.

(e) SIMILARITY OF APPEARANCE CASES.—The Secretary may, by regulation of commerce or taking, and to the extent he deems advisable, treat any species as an endangered species or threatened species even though it is not listed pursuant to section 4 of this Act if he finds that—

(f)(1) RECOVERY PLANS.—The Secretary shall develop and implement plans (hereinafter in this subsection referred to as "recovery plans") for the conservation and survival of endangered species and threatened species listed pursuant to this section, unless he finds that such a plan will not promote the conservation of the species . . .

(g) MONITORING.—(1) The Secretary shall implement a system in cooperation with the States to monitor effectively for not less than five years the status of all species which have recovered to the point at which the measures provided pursuant to this Act are no longer necessary and which, in accordance with the provisions of this section, have been removed from either of the lists published under subsection (c). (2) The Secretary shall make prompt use of the authority under paragraph 7 of subsection (b) of this section to prevent a significant risk to the well being of any such recovered species.

Sec. 6. Land Acquisition

The Secretary, and the Secretary of Agriculture with respect to the National Forest System, shall establish and implement a program to conserve fish, wildlife, and plants, including those which are listed as endangered species or threatened species pursuant to section 4 of this Act. To carry out such a program, the appropriate Secretary—

(1) shall utilize the land acquisition and other authority under the Fish and Wildlife Act of 1956, as amended, the Fish and Wildlife Coordination Act, as amended, and the Migratory Bird Conservation Act, as appropriate; and

(2) is authorized to acquire by purchase, donation, or otherwise, lands, waters, or interests therein, and such authority shall be in addition to any other land acquisition authority vested in him.

(b) ACQUISITIONS.—Funds made available pursuant to the Land and Water Conservation Fund Act of 1965, as amended, may be used for the purpose of acquiring lands, waters, or interest therein under subsection (a) of this section.

SEC. 7. (a)Federal Agencies Actions and Consultations.—

(1) The Secretary shall review other programs administered by him and utilize such programs in furtherance of the purposes of this Act. All other Federal agencies shall, in consultation with and with the assistance of the Secretary, utilize their authorities in furtherance of the purposes of this Act by carrying out programs for the conservation of endangered species and threatened species listed pursuant to section 4 of this Act.

(2) Each Federal agency shall, in consultation with and with the assistance of the Secretary, insure that any action authorized, funded, or carried out by such agency (hereinafter in this section referred to as an "agency action") is not likely to jeopardize the continued existence of any endangered species or threatened species or result in the destruction or adverse modification of habitat of such species which is determined by the Secretary, after consultation as appropriate with affected States, to be critical, unless such agency has been granted an exemption for such action by the Committee pursuant to subsection (h) of this section. In fulfilling the requirements of this paragraph each agency shall use the best scientific and commercial data available.

(3) Subject to such guidelines as the Secretary may establish, a Federal agency shall consult with the Secretary on any prospective agency action at the request of, and in cooperation with, the prospective permit or license applicant if the applicant has reason to believe that an endangered species or a threatened species may be present in the area affected by his project and that implementation of such action will likely affect such species.

(4) Each Federal agency shall confer with the Secretary on any agency action which is likely to jeopardize the continued existence of any species proposed to be listed under section 4 or result in the destruction or adverse modification of critical habitat proposed to be designated for such species. This paragraph does not require a limitation on the commitment of resources as described in subsection (d).

(c) BIOLOGICAL ASSESSMENT.—(1) To facilitate compliance with the requirements of subsection (a)(2), each Federal agency shall, with respect to any agency action of such agency for which no contract for construction has been entered into and for which no construction has begun on the date of enactment of the Endangered Species Act Amendments of 1978, request of the Secretary information whether any species which is listed or proposed to be listed may be present in the area of such proposed action. If the Secretary advises, based on the best scientific and commercial data available, that such species may be present, such agency shall conduct a biological assessment for the purpose of identifying any endangered species or threatened species which is likely to be affected by such action . . .

Sec. 9. Prohibited Acts

a) GENERAL.—(1) Except as provided in sections 6(g)(2) and 10 of this Act, with respect to any endangered species of fish or wildlife listed pursuant to section 4 of this Act it is unlawful for any person subject to the jurisdiction of the United States to—

(A) import any such species into, or export any such species from the United States;

(B) take any such species within the United States or the territorial sea of the United States;

(C) take any such species upon the high seas;

(D) possess, sell, deliver, carry, transport, or ship, by any means whatsoever, any such species taken in violation of subparagraphs (B) and (C);

(E) deliver, receive, carry, transport, or ship in interstate or foreign commerce, by any means whatsoever and in the course of a commercial activity, any such species;

(F) sell or offer for sale in interstate or foreign commerce any such species; or

(G) violate any regulation pertaining to such species or to any threatened species of fish or wildlife listed pursuant to section 4 of this Act and promulgated by the Secretary pursuant to authority provided by this Act.

(2) Except as provided in sections 6(g)(2) and 10 of this Act, with respect to any endangered species of plants listed pursuant to section 4 of this Act, it is unlawful for any person subject to the jurisdiction of the United States to—

(A) import any such species into, or export any such species from, the United States;

(B) remove and reduce to possession any such species from areas under Federal jurisdiction; maliciously damage or destroy any such species on any such area; or remove, cut, dig up, or damage or destroy any such species on any other area in knowing violation of any law or regulation of any State or in the course of any violation of a State criminal trespass law;

(C) deliver, receive, carry, transport, or ship in interstate or foreign commerce, by any means whatsoever and in the course of a commercial activity, any such species;

(D) sell or offer for sale in interstate or foreign commerce any such species; or

(E) violate any regulation pertaining to such species or to any threatened species of plants listed pursuant to section 4 of this Act and promulgated by the Secretary pursuant to authority provided by this Act.

Sec. 10. Exceptions

(a) PERMITS.—(1) The Secretary may permit, under such terms and conditions as he shall prescribe—

(2)(A) No permit may be issued by the Secretary authorizing any taking referred to in paragraph (1)(B) unless the applicant therefor submits to the Secretary a conservation plan that specifies—

(i) the impact which will likely result from such taking;

(ii) what steps the applicant will take to minimize and mitigate such impacts, and the funding that will be available to implement such steps;

(iii) what alternative actions to such taking the applicant considered and the reasons why such alternatives are not being utilized; and

(iv) such other measures that the Secretary may require as being necessary or appropriate for purposes of the plan.

(B) If the Secretary finds, after opportunity for public comment, with respect to a permit application and the related conservation plan that—

(i) the taking will be incidental;

(ii) the applicant will, to the maximum extent practicable, minimize and mitigate the impacts of such taking;

(iii) the applicant will ensure that adequate funding for the plan will be provided;

(iv) the taking will not appreciably reduce the likelihood of the survival and recovery of the species in the wild; and

(v) the measures, if any, required under subparagraph (A) (iv) will be met; and he has received such other assurances as he may require that the plan will be implemented, the Secretary shall issue the permit. The permit shall contain such terms and conditions as the Secretary deems necessary or appropriate to carry out the purposes of this paragraph, including, but not limited to, such reporting requirements as the Secretary deems necessary for determining whether such terms and conditions are being complied with. (C) The Secretary shall revoke a permit issued under this paragraph if he finds that the permittee is not complying with the terms and conditions of the permit.

Sec. 11. Penalties and Enforcement

(a) CIVIL PENALTIES.—(1) Any person who knowingly violates, and any person engaged in business as an importer or exporter of fish, wildlife, or plants who violates, any provision of this Act, . . . may be assessed a civil penalty by the Secretary of not more than $ 25,000 for each violation. Any person who knowingly violates, and any person engaged in business as an importer or exporter of fish, wildlife, or plants who violates, any provision of any other regulation issued under this Act may be assessed a civil penalty by the Secretary of not more than $ 12,000 for each such violation. Any person who otherwise violates any provision of this Act, or any regulation, permit, or certificate issued hereunder, may be assessed a civil penalty by the Secretary of not more than $500 for each such violation. No penalty may be assessed under this subsection unless such person is given notice and opportunity for a hearing with respect to such violation. Each violation shall be a separate offense.

(g) CITIZEN SUITS.—(1) Except as provided in paragraph (2) of this subsection any person may commence a civil suit on his own behalf—

(A) to enjoin any person, including the United States and any other governmental instrumentality or agency (to the extent permitted by the eleventh amendment to the Constitution), who is alleged to be in violation of any provision of this Act or regulation issued under the authority thereof; or

(B) to compel the Secretary to apply, pursuant to section 6(g)(2)(B)(ii) of this Act, the prohibitions set forth in or authorized pursuant to section 4(d) or section 9(a)(1)(B) of this Act with respect to the taking of any resident endangered species or threatened species within any State; or (C) against the Secretary where there is alleged a failure of the Secretary to perform any act or duty under section 4 which is not discretionary with the Secretary. The district courts shall have jurisdiction, without regard to the amount in controversy or the citizenship of the parties, to enforce any such provision or regulation, or to order the Secretary to perform such act or duty, as the case may be. In any civil suit commenced under subparagraph (B) the district court shall compel the Secretary to apply the prohibition sought if the court finds that the allegation that an emergency exists is supported by substantial evidence.

(3)(A) Any suit under this subsection may be brought in the judicial district in which the violation occurs.

(B) In any such suit under this subsection in which the United States is not a party, the Attorney General, at the request of the Secretary, may intervene on behalf of the United States as a matter of right.

(4) The court, in issuing any final order in any suit brought pursuant to paragraph (1) of this subsection, may award costs of litigation (including reasonable attorney and expert witness fees) to any party, whenever the court determines such award is appropriate.

(5) The injunctive relief provided by this subsection shall not restrict any right which any person (or class of persons) may

have under any statute or common law to seek enforcement of any standard or limitation or to seek any other relief (including relief against the Secretary or a State agency).

Source: Endangered Species Act of 1973. U.S. Code 16 (1973): §§ 1531 et seq.

Tennessee Valley Authority v. Hill (1978)

Tennessee Valley Authority v. Hill tested the power and limits of the Endangered Species Act (1973). The Supreme Court ruled that the construction of Tellico Dam must be stopped because a fish, the snail darter, would be eradicated by the completion of the dam. Although there is a suggestion that the Court disliked the implications of the Endangered Species Act, it found it constitutional and would not rule in favor of completing the dam, despite the TVA's plea to use "common sense;" that would appropriate power properly contained in Congress.

MR. CHIEF JUSTICE BURGER delivered the opinion of the Court.

The questions presented in this case are (a) whether the Endangered Species Act of 1973 requires a court to enjoin the operation of a virtually completed federal dam—which had been authorized prior to 1973—when, pursuant to authority vested in him by Congress, the Secretary of the Interior has determined that operation of the dam would eradicate an endangered species; and (b) whether continued congressional appropriations for the dam after 1973 constituted an implied repeal of the Endangered Species Act, at least as to the particular dam.

I

The Little Tennessee River originates in the mountains of northern Georgia and flows through the national forest lands of North Carolina into Tennessee, where it converges with the Big Tennessee River near Knoxville. The lower 33 miles of the Little Tennessee takes the river's clear, free-flowing waters through an area of great natural beauty. Among other environmental amenities, this stretch of river is said to contain abundant trout. Considerable historical importance attaches to the areas immediately adjacent to this portion of the Little Tennessee's banks. To the south of the river's edge lies Fort Loudon, established in 1756 as England's southwestern outpost in the French and Indian War. Nearby are also the ancient sites of several native American villages, the archeological stores of which are to a large extent unexplored. These include the Cherokee towns of Echota and Tennase, the former being the sacred capital of the Cherokee Nation as early as the 16th century and the latter providing the linguistic basis from which the State of Tennessee derives its name.

In this area of the Little Tennessee River the Tennessee Valley Authority, a wholly owned public corporation of the United States, began constructing the Tellico Dam and Reservoir Project in 1967, shortly after Congress appropriated initial funds for its development. Tellico is a multipurpose regional development project designed principally to stimulate shoreline development, generate sufficient electric current to heat 20,000 homes, and provide flatwater recreation and flood control, as well as improve economic conditions in "an area characterized by underutilization of human resources and outmigration of young people." Hearings on Public Works for Power and Energy Research Appropriation Bill, 1977, before a Subcommittee of the House Committee on Appropriations. Of particular relevance to this case is one aspect of the project, a dam which TVA determined to place on the Little Tennessee, a short distance from where the river's waters meet with the Big Tennessee. When fully operational, the dam would impound water covering some 16,500 acres—much of which represents valuable and productive farmland—thereby converting the river's shallow, fast-flowing waters into a deep reservoir over 30 miles in length.

The Tellico Dam has never opened, however, despite the fact that construction has been virtually completed and the dam is essentially ready for operation. Although Congress has appropriated monies for Tellico every year since 1967, progress was delayed, and ultimately stopped, by a tangle of lawsuits and administrative proceedings. After unsuccessfully urging TVA to consider alternatives to damming the Little Tennessee, local citizens and national conservation groups brought suit in the District Court, claiming that the project did not conform to the requirements of the National Environmental Policy Act of 1969 (NEPA). After finding TVA to be in violation of NEPA, the District Court enjoined the dam's completion pending the filing of an appropriate environmental impact statement. The injunction remained in effect until late 1973, when the District Court concluded that TVA's final environmental impact statement for Tellico was in compliance with the law.

A few months prior to the District Court's decision dissolving the NEPA injunction, a discovery was made in the waters of the Little Tennessee which would profoundly affect the Tellico Project. Exploring the area around Coytee Springs, which is about seven miles from the mouth of the river, a University of Tennessee ichthyologist, Dr. David A. Etnier, found a previously unknown species of perch, the snail darter, or Percina (Imostoma) tanasi. This three-inch, tannish-colored fish, whose numbers are estimated to be in the range of 10,000 to 15,000, would soon engage the attention of environmentalists, the TVA, the Department of the Interior, the Congress of the United States, and ultimately the federal courts, as a new and additional basis to halt construction of the dam.

Until recently the finding of a new species of animal life would hardly generate a cause celebre. This is particularly so in the case of darters, of which there are approximately 130 known species, 8 to 10 of these having been identified only in the last five years. The moving force behind the snail darter's sudden fame came some four months after its discovery, when the Congress passed the Endangered Species Act of 1973 (Act).

This legislation, among other things, authorizes the Secretary of the Interior to declare species of animal life "endangered" and to identify the "critical habitat" of these creatures. . . .

II

We begin with the premise that operation of the Tellico Dam will either eradicate the known population of snail darters or destroy their critical habitat. Petitioner does not now seriously dispute this fact. In any event, under 4 (a) (1) of the Act, 87 Stat. 886, 16 U.S.C. 1533 (a) (1) (1976 ed.), the Secretary of the Interior is vested with exclusive authority to determine whether a species such as the snail darter is "endangered" or "threatened" and to ascertain the factors which have led to such a precarious existence. By 4 (d) Congress has authorized— indeed commanded—the Secretary to "issue such regulations as he deems necessary and advisable to provide for the conservation of such species." As we have seen, the Secretary promulgated regulations which declared the snail darter an endangered species whose critical habitat would be destroyed by creation of the Tellico Reservoir. Doubtless petitioner would prefer not to have these regulations on the books, but there is no suggestion that the Secretary exceeded his authority or abused his discretion in issuing the regulations. Indeed, no judicial review of the Secretary's determinations has ever been sought and hence the validity of his actions are not open to review in this Court.

Starting from the above premise, two questions are presented: (a) would TVA be in violation of the Act if it completed and operated the Tellico Dam as planned? (b) if TVA's actions would offend the Act, is an injunction the appropriate remedy for the violation? For the reasons stated hereinafter, we hold that both questions must be answered in the affirmative.

(A)

It may seem curious to some that the survival of a relatively small number of three-inch fish among all the countless millions of species extant would require the permanent halting of a virtually completed dam for which Congress has expended more than $100 million. The paradox is not minimized by the fact that Congress continued to appropriate large sums of public money for the project, even after congressional Appropriations Committees were apprised of its apparent impact upon the survival of the snail darter. We conclude, however, that the explicit provisions of the Endangered Species Act require precisely that result.

One would be hard pressed to find a statutory provision whose terms were any plainer than those in 7 of the Endangered Species Act. Its very words affirmatively command all federal agencies "to insure that actions authorized, funded, or carried out by them do not jeopardize the continued existence" of an endangered species or "result in the destruction or modification of habitat of such species. . . ." This language admits of no exception. Nonetheless, petitioner urges, as do the dissenters, that the Act cannot reasonably be interpreted as applying to a federal project which was well under way when Congress passed the Endangered Species Act of 1973. To sustain that position, however, we would be forced to ignore the ordinary meaning of plain language. It has not been shown, for example, how TVA can close the gates of the Tellico Dam without "carrying out" an action that has been "authorized" and "funded" by a federal agency. Nor can we understand how such action will "insure" that the snail darter's habitat is not disrupted. Accepting the Secretary's determinations, as we must, it is clear that TVA's proposed operation of the dam will have precisely the opposite effect, namely the eradication of an endangered species.

Concededly, this view of the Act will produce results requiring the sacrifice of the anticipated benefits of the project and of many millions of dollars in public funds. But examination of the language, history, and structure of the legislation under review here indicates beyond doubt that Congress intended endangered species to be afforded the highest of priorities. . . .

As it was finally passed, the Endangered Species Act of 1973 represented the most comprehensive legislation for the preservation of endangered species ever enacted by any nation. Its stated purposes were "to provide a means whereby the ecosystems upon which endangered species and threatened species depend may be conserved," and "to provide a program for the conservation of such . . . species. . . ." In furtherance of these goals, Congress expressly stated in 2 (c) that "all Federal departments and agencies shall seek to conserve endangered species and threatened species. . . ." Lest there be any ambiguity as to the meaning of this statutory directive, the Act specifically defined "conserve" as meaning "to use and the use of all methods and procedures which are necessary to bring any endangered species or threatened species to the point at which the measures provided pursuant to this chapter are no longer necessary." Aside from 7, other provisions indicated the seriousness with which Congress viewed this issue: Virtually all dealings with endangered species, including taking, possession, transportation, and sale, were prohibited, except in extremely narrow circumstances. The Secretary was also given extensive power to develop regulations and programs for the preservation of endangered and threatened species. Citizen involvement was encouraged by the Act, with provisions allowing interested persons to petition the Secretary to list a species as endangered or threatened, and bring civil suits in United States district courts to force compliance with any provision of the Act. . . .

It is against this legislative background that we must measure TVA's claim that the Act was not intended to stop operation of a project which, like Tellico Dam, was near completion when an endangered species was discovered in its path. While there is no discussion in the legislative history of precisely this problem, the totality of congressional action makes it abundantly clear that the result we reach today is wholly in accord with both the words of the statute and the intent of Congress. The plain intent of Congress in enacting this statute was to halt and reverse the trend toward species extinction, whatever the cost. This is reflected not only in the stated policies of the Act, but in literally every section of the statute. All persons, including

federal agencies, are specifically instructed not to "take" endangered species, meaning that no one is "to harass, harm, pursue, hunt, shoot, wound, kill, trap, capture, or collect" such
life forms. Agencies in particular are directed by 2 (c) and 3
(2) of the Act to "use . . . all methods and procedures which
are necessary" to preserve endangered species. In addition, the
legislative history undergirding 7 reveals an explicit congressional decision to require agencies to afford first priority to
the declared national policy of saving endangered species. The
pointed omission of the type of qualifying language previously
included in endangered species legislation reveals a conscious
decision by Congress to give endangered species priority over
the "primary missions" of federal agencies. . . .

(B)

Having determined that there is an irreconcilable conflict between operation of the Tellico Dam and the explicit provisions
of 7 of the Endangered Species Act, we must now consider
what remedy, if any, is appropriate. It is correct, of course, that
a federal judge sitting as a chancellor is not mechanically obli-
gated to grant an injunction for every violation of law. . . .

But these principles take a court only so far. Our system of
government is, after all, a tripartite one, with each branch having certain defined functions delegated to it by the Constitution. While "[i]t is emphatically the province and duty of the
judicial department to say what the law is," *Marbury v. Madison*
(1803), it is equally—and emphatically—the exclusive province of the Congress not only to formulate legislative policies
and mandate programs and projects, but also to establish their
relative priority for the Nation. Once Congress, exercising its
delegated powers, has decided the order of priorities in a given
area, it is for the Executive to administer the laws and for the
courts to enforce them when enforcement is sought.

Here we are urged to view the Endangered Species Act "reasonably," and hence shape a remedy "that accords with some
modicum of common sense and the public weal." But is that

our function? We have no expert knowledge on the subject of endangered species, much less do we have a mandate from the people to strike a balance of equities on the side of the Tellico Dam. Congress has spoken in the plainest of words, making it abundantly clear that the balance has been struck in favor of affording endangered species the highest of priorities, thereby adopting a policy which it described as "institutionalized caution." . . .

We agree with the Court of Appeals that in our constitutional system the commitment to the separation of powers is too fundamental for us to pre-empt congressional action by judicially decreeing what accords with "common sense and the public weal." Our Constitution vests such responsibilities in the political branches.

Affirmed.

Source: *Tennessee Valley Auth. v. Hill*, 437 U.S. 153 (1978).

Testimony on Reintroducing Wolves (1995)

In the early 1990s, Interior Department officials in the Clinton administration approved a plan to reintroduce gray wolves into the Rocky Mountains, where they had been extirpated decades earlier by farmers and livestock owners who viewed them as a vicious predator that threatened their livelihoods. Specifically, the wolf recovery scheme spearheaded by the U.S. Fish and Wildlife Service proposed to release captured gray wolves from Canada into Yellowstone National Park and the remote valleys of central Idaho's Frank Church–River of No Return Wilderness. The legal authority for this initiative came from the Endangered Species Act (ESA). The USFS plan, however, triggered angry rebukes from rural landowners in the regions surrounding these public lands, as well as from their elected representatives in Washington, D.C., and the state capitols of Wyoming and Idaho. Conservative Republicans opposed to the reintroduction plan quickly convened congressional hearings in Washington in an effort to scuttle the reintroduction. One of the private citizens who spoke out against the wolf recovery effort was Robert Sears, representing the Idaho Cattle Association.

I appreciate the opportunity to appear here. I represent not only the Idaho Cattle Association but the Idaho Wool Growers Association as I testify before this Committee today.

It is apparent to anyone who lives in the more remote areas of our western States that cattle and sheepmen have a distinct fear of having wolves, bears, and other predators in direct proximity to their livestock. This has been the case since the dawn of recorded history. One needs but to recall the biblical records of the lives of Cain, David, and the Good Shepherd, and others as examples of the constant vigil these individuals keep over their livestock and of the need to slay the predators that threaten the herds and the flocks. By the way, our 3,000,000 animal herd of sheep of a few years back has now dwindled to 225,000 partly because of Government action, partly because of imported lamb, and partly because of coyotes, and we certainly don't need wolves to add to the reduction of those numbers.

With this in mind, I assure you that the herdsmen and shepherds of today are no less concerned than their counterparts throughout recorded history with the thought of having these vicious predators nearby while the cattle and sheep they depend upon for their livelihood graze on the meadows and hillsides.

Today's herdsmen and shepherds trying to survive in the modern world on lands that were passed down to them for several generations by ancestors who, through the years of effort, succeeded in eliminating what was recognized as a significant threat to their livelihood, that being the wolves and the bears, are now faced with the prospect of having those same predators reintroduced to the land by that referred-to menace, the wolf in sheep's clothing. This menace, of course, was represented by the Federal Fish and Wildlife Service under the direction of the Secretary of the Interior . . . [who are] justifiably suspect by those I represent.

Nevertheless, some cattle and sheep owners in Idaho, against their better judgment, perplexed and bewildered by the burning desire of preservationists and conservationist groups from the east to return these animals to their backyards, agreed to serve on the congressionally-appointed Wolf Management Committee to develop a plan whereby a nonessential experimental population of wolves could be reintroduced into the Frank Church Wilderness Area of central Idaho.

This committee produced such a plan and presented it, I believe, to this Committee, where it was pigeonholed because of opposition of some of the environmental groups and never acted upon. Subsequently the Fish and Wildlife Service prepared an environmental impact statement on which numerous comments were submitted by our members and others presenting the essentials of the original management plan that included the right to protect their livestock and not only their livestock but their guard dogs and their herd dogs and those animals with which they are closely associated, many of them more importantly than the loss of a cow or a sheep and their pets from being attacked by these vicious predators, making the agency responsible for their actions, namely the reintroduction and for the subsequent financial losses incurred by the owners of those domestic animals. Most of these reasonable safeguards were ignored in the final wolf recovery environmental impact statement, making it impossible for reasonable and prudent livestock producers to support the process. One avenue for obtaining this protection did, however, still exist, the opportunity to participate in developing a State wolf management plan that could be adopted by the State by the Fish and Wildlife Service, allowing the Idaho Department of Fish and Game to provide the management of the reintroduced, nonessential, experimental population of wolves.

Once again, livestock producer representatives worked with others to develop a plan that provided for a growing population of wolves in central Idaho and reasonable assurance of the right to protect one's domestic animals and provide for just compensation for actual animal losses. These essential elements of the plan were rejected by the U.S. Fish and Wildlife Service along with one other very critical element of the plan, which is the statutory right of the Idaho State Legislature to maintain control over the actions of the Idaho Fish and Game Department in managing these wolves.

We have been assured by the U.S. Fish and Wildlife Service that the wolves will be retained under the nonessential experimental status. However, as I speak, the Sierra Club and others have lawsuits in Federal courts calling for elimination of this status. The U.S. Fish and Wildlife Service then assures us that should this happen they will remove the wolves from the area. However, since one wolf was killed by the dart process and the gathering process, it is entirely probable that a subsequent lawsuit by animal rights groups would keep U.S. Fish and Wildlife Service from keeping this promise.

The bottom line is that every elected official in the State of Idaho Capitol Building, 75 percent of the members of our Idaho legislature, and the entire Idaho congressional delegation requested that Interior Secretary Babbitt halt his plans to transport wolves into central Idaho until such time as the . . . legitimate concerns of our citizens could be properly dealt with in a workable wolf management plan. I do not know if the letters requesting this action reached the Secretary before he left Washington for Yellowstone Park where he personally participated in the first release of wolves in that location. I would like to give him the benefit of the doubt in regard to those first four wolves that came into central Idaho. Perhaps he was unaware of the concerns of our citizens and our legislature. However, I cannot extend the same doubt to the apparent disregard for those express concerns in subsequent releases of 11 more wolves several days later.

This is not the first time the Secretary has shown his apparent lack of concern for the wishes of our State's elected officials. He has been a party to a number of such actions in the past two years, including total disregard of the wishes of our recently retired governor and former Secretary of Interior Cecil Andrus relative to a new Air Force training range also supported by ranchers who graze livestock in the area.

We would ask Congress to intercede in this matter and prohibit the Secretary and U.S. Fish and Wildlife Service from any further reintroduction of wolves in the State of Idaho and to further instruct him to negotiate in good faith with the State of Idaho in the development of a realistic, workable management plan or, as an alternative, get the wolves out of our backyard. Not to do so is tantamount to inviting international terrorist groups to bring small detachments of trainees into the area, allowing them to practice their activities on the unsuspecting local communities and then prohibiting the locals from protecting themselves from these killers. Such actions are unconscionable.

We would further request that Congress take timely action to proceed on reauthorization of the Endangered Species Act, therein providing some much needed safeguards that recognize the right of human beings to exist in the presence of other species in this land and place reasonable priorities for the protection of their human rights somewhat above or at least on an equal footing with wolves, bears, salmon, and the now infamous Bruneau Hotspring Snail, also an Idaho resident.

The taxpayer burden on this reintroduction has, we believe, been seriously underestimated. The net economic value to the central Idaho area reported in the EIS at $8.4 million is ludicrous. Mr. Bangs, the U.S. Fish and Wildlife Service project chairman for the EIS, has with a straight face told me that this estimate is based largely upon anticipated tourist expenditures from those drawn to the area in anticipation of seeing a wolf. Can you honestly believe that tourists are going to buy $8.4 million worth of T-shirts, sculptures, and photo prints of wolves in central Idaho? This is one of the most ridiculous examples of bureaucratic hoodwinking I have ever heard.

Please consider the private property rights of Idahoans and the rights of Idaho State Government in managing the affairs within its border. Halt this activity until proper safeguards can be worked out and put into place, or halt it permanently.

I thank you for your consideration.

Source: Statement of Robert Sears, Idaho Cattle Association. In Introducing Gray Wolves in Yellowstone and Idaho: Oversight Hearing before the Committee on Resources, House of Representatives, One Hundred Fourth Congress, First Session, on Federal Efforts to Introduce Canadian Gray Wolves into Yellowstone National Park and the Central Idaho Wilderness, January 26, 1995. Washington, DC: Government Printing Office, 1995, pp. 58–60.

Examining the Endangered Species Act (2014)

Chairman James Lankford (R-OK) hosted this exchange at a hearing on the Endangered Species Act in February 2014. Also involved were Representative Cynthia Lummis (R-WY), Counselor Michael Bean (Fish and Wildlife and Parks, Department of the Interior) and Representative Rob Woodall (R-GA).

Mr. Lankford. The ESA was enacted to conserve habitats and species that are considered endangered or threatened. President Nixon signed it into law with the support of 99 percent of Congress. At the time, there were high expectations for the Endangered Species Act, President Nixon saying this new law will protect an irreplaceable part of our national heritage and threatened wildlife.

However, over the years, some flaws of the Endangered Species Act have surfaced. There is a significant concern that some are using the act to advance other policy goals, such as stopping development, instead of for its intended purpose of protecting threatened animal and plant species.

Concerns also abound over whether or not the law gives the implementing agencies enough time to properly process the candidates for species listing. In one instance, Fish and Wildlife

Service was asked in a petition to examine 374 separate aquatic species, all from 1 petition, in the statutory 90-day timeframe. As a result, the Agency admitted that it was only able to conduct cursory reviews of the information in their files and the literature cited in the petition.

This put the Agencies in a very difficult position: Process the enormous work brought in by a petition within 90 days or face a lawsuit for missing the deadline from the same groups bringing the petition in the first place.

The mass amount of petitions led to a transition toward sue-and-settle agreements. Whether by choice or not, the Federal Government faces lawsuits that are very often settled to the financial benefit of environmental groups and their lawyers. In many of these cases, States and other affected stakeholders are not even aware of the negotiations or what is being discussed until they are resolved.

Also, there have been instances where much of the basis of these settlements remains sealed. Thus, communities and stakeholders affected by these listings don't have a full view of what all occurred. In general, the lack of transparency of the data used to justify a species' listing remains a major problem. In some cases, data gathered at taxpayer expense has not been publicly released.

Transparency is essential to public faith in government. The less information the public has to understand the Endangered Species Act and how it is carried out, the less support the act will have, and it will be even more difficult to process in the future.

The general success rate of the ESA has also come under criticism, as well: only a 2 percent recovery rate of the approximately 2,100 species listed on the endangered/threatened list since 1973. As I discussed previously, we have seen how we get species on the list. However, the above statistic begs the question, how do species graduate off the list? Is 2 percent enough for success?

Like all Federal agencies in this time of belt-tightening, Fish and Wildlife Service and NOAA Fisheries have finite resources.

They are spending all their time and resources getting species on the list. It is unclear if they are able to spend the time necessary and the finances necessary to get species off the list, which was the reason this law was passed in the first place 40 years ago.

Some claim that success can be measured by adding species to the list, as their prospects will benefit once they get there. I hope that is the case. However, the goal of the law enacted 40 years ago was to rehabilitate species and to move them off the list, not perpetual staying on it.

If Americans are going to have faith in the Endangered Species Act, they need to see how it works and that it works at all. Constantly heaping more species on the listings while barely moving any off of it will undermine that faith and raise questions about the act's effectiveness.

We also have to deal with the issues of: How do we determine if the act is being effective? And when things are moved off, are they moved off because of habitat or because of population numbers? Are those goals set in advance? And do the different communities even know how to have those goals achieved at all?

. . .

Mrs. Lummis. Okay. Well, let me ask it this way: Do you think science has been static since 1973?

Mr. Bean. Of course not.

Mrs. Lummis. Do you think that people's environmental ethic has been static since 1973?

Mr. Bean. Probably not.

Mrs. Lummis. Do you think that people in general are more attuned to their stewardship responsibilities to the environment than they were in 1973?

Mr. Bean. Probably so.

Mrs. Lummis. I think so, too. In fact, I think it has become embedded, it is cultural now, much more so than it was when the Endangered Species Act was passed. I think that the culture has grown in its sensitivity and its stewardship obligations to species, to clean water, clean air, clean land. And I think that is why things like our compliance with the Kyoto protocols for clean air have been met. And we are the only country that met those Kyoto protocols, even though we didn't sign on to the Kyoto protocols.

Americans have a marvelous stewardship and an environmental sensitivity that is cultural; it is embedded. And, to that extent, litigation, in my opinion, that puts briefcases in courtrooms but not species on conserved habitat isn't the answer in the 21st century. To me, the answer in the 21st century is boots-on-the-ground conservation by people who are culturally attuned to preserve species, be they tribal members or State government employees or private landowners working together to conserve species.

So to take an act that passed in 1973 and was last amended in 1988, where the people, the culture has gone far beyond the ethos of the act, and expect that act and its litigation-driven model to be the way we should administer the law in the 21st century is a lot like driving an Edsel in 2014 and thinking that it ought to perform like a 2014 car. The performance of automobiles is better. The performance of the American people with regard to science and culture and the ethics of species conservation have improved.

So I would really like to see the Endangered Species Act updated to acquaint it with and harmonize it with the culture and the ethos and the ethics and the stewardship that the American people are quite capable of providing. It doesn't need to be done in the courtroom anymore. Those funds that are so difficult to come by can be spent on habitat conservation and boots-on-the-ground species recovery without lawyers in the courtroom earning the money and taking that precious financial resource that is so hard to come by away from the very species that the Endangered Species Act was designed to protect.

Mr. Woodall. Mr. Chairman, if I could follow up on that? I want to ask, because listening to both Ms. Lummis and the chairman, it felt oddly adversarial to me. I am thinking, for Pete's sakes, the chairman's talking about millions of dollars that are being spent that are not directed at something that we have come together on and tried to unify our might to solve but directed towards ambiguities.

Ms. Lummis doesn't just live this every day back home but, you know, isn't talking through her hat when she talks about a conservation ethos. And, obviously, things have changed over the last 40 years. Obviously, what President Nixon envisioned is not where we are today. Are we close, are we further? We could have that conversation, but, obviously, we are not exactly where folks thought we would be 40 years later.

Why does it feel adversarial? Why isn't it a big Kumbayah session to say, let's make some changes and let's refocus our resources on those most critical missions?

I can't think of the last time I was involved in an ESA problem-solving session that was on its way to fruition. I can think of many ESA arguments that I have been involved in. Tell me why that is. Why aren't we moving closer to a common goal today?

Mr. Bean. Well, sir, I will be happy to offer my own experience in answer to your question.

My own experience is I have worked with landowners in your State; I mentioned the forest landowners in the Red Hills area. I have worked with forest landowners in North Carolina in the Sandhills area. I have worked in ranchland in Texas. In particular, I mentioned to Mr. Lankford yesterday a gentleman named Bob Long, who was chairman of the Republican Party of Bastrop County, Texas—local bank president, fundamentalist minister, extreme conservative, but somebody who was willing to manage his land to help recover an endangered amphibian called the Houston toad.

And what I learned from that work with him and those other landowners is that a lot of this acrimony or contention that has been talked about today in this room doesn't really exist at that level. People are willing to roll up their sleeves and work together with the Fish and Wildlife Service, with the organization for which I work which Mrs. Lummis mentioned. And one doesn't get that sense often out on the ground talking to people where these efforts are ongoing.

So I can only answer based on my experience, but my experience is that when you offer landowners an opportunity to work constructively with the Fish and Wildlife Service in a way that each understands the needs of the others and tries to accommodate them, you can have success.

Mr. Woodall. I am afraid you are making my point exactly. That is my experience on the ground, too.

So when the chairman says he sees millions of dollars being wasted on efforts that we are not directing together, why aren't we equally incensed about that?

When Ms. Lummis says that there are dollars being errantly directed to litigation instead of mitigation, and you talk about your successful experiences one-on-one on the ground, why aren't we rushing to agree with Ms. Lummis and talk about proposed changes to the statute to foster what is the most hard-fought commodity in this Nation, not the all-precious and incredibly too limited American dollar, but the all-precious and incredibly limited trust that goes between citizens and their government?

What you say I will stipulate is true. So what next? Why isn't the next conversation, then, that collaborative sitting around the table making changes to the statute to amplify those successes and mitigate these failures?

Mr. Bean. Well, sir, perhaps the answer is that all the examples I gave—or none of the examples I gave required amending the law. All of the examples I gave required creatively interpreting and applying the law.

And I think what this act has shown, despite the fact that it has remained unchanged by Congress since 1988, it has been changed substantially by the Fish and Wildlife Service in its implementation, in its use of new tools that didn't exist in 1973 or 1988 in order to engage landowners as partners, in order to better engage States, in order to make use of the flexible authorities I described.

The act has been, in my judgment, remarkably flexible and adaptive. I don't for a minute mean to suggest that there aren't controversies, but as I tried to make the point with respect to the Oregon chub at the outset, most of the species most of the time don't generate those controversies. Progress is being made without lots of headlines, without lots of heat, without lots of rancor.

Mr. Woodall. If I could just take one last stab at it. You are absolutely right; the successes that you mentioned don't require changing the statute at all, but the failures that my colleagues mentioned did.

I don't know why it is that somehow we have to choose between having both the successes and the failures or having neither the success nor the failures. I don't think that is the world that we live in. I think we can have the successes, and even greater successes, and eliminate those failures.

But, again, just one last effort: Am I wrong about that? Again, you are talking about successes that don't require changes. My colleagues are talking about failures that do require changes. Why aren't we coming together around eliminating the failures and amplifying the successes?

Mr. Bean. We may have a disagreement about the failures. In Mr. Lankford's case, I don't think the money that is being spent is being wasted. I think the money is being invested to find out what the status of the lesser prairie chicken really is. And I think that will be very helpful to us in deciding whether we need to protect it and, if so, how we need to protect it.

So I don't for a minute suggest that it isn't oftentimes difficult and sometimes expensive in order to get answers to these questions, but I think investing in finding out the answers is not necessarily a waste of resources or money or time.

Source: Hearing before the Subcommittee on Energy Policy, Health Care, and Entitlements of the Committee on Oversight and Government Reform, House of Representatives. 113th Congress, 2nd Session. February 27, 2014. Washington, DC: Government Printing Office, 2014. https://www.govinfo.gov/content/pkg/CHRG-113hhrg87950/html/CHRG-113hhrg87950.htm.

Executive Order Promoting Energy Independence and Economic Growth (2017)

President Donald Trump began dismantling efforts to curb greenhouse gases on March 28, 2017, with an executive order directing the Environmental Protection Agency (EPA) to review, suspend, revise or rescind the Clean Power Plan rule established by President Obama and stayed by the Supreme Court in February 2016. (The Obama rule, designed to lower carbon dioxide emissions to fight global warming, would have closed hundreds of coal-fired power plants, frozen construction of new plants, and replaced them with new wind and solar farms.) The Trump order also directed federal agencies to review all existing regulations, orders, guidance documents, and policies that "burden the development and use" of domestically produced energy resources, disband the White House Council on Environmental quality, and lift the Department of Interior's moratorium on new coal leases on federal land. (On June 1, 2017, President Trump continued his efforts to roll back climate change policy with an announcement that the United States would withdraw from the Paris climate accord.)

By the authority vested in me as President by the Constitution and the laws of the United States of America, it is hereby ordered as follows:

Section 1. Policy. (a) It is in the national interest to promote clean and safe development of our Nation's vast energy resources, while at the same time avoiding regulatory burdens that unnecessarily encumber energy production, constrain economic growth, and prevent job creation. Moreover, the prudent development of these natural resources is essential to ensuring the Nation's geopolitical security.

(b) It is further in the national interest to ensure that the Nation's electricity is affordable, reliable, safe, secure, and clean, and that it can be produced from coal, natural gas, nuclear material, flowing water, and other domestic sources, including renewable sources.

(c) Accordingly, it is the policy of the United States that executive departments and agencies (agencies) immediately review existing regulations that potentially burden the development or use of domestically produced energy resources and appropriately suspend, revise, or rescind those that unduly burden the development of domestic energy resources beyond the degree necessary to protect the public interest or otherwise comply with the law.

(d) It further is the policy of the United States that, to the extent permitted by law, all agencies should take appropriate actions to promote clean air and clean water for the American people, while also respecting the proper roles of the Congress and the States concerning these matters in our constitutional republic.

(e) It is also the policy of the United States that necessary and appropriate environmental regulations comply with the law, are of greater benefit than cost, when permissible, achieve environmental improvements for the American people, and are developed through transparent processes that employ the best available peer-reviewed science and economics.

Sec. 2. Immediate Review of All Agency Actions that Potentially Burden the Safe, Efficient Development of Domestic Energy Resources. (a) The heads of agencies shall review all existing regulations, orders, guidance documents, policies, and any other similar agency actions (collectively, agency actions) that potentially burden the development or use of domestically produced energy resources, with particular attention to oil, natural gas, coal, and nuclear energy resources. Such review shall not include agency actions that are mandated by law, necessary for the public interest, and consistent with the policy set forth in section 1 of this order.

(b) For purposes of this order, "burden" means to unnecessarily obstruct, delay, curtail, or otherwise impose significant costs on the siting, permitting, production, utilization, transmission, or delivery of energy resources.

. . .

Sec. 3. Rescission of Certain Energy and Climate-Related Presidential and Regulatory Actions. (a) The following Presidential actions are hereby revoked:

(i) Executive Order 13653 of November 1, 2013 (Preparing the United States for the Impacts of Climate Change);

(ii) The Presidential Memorandum of June 25, 2013 (Power Sector Carbon Pollution Standards);

(iii) The Presidential Memorandum of November 3, 2015 (Mitigating Impacts on Natural Resources from Development and Encouraging Related Private Investment); and

(iv) The Presidential Memorandum of September 21, 2016 (Climate Change and National Security).

(b) The following reports shall be rescinded:

(i) The Report of the Executive Office of the President of June 2013 (The President's Climate Action Plan); and

(ii) The Report of the Executive Office of the President of March 2014 (Climate Action Plan Strategy to Reduce Methane Emissions).

(c) The Council on Environmental Quality shall rescind its final guidance entitled "Final Guidance for Federal Departments and Agencies on Consideration of Greenhouse Gas Emissions and the Effects of Climate Change in National Environmental Policy Act Reviews," which is referred to in "Notice of Availability," 81 Fed. Reg. 51866 (August 5, 2016).

. . .

Sec. 4. Review of the Environmental Protection Agency's "Clean Power Plan" and Related Rules and Agency Actions. (a) The Administrator of the Environmental Protection Agency (Administrator) shall immediately take all steps necessary to review the final rules set forth in subsections (b)(i) and (b)(ii) of this section, and any rules and guidance issued pursuant to them, for consistency with the policy set forth in section 1 of this order and, if appropriate, shall, as soon as practicable, suspend, revise, or rescind the guidance, or publish for notice and comment proposed rules suspending, revising, or rescinding those rules. In addition, the Administrator shall immediately take all steps necessary to review the proposed rule set forth in subsection (b)(iii) of this section, and, if appropriate, shall, as soon as practicable, determine whether to revise or withdraw the proposed rule.

(b) This section applies to the following final or proposed rules:

    (i)   The final rule entitled "Carbon Pollution Emission Guidelines for Existing Stationary Sources: Electric Utility Generating Units," 80 Fed. Reg. 64661 (October 23, 2015) (Clean Power Plan);

    (ii) The final rule entitled "Standards of Performance for Greenhouse Gas Emissions from New, Modified, and Reconstructed Stationary Sources: Electric Utility Generating Units," 80 Fed. Reg. 64509 (October 23, 2015); and

    (iii) The proposed rule entitled "Federal Plan Requirements for Greenhouse Gas Emissions From Electric Utility Generating Units Constructed on or Before January 8, 2014; Model Trading Rules; Amendments to Framework Regulations; Proposed Rule," 80 Fed. Reg. 64966 (October 23, 2015).

(c) The Administrator shall review and, if appropriate, as soon as practicable, take lawful action to suspend, revise, or rescind, as appropriate and consistent with law, the "Legal Memorandum Accompanying Clean Power Plan for Certain Issues," which was published in conjunction with the Clean Power Plan.

. . .

(d) The Administrator shall promptly notify the Attorney General of any actions taken by the Administrator pursuant to this order related to the rules identified in subsection (b) of this section so that the Attorney General may, as appropriate, provide notice of this order and any such action to any court with jurisdiction over pending litigation related to those rules, and may, in his discretion, request that the court stay the litigation or otherwise delay further litigation, or seek other appropriate relief consistent with this order, pending the completion of the administrative actions described in subsection (a) of this section.

Sec. 5. Review of Estimates of the Social Cost of Carbon, Nitrous Oxide, and Methane for Regulatory Impact Analysis. (a) In order to ensure sound regulatory decision making, it is essential that agencies use estimates of costs and benefits in their regulatory analyses that are based on the best available science and economics.

(b) The Interagency Working Group on Social Cost of Greenhouse Gases (IWG), which was convened by the Council of Economic Advisers and the OMB Director, shall be disbanded, and the following documents issued by the IWG shall be withdrawn as no longer representative of governmental policy:

(i) Technical Support Document: Social Cost of Carbon for Regulatory Impact Analysis Under Executive Order 12866 (February 2010);

(ii) Technical Update of the Social Cost of Carbon for Regulatory Impact Analysis (May 2013);

(iii) Technical Update of the Social Cost of Carbon for Regulatory Impact Analysis (November 2013);

(iv) Technical Update of the Social Cost of Carbon for Regulatory Impact Analysis (July 2015);

(v) Addendum to the Technical Support Document for Social Cost of Carbon: Application of the Methodology to Estimate the Social Cost of Methane and the Social Cost of Nitrous Oxide (August 2016); and

(vi) Technical Update of the Social Cost of Carbon for Regulatory Impact Analysis (August 2016).

(c) Effective immediately, when monetizing the value of changes in greenhouse gas emissions resulting from regulations, including with respect to the consideration of domestic versus international impacts and the consideration of appropriate discount rates, agencies shall ensure, to the extent permitted by law, that any such estimates are consistent with the guidance contained in OMB Circular A-4 of September 17, 2003 (Regulatory Analysis), which was issued after peer review and public comment and has been widely accepted for more than a decade as embodying the best practices for conducting regulatory cost-benefit analysis.

Sec. 6. Federal Land Coal Leasing Moratorium. The Secretary of the Interior shall take all steps necessary and appropriate to amend or withdraw Secretary's Order 3338 dated January 15, 2016 (Discretionary Programmatic Environmental Impact Statement (PEIS) to Modernize the Federal Coal Program), and to lift any and all moratoria on Federal land coal leasing activities related to Order 3338. The Secretary shall commence Federal coal leasing activities consistent with all applicable laws and regulations.

Sec. 7. Review of Regulations Related to United States Oil and Gas Development. (a) The Administrator shall review the final rule entitled "Oil and Natural Gas Sector: Emission Standards for New, Reconstructed, and Modified Sources," 81 Fed. Reg. 35824 (June 3, 2016), and any rules and guidance issued pursuant to it, for consistency with the policy set forth in section 1 of this order and, if appropriate, shall, as soon as practicable, suspend, revise, or rescind the guidance, or publish for notice and comment proposed rules suspending, revising, or rescinding those rules.

(b) The Secretary of the Interior shall review the following final rules, and any rules and guidance issued pursuant to them, for consistency with the policy set forth in section 1 of this order and, if appropriate, shall, as soon as practicable, suspend, revise, or rescind the guidance, or publish for notice and comment proposed rules suspending, revising, or rescinding those rules:

(i) The final rule entitled "Oil and Gas; Hydraulic Fracturing on Federal and Indian Lands," 80 Fed. Reg. 16128 (March 26, 2015);

(ii) The final rule entitled "General Provisions and Non-Federal Oil and Gas Rights," 81 Fed. Reg. 77972 (November 4, 2016);

(iii) The final rule entitled "Management of Non Federal Oil and Gas Rights," 81 Fed. Reg. 79948 (November 14, 2016); and

(iv) The final rule entitled "Waste Prevention, Production Subject to Royalties, and Resource Conservation," 81 Fed. Reg. 83008 (November 18, 2016).

. . .

Source: Executive Order 13783, 82 Federal Register 16093, signed March 28, 2017; published March 31, 2017.

U.S. Withdrawal from the Paris Climate Accord (2017)

Despite pressure to remain in the Paris Accord on Climate Change from businesses and corporations (including ExxonMobil, Conoco Phillips, and GE), a gift from Pope Francis of his Encyclical on Climate Change, and support by a majority of Americans, President Trump issued an executive order to pull out of the Paris agreement on June 1, 2017, joining only Syria and Nicaragua as countries not included in the agreement. In this statement given at the White House, Trump explains his reasoning.

. . . Therefore, in order to fulfill my solemn duty to protect America and its citizens, the United States will withdraw from the Paris Climate Accord thank you, thank you—but begin negotiations to reenter either the Paris Accord or a really entirely new transaction on terms that are fair to the United States, its businesses, its workers, its people, its taxpayers. So we're getting out. But we will start to negotiate, and we will see if we can make a deal that's fair. And if we can, that's great. And if we can't, that's fine.

As President, I can put no other consideration before the wellbeing of American citizens. The Paris Climate Accord is simply the latest example of Washington entering into an agreement that disadvantages the United States to the exclusive benefit of other countries, leaving American workers—who I love—and taxpayers to absorb the cost in terms of lost jobs, lower wages, shuttered factories, and vastly diminished economic production.

Thus, as of today, the United States will cease all implementation of the non-binding Paris Accord and the draconian financial and economic burdens the agreement imposes on our country. This includes ending the implementation of the nationally determined contribution and, very importantly, the Green Climate Fund which is costing the United States a vast fortune.

Compliance with the terms of the Paris Accord and the onerous energy restrictions it has placed on the United States could cost America as much as 2.7 million lost jobs by 2025 according to the National Economic Research Associates. This includes 440,000 fewer manufacturing jobs—not what we need—believe me, this is not what we need—including automobile jobs, and the further decimation of vital American industries on which countless communities rely. They rely for so much, and we would be giving them so little.

According to this same study, by 2040, compliance with the commitments put into place by the previous administration would cut production for the following sectors: paper down 12 percent; cement down 23 percent; iron and steel down 38 percent; coal—and I happen to love the coal miners—down

86 percent; natural gas down 31 percent. The cost to the economy at this time would be close to $3 trillion in lost GDP and 6.5 million industrial jobs, while households would have $7,000 less income and, in many cases, much worse than that.

Not only does this deal subject our citizens to harsh economic restrictions, it fails to live up to our environmental ideals. As someone who cares deeply about the environment, which I do, I cannot in good conscience support a deal that punishes the United States—which is what it does—the world's leader in environmental protection, while imposing no meaningful obligations on the world's leading polluters.

For example, under the agreement, China will be able to increase these emissions by a staggering number of years—13. They can do whatever they want for 13 years. Not us. India makes its participation contingent on receiving billions and billions and billions of dollars in foreign aid from developed countries. There are many other examples. But the bottom line is that the Paris Accord is very unfair, at the highest level, to the United States.

Further, while the current agreement effectively blocks the development of clean coal in America—which it does, and the mines are starting to open up. We're having a big opening in two weeks. Pennsylvania, Ohio, West Virginia, so many places. A big opening of a brand-new mine. It's unheard of. For many, many years, that hasn't happened. They asked me if I'd go. I'm going to try.

China will be allowed to build hundreds of additional coal plants. So we can't build the plants, but they can, according to this agreement. India will be allowed to double its coal production by 2020. Think of it: India can double their coal production. We're supposed to get rid of ours. Even Europe is allowed to continue construction of coal plants.

In short, the agreement doesn't eliminate coal jobs, it just transfers those jobs out of America and the United States, and ships them to foreign countries.

This agreement is less about the climate and more about other countries gaining a financial advantage over the United States. The rest of the world applauded when we signed the Paris Agreement—they went wild; they were so happy—for the simple reason that it put our country, the United States of America, which we all love, at a very, very big economic disadvantage. A cynic would say the obvious reason for economic competitors and their wish to see us remain in the agreement is so that we continue to suffer this self-inflicted major economic wound. We would find it very hard to compete with other countries from other parts of the world.

We have among the most abundant energy reserves on the planet, sufficient to lift millions of America's poorest workers out of poverty. Yet, under this agreement, we are effectively putting these reserves under lock and key, taking away the great wealth of our nation—it's great wealth, it's phenomenal wealth; not so long ago, we had no idea we had such wealth—and leaving millions and millions of families trapped in poverty and joblessness.

The agreement is a massive redistribution of United States wealth to other countries. At 1 percent growth, renewable sources of energy can meet some of our domestic demand, but at 3 or 4 percent growth, which I expect, we need all forms of available American energy, or our country will be at grave risk of brownouts and blackouts, our businesses will come to a halt in many cases, and the American family will suffer the consequences in the form of lost jobs and a very diminished quality of life.

Even if the Paris Agreement were implemented in full, with total compliance from all nations, it is estimated it would only produce a two-tenths of one degree—think of that; this much—Celsius reduction in global temperature by the year 2100. Tiny, tiny amount. In fact, 14 days of carbon emissions from China alone would wipe out the gains from America—and this is an incredible statistic—would totally wipe out the gains from America's expected reductions in the year 2030, after we have had to spend billions and billions of dollars, lost jobs, closed factories, and suffered much higher energy costs for our businesses and for our homes.

As the *Wall Street Journal* wrote this morning: "The reality is that withdrawing is in America's economic interest and won't matter much to the climate." The United States, under the Trump administration, will continue to be the cleanest and most environmentally friendly country on Earth. We'll be the cleanest. We're going to have the cleanest air. We're going to have the cleanest water. We will be environmentally friendly, but we're not going to put our businesses out of work and we're not going to lose our jobs. We're going to grow; we're going to grow rapidly.

And I think you just read—it just came out minutes ago, the small business report—small businesses as of just now are booming, hiring people. One of the best reports they've seen in many years.

I'm willing to immediately work with Democratic leaders to either negotiate our way back into Paris, under the terms that are fair to the United States and its workers, or to negotiate a new deal that protects our country and its taxpayers.

So if the obstructionists want to get together with me, let's make them non-obstructionists. We will all sit down, and we will get back into the deal. And we'll make it good, and we won't be closing up our factories, and we won't be losing our jobs. And we'll sit down with the Democrats and all of the people that represent either the Paris Accord or something that we can do that's much better than the Paris Accord. And I think the people of our country will be thrilled, and I think then the people of the world will be thrilled. But until we do that, we're out of the agreement.

I will work to ensure that America remains the world's leader on environmental issues, but under a framework that is fair and where the burdens and responsibilities are equally shared among the many nations all around the world.

No responsible leader can put the workers—and the people—of their country at this debilitating and tremendous disadvantage. The fact that the Paris deal hamstrings the United States, while empowering some of the world's top polluting countries, should dispel any doubt as to the real reason why foreign lobbyists wish to keep our magnificent country tied up and bound down by this agreement: It's to give their country an economic edge over the United States. That's not going to happen while I'm President. I'm sorry.

My job as President is to do everything within my power to give America a level playing field and to create the economic, regulatory and tax structures that make America the most prosperous and productive country on Earth, and with the highest standard of living and the highest standard of environmental protection.

Our tax bill is moving along in Congress, and I believe it's doing very well. I think a lot of people will be very pleasantly surprised. The Republicans are working very, very hard. We'd love to have support from the Democrats, but we may have to go it alone. But it's going very well.

The Paris Agreement handicaps the United States economy in order to win praise from the very foreign capitals and global activists that have long sought to gain wealth at our country's expense. They don't put America first. I do, and I always will.

The same nations asking us to stay in the agreement are the countries that have collectively cost America trillions of dollars through tough trade practices and, in many cases, lax contributions to our critical military alliance. You see what's happening. It's pretty obvious to those that want to keep an open mind.

At what point does America get demeaned? At what point do they start laughing at us as a country? We want fair treatment for its citizens, and we want fair treatment for our taxpayers. We don't want other leaders and other countries laughing at us anymore. And they won't be. They won't be.

I was elected to represent the citizens of Pittsburgh, not Paris. I promised I would exit or renegotiate any deal which fails to serve America's interests. Many trade deals will soon be under renegotiation. Very rarely do we have a deal that works for this country, but they'll soon be under renegotiation. The process has begun from day one. But now we're down to business.

Beyond the severe energy restrictions inflicted by the Paris Accord, it includes yet another scheme to redistribute wealth out of the United States through the so-called Green Climate Fund—nice name—which calls for developed countries to send $100 billion to developing countries all on top of America's existing and massive foreign aid payments. So we're going to be paying billions and billions and billions of dollars, and we're already way ahead of anybody else. Many of the other countries haven't spent anything, and many of them will never pay one dime.

The Green Fund would likely obligate the United States to commit potentially tens of billions of dollars of which the United States has already handed over $1 billion—nobody else is even close; most of them haven't even paid anything—including funds raided out of America's budget for the war against terrorism. That's where they came. Believe me, they didn't come from me. They came just before I came into office. Not good. And not good the way they took the money.

In 2015, the United Nation's departing top climate officials reportedly described the $100 billion per year as "peanuts," and stated that "the $100 billion is the tail that wags the dog." In 2015, the Green Climate Fund's executive director reportedly stated that estimated funding needed would increase to $450 billion per year after 2020. And nobody even knows where the money is going to. Nobody has been able to say, where is it going to?

Of course, the world's top polluters have no affirmative obligations under the Green Fund, which we terminated. America is $20 trillion in debt. Cash-strapped cities cannot hire enough police officers or fix vital infrastructure. Millions of our citizens are out of work. And yet, under the Paris Accord, billions of dollars that ought to be invested right here in America will be sent to the very countries that have taken our factories and our jobs away from us. So think of that.

There are serious legal and constitutional issues as well. Foreign leaders in Europe, Asia, and across the world should not have more to say with respect to the U.S. economy than our own citizens and their elected representatives. Thus, our withdrawal from the agreement represents a reassertion of America's sovereignty. Our Constitution is unique among all the nations of the world, and it is my highest obligation and greatest honor to protect it. And I will.

Staying in the agreement could also pose serious obstacles for the United States as we begin the process of unlocking the restrictions on America's abundant energy reserves, which we have started very strongly. It would once have been unthinkable that an international agreement could prevent the United States from conducting its own domestic economic affairs, but this is the new reality we face if we do not leave the agreement or if we do not negotiate a far better deal.

The risks grow as historically these agreements only tend to become more and more ambitious over time. In other words, the Paris framework is a starting point—as bad as it is—not an end point. And exiting the agreement protects the United States from future intrusions on the United States' sovereignty and massive future legal liability. Believe me, we have massive legal liability if we stay in.

As President, I have one obligation, and that obligation is to the American people. The Paris Accord would undermine our economy, hamstring our workers, weaken our sovereignty, impose unacceptable legal risks, and put us at a permanent disadvantage to the other countries of the world. It is time to exit the Paris Accord and time to pursue a new deal that protects the environment, our companies, our citizens, and our country.

It is time to put Youngstown, Ohio, Detroit, Michigan, and Pittsburgh, Pennsylvania—along with many, many other locations within our great country—before Paris, France. It is time to make America great again.

Source: Trump, Donald. 2017, June 1. "Statement by President Trump on the Paris Climate Accord." White House, Office of the Press Secretary. https://www.whitehouse.gov/the-press-office/2017/06/01/statement-president-trump-paris-climate-accord.

Introduction

A majority of Americans are concerned about the loss of bio-diversity and declines and possible extinction of endangered species. Because of this interest there are abundant videos and films, books, articles, reports, and Internet information on the topic. No list, therefore, can be complete in the limited space offered here. The items selected are some classic sources and recent information about the status of biodiversity and endangered species and the controversies surrounding the Endangered Species Act (ESA) and climate change. Each source contains a brief summary of the main theme and what to expect in the selection.

Books

Abbey, Edward. 1968. *Desert Solitaire: A Season in the Wilderness.* New York: Random House, Inc.

> As the only ranger, Abbey spent two lonely, reflective summers in Arches National Monument in Utah (now a national park) in the late 1950s. In 18 essays, he offers his appreciation for the harsh environment and his joy in discovering the beauty and solitude of the wilderness. Besides self-discovery, Abbey engages in critiques of modern

Protesters outside the White House respond to President Donald Trump's June 1, 2017, announcement that the United States is withdrawing from the Paris climate change accord. (AP Photo/Susan Walsh)

Western civilization, U.S. politics, and the decline of America's environment. The book has become a cult classic for environmental activists and to those who simply cherish the beauty of wilderness.

Ackerman, Diane. 1995. *The Rarest of the Rare: Vanishing Animals, Timeless Worlds*. New York: Random House.

Ackerman writes in beautiful prose of her personal odyssey to witness and explore the status of some of the rarest animals and ecosystems before they vanish. She focuses on three endangered species (monk seals, short-tailed albatrosses, and golden lion tamarins), two vanishing ecosystems (the Amazon and the Florida scrublands), and the migration of monarch butterflies.

Adler, Jonathan, ed. 2011. *Rebuilding the Ark: New Perspectives on Endangered Species Act Reform*. Washington, DC: AEI Press.

A professor of law at Case Western Reserve University, Adler leads a group of law experts in evaluating successes and failures of the ESA. The lawyers evaluate avenues for reform and methods to provide incentives for better conservation on private land. The book also considers how the ESA can be used to address the threat of climate change that will affect so many species.

Bauer, Donald C., and Irvin, Wm. Robert, eds. 2010. *Endangered Species Act: Law, Policy, and Perspectives*, Second Edition. American Bar Association Section of Environment, Energy, and Resources.

The many authors in 19 chapters lead the reader through the historical background and important issues surrounding the ESA. The authors provide detailed explanations about various sections of the law and explain how court cases have helped clarify and modify the law. Although informative, the chapters are not an easy read, and the book may be best used as a reference source.

Darwin, Charles. 1979. *On the Origin of Species.* New York: Avenel Books.

> Anyone who is interested in the history and thought behind the theory of natural selection and its place in understanding evolution must read this book.

Duncan, Dayton, and Burns, Ken. 2009. *National Parks: America's Best Idea.* New York: Knopf.

> This book offers a beautifully illustrated history of America's national parks and five extended interviews with people whose lives have been shaped by their experiences in the parks.

Fischer, Hank. 2003. *Wolf Wars: The Remarkable Inside Story of the Restoration of Wolves of Yellowstone.* Missoula, MT: Fischer Outdoor Discoveries, LLC.

> Although some conservationists said it could not be done, Fischer persevered and was instrumental in the reintroduction of the gray wolf into Yellowstone National Park. The book is an account of the politics and struggle to return the wolves to their former habitat in the Rocky Mountain states of Wyoming and Idaho.

Fraser, Caroline. 2009. *Rewilding the World: Dispatches from the Conservation Revolution.* New York: Henry Holt and Company, LLC.

> *Rewilding* is a gripping account of the environmental crusade to save the world's most endangered species by restoring habitats, reviving migration corridors, and reestablishing predators. The author traveled with wildlife biologists and conservationists to report their scientific discoveries and grassroot actions.

Gallagher, Nora, and Myers, Lisa, eds. 2016. *Patagonia's Tools for Grassroots Activists: Best Practices for Success in the Environmental Movement.* Ventura, CA: Patagonia.

> Since 1994, Patagonia, a successful sportswear company, has sponsored a biannual "Tools Conference" attended

by environmental activists to learn techniques to become more effective. The book is a collection of essays written by respected experts who were presenters at the conferences. The essays offer advice and best practices for fund-raising, marketing, communication, grassroots advocacy, and campaign strategies. A case study accompanies each chapter to demonstrate the principles in action.

Goodall, Jane, Maynard, Thane, and Hudson, Gail. 2009. *Hope for Animals and Their World: How Endangered Species Are Being Rescued from the Brink*. New York: Grand Central Publishing.

This book differs from most books on the environment and endangered species by taking a positive viewpoint. Goodall features species that have been recovered or are on their way to recovery. She describes the huge effort made by scientists and conservationists to bring imperiled species back from the brink such as the California condor, whooping crane, and black-footed ferret. Also included are species thought extinct and rediscovered. To Goodall, it is never too late. The book is easy to read and is enhanced by two sections of beautiful photos of plants and animals.

Gore, Al. 2006. *An Inconvenient Truth: The Planetary Emergency of Global Warming and What We Can Do about It*. New York: Rodale.

The book is based on the ground-breaking film produced by Al Gore to awaken the U.S. public to the consequences of greenhouse gas emissions perpetuated by human activities and the resulting global warming and climate change. The book reports the research of the top climate scientists from around the world. It is very readable with many pictures, graphs, illustrations, and personal anecdotes.

Anyone who wishes to understand the basics of climate change should read this book.

Gore, Al. 2017. *An Inconvenient Sequel: Truth to Power*. New York: Rodale.

In his new documentary and book former vice president Al Gore follows his 2006 film and book about climate change with the news that, although the situation has only become worse, the impact of extreme weather is making climate change harder to deny.

Klein, Naomi. 2014. *This Changes Everything*. New York: Simon & Schuster.

This provocative, but very readable, book exposes the myths surrounding climate change and argues that climate change is a civilization wake-up call delivered in fires, floods, storms, and droughts. The United States and world face a huge transition in the economic model of capitalism if they are to stop the war against life on Earth.

Kolbert, Elizabeth. 2014. *The Sixth Extinction: An Unnatural History*. New York: Henry Holt and Company.

There have been five mass extinctions in the history of the Earth. As far as is known, all of these extinctions were from natural causes. In contrast, there is a sixth mass extinction occurring today as a result of human activities. Kolbert draws on scientific research to explain how and why this extinction is happening. She brings the reader closer to the species affected by featuring species already gone and others that are facing extinction.

Leopold, Aldo. 2013. *A Sand County Almanac & Other Writings on Ecology and Conservation*. New York: Oxford University Press.

The book consists of complete publication of Leopold's writings and letters from over a 40-year period. It includes

Leopold's classic, *A Sand County Almanac*, in which he beautifully details the monthly changes to a farm in Wisconsin. (See Profile of Leopold for more information.)

Lovejoy, Thomas E., and Hannah, Lee. 2005. *Climate Change and Biodiversity.* New Haven: Yale University Press.

The book is an easy read with many pictures and some graphs. It is an edited volume consisting of 24 chapters written by experts on all aspects of climate change ranging from tropical responses to climate change to freshwater ecosystems. The six sections of the book include: "Present Changes, Learning from the Past, Understanding the Future, Conservation Responses and Policy Responses." (See essay on the Amazon by Lovejoy in the Perspectives section of this book.)

Mann, Michael, and Toles, Tom. 2016. *The Madhouse Effect: How Climate Change Denial Is Threatening Our Planet, Destroying Our Politics, and Driving Us Crazy.* New York: Columbia University Press.

Mann, an award-winning climate scientist, and Toles, a Pulitzer Prize–winning cartoonist, join forces to offer a fun, but informative, book on climate change with the goal to motivate the reader into action. The book begins with a good explanation of how the scientific process works and the basic science underlying climate change. The authors explore reasons to care about climate change and how political figures have confused the public by attacking science and refusing to acknowledge the problem even exists.

Mayr, Ernst. 1982. *The Growth of Biological Thought: Diversity, Evolution and Inheritance.* Cambridge, MA: Harvard University Press.

This is a classic and highly recommended book about the history and development of biological thought by one of the 20th century's leading evolutionary biologists. Mayr synthesizes three major concepts in contemporary biology: the classification of life forms, evolution of the species, and inheritance and variation of characteristics.

McKibben, Bill. 2013. *Oil and Honey: The Education of an Unlikely Activist*. New York: Henry Holt and Company.

McKibben offers a memoir about his grassroots activism to stop approval of the Keystone pipeline and his personal endeavor to become closer to sustainable living by becoming a beekeeper. He describes his journey from a writer and journalist to staging a protest at the White House and ending up in jail. The book could be used as a model for personal activism from the smallest to the largest endeavors.

Mech, L. David, and Boitani, Luigi, eds. 2003. *Wolves: Behavior, Ecology, and Conservation*. Chicago: Chicago University Press.

This scholarly book is edited by long-term wolf biologists with the goal to provide a comprehensive review of wolf biology, behavior, and conservation. The authors of each of the 13 chapters are research scientists and natural resource managers who deeply care about their subject. The chapters are packed with information about wolves and can be used as a scientific resource.

Middleton, Susan, and Littschwager, David. 1994. *Witness: Endangered Species of North America*. San Francisco: Chronicle Books.

One-hundred beautifully photographed species of North American plants and animals on the verge of extinction are featured in this book. Besides the stunning photographs, the book contains an introduction by E. O. Wilson, a biography of each species, a resource guide, and an essay on the ESA.

National Academy of Science. 1999. *Science and Creationism: A View from the National Academy of Science*, Second Edition. Washington, DC: National Academy Press. Available to download free online, http://www.nap.edu/download/6024/.

> Chaired by Francisco Ayala, a prominent evolutionary biologist, the Steering Committee on Science and Creationism of the National Academy of Science presents a summary of key aspects of the most important evidence supporting evolution. The book also describes positions taken by advocates of creation science and presents an analysis of these claims.

Neme, Laurel, A. 2009. *Animal Investigators: How the World's First Wildlife Forensics Lab Is Solving and Saving Endangered Species*. New York: Scribner.

> This book is about wildlife CSI and the work done in the U.S. Fish Wildlife Services' Forensics Laboratory in Ashland, Oregon. The scientific information in the book follows samples from various wildlife species through the lab process that helps law enforcement officers solve crimes. For instance, in an investigation of a dead walrus, the scientists must determine whether the animal died naturally or was illegally poached. Bear bile is in demand in Asian countries to sell for more than heroin. Pig bile, however, is often substituted for bear pile. It is the lab's job to determine the difference.

Oldfield, Sara, ed. 2003. *The Trade in Wildlife: Regulation for Conservation*. New York: Earthscan Publications.

> Contributors to chapters in this edited volume have been on the front lines to stop the illegal trafficking of endangered species. They debate about the ethical, biological, and socioeconomic issues that arise in attempts to regulate the wildlife trade and why the regulation of the trade in wildlife is failing. Increased numbers of plant and animal species are threatened with extinction, despite improved

understanding of the issues and management of global trade. Why this occurs and how to halt it is discussed.

Otto, Shawn. 2016. *The War on Science*. Minneapolis, MN: Milkweed Editions.

Otto makes the case for science and how it is important for a successful democracy. The book is carefully researched and is especially strong in explanations of the scientific process. The history of modern science politics, rise in authoritarianism, attacks on climate change, and bias in the media are discussed. The last chapter offers solutions.

Plater, Zygmunt J.B. 2013. *The Snail Darter and the Dam: How Pork-Barrel Politics Endangered a Little Fish and Killed a River*. New Haven: Yale University Press.

Plater, a lead attorney representing the citizens defending the endangered snail darter threatened by the Tellico dam, provides an inside story of the Tellico dam and the snail darter case. The book describes the political maneuvering of the U.S. Congress and offers a detailed account of the six-year crusade against final construction of the dam.

Quammen, David. 1996. *The Song of the Dodo: Island Biogeography in an Age of Extinctions*. New York: Scribner.

Why islands often suffer high rates of extinction is explored in this book. The book is part scientific explanation and part travelogue. Quammen traces the origins of island biogeography from Darwin and Wallace to more modern interpretations and provides lessons in evolution, biodiversity, and how scientists think and argue over the application of ecological theory. He explains why the theory of island biogeography greatly influenced the discipline of ecology and became a cornerstone of conservation biology.

Roman, Joe. 2011. *Listed: Dispatches from America's Endangered Species Act.* Cambridge, MA: Harvard University Press.
Roman provides a comprehensive view of the history, implementation, and positive outcomes of the ESA. His writing style is an easy read with many examples of threatened species and the people who worked to save them. Roman challenges the belief that protecting biodiversity is too costly and explains why extinctions should matter to everyone. References in the Notes section at the end of the book provide additional sources.

Ruse, Michael. 2013. *Darwin and Evolutionary Thought.* Cambridge, UK: Cambridge University Press.
This is an edited volume of 65 essays written by experts covering every aspect of Charles Darwin's life and influence. The goal of the volume is to provide a full sense of scholarship on Darwin and his importance to biology. The essays cover the history, evidence for every aspect of evolution, and discussions of the ongoing controversy.

Sartore, Joel. 2010. *Rare: Portraits of America's Endangered Species.* Washington, DC: National Geographic Society.
A gorgeous book by a National Geographic photographer, the book features species on the brink of extinction as well as species that have been recovered. The purpose of the book is to stimulate action to prevent species from being lost forever.

Schneider, Jacqueline L. 2012. *Sold into Extinction: The Global Trade in Endangered Species.* Santa Barbara, CA: ABC-CLIO.
This is a book about forensics and criminology in the fight against illegal trafficking in endangered species. Schneider explores the extensive illegal market of endangered species and presents revealing case studies of terrestrial, marine, plant, and avian species.

Smith, Douglas W., and Ferguson, Gary. 2005. *Decade of the Wolf: Returning the Wild to Yellowstone*. Guilford, CT: The Lyons Press.

> Doug Smith is the biologist who was head of the Yellowstone Recovery Project and was involved with introduction of the gray wolf into Yellowstone since its inception. He gives a firsthand account of the capturing of the Canadian wolves and their transfer to acclimation pens in Yellowstone and subsequent release. The case histories of six wolves illustrate the dynamics of wolf existence. The book also has a section of beautiful color photographs of wolves, their habitat, and some of the researchers who worked with them.

Stanford Environmental Law Society. 2001. *The Endangered Species Act*. Stanford: Stanford University Press.

> This is the ESA from a legal point of view. One of the more interesting chapters is the one on international aspects of the ESA.

Stein, Bruce A., Kutner, Lynn S., and Adams, Jonathan S. 2000. *Precious Heritage: The Status of Biodiversity in the United States*. New York: Oxford University Press. 416 p.

> A quarter century of information on U.S. biodiversity, documented by the Natural Heritage Network of the Nature Conservancy, is documented in this richly illustrated volume. The book considers how ecosystems are faring, what is threatening them, and what is needed to protect the nation's remaining natural inheritance.

Stolzenburg, William. 2008. *Where the Wild Things Were: Life, Death, and Ecological Wreckage in a Land of Vanishing Predators*. New York: Bloomsbury.

> Wildlife journalist Stolzenburg examines the delicate balance between predator and prey and explains the critical

role of predators in the preservation of biodiversity. The book is replete with examples of the damage that is done when predators are removed and natural balances disrupted.

Switzer, Jacqueline Vaughan. 2003. *Environmental Activism: A Reference Handbook*. Santa Barbara: ABC-CLIO.

Switzer offers a balanced presentation chronicling both the major events that sparked environmental activism and the nature of that activism in the past century.

Thelander, Carl G., ed. 1994. *Life on the Edge: A Guide to California's Endangered Natural Resources*. Santa Cruz, CA: Biosystems Books.

California's 115 threatened wildlife species are individually featured in chapters written by the biologists who study them. The biology, range, conservation efforts, and recovery are outlined for each species. The book is beautifully illustrated with color and black and white photos. Although some of the information is out of date, the book is still a treasure trove of information about the biodiversity of California.

Williams, Terry Tempest. 2016. *The Hour of Land: A Personal Topography of America's National Parks*. New York: Farrar, Straus, Giroux.

Williams pens essays of her personal journey in 12 national parks and monuments to bring alive the beauty and essence of each place.

Wilson, Edward O. 1992. *The Diversity of Life*. Cambridge, MA: Harvard University Press.

In his clear writing style, Wilson explains how life on Earth evolved and the value of biodiversity. He describes the events that have disrupted biodiversity over the last several hundred years with the last five chapters of the book devoted to the human impact.

Wilson, E. O. 2016. *Half-Earth: Our Planet's Fight for Life*. New York: Liveright.

> This is the most recent in a series of books written by Wilson to warn of the loss of biodiversity and endangerment of Earth's species. He offers a solution to preserving the biodiversity of the planet. He believes the magnitude of the problem is too big for the piecemeal approach. Instead, to save species we must dedicate half of the Earth's surface to nature.

Articles, Comments, and Hearings

Briggs, John C. 2014. "Global Diversity Gain Is Concurrent with Declining Population Sizes." *Biodiversity Journal* 5: 447–452. https://www.researchgate.net/publication/232849602_Global_species_diversity.

> Briggs claims that the rate and extent of extinctions are overrated because they are based on indirect evidence. Direct evidence using extinction records shows no evidence for unusually high rates of extinction. There are, however, numerous small populations that require rescue via conservation activity.

Buse, John, 2015. "A Different Perspective on the Endangered Species Act at 40: Responding to Damien M. Schiff." *Environs: Environmental Law and Policy Journal* 38: 145–16. https://www.biologicaldiversity.org/publications/papers/Buse_ESA40_2015.pdf.

> This article is a counterargument to the criticisms of the ESA by Damian Schiff referenced later in the chapter. Buse systematically discounts Schiff's argument about the ESA and provides a different, more positive perspective of assessment of the ESA for the last 40 years.

Center for Biological Diversity (CBD). 2011. "A Future for All: A Blueprint for Strengthening the Endangered Species Act."

https://www.biologicaldiversity.org/campaigns/esa/pdfs/A-Future-for-All.pdf.

> The CBD proposes a set of recommendations to strengthen the ESA that includes increased funding, streamlined internal agency review, and revised regulations for listing species.

Committee on Science, Space, & Technology. 2017, March 29. "Climate Science: Assumptions, Policy Implications, and Scientific Method." https://science.house.gov/legislation/hearings/full-committee-hearing-climate-science-assumptions-policy-implications-and.

> Transcripts of testimony before the U.S. House of Representative's Committee on Science and Technology, convened by Lamar Smith (R-Texas, a climate change denier), on climate change and the scientific method by three scientists who question climate change research and a well-known climate scientist are provided. According to Smith, the panel was to examine the scientific methods underlying climate data, because "too often scientists ignore the basic tenants of science in order to justify their claims." The testimony provides a view of the politics (with some data) on both sides of the issue.

Dirzo, Rodolfo, Young, Hillary S., Galetti, Mauro, Ceballos, Gerado, Isaac, Nick J. B., and Collen, Ben. 2014. "Defaunation in the Anthropocene." *Science* 345: 401–406. http://science.sciencemag.org/content/345/6195/401.

> This review article is part of a special issue in *Science* magazine on vanishing fauna because of human impact. Since 1500, 322 species have become extinct and many populations are in decline as part of the sixth mass extinction.

Dwyer, Lynn E., Murphy, Dennis D., and Ehrlich, Paul R. 1995. "Property Rights Case Law and the Challenge to the

Endangered Species Act." *Conservation Biology* 9: 725–741.
http://www.life.illinois.edu/ib/451/Dwyer%20(1995).pdf.
> In 1995, there was a strong movement in Congress to deny reauthorization of the ESA based on interpretation of Fifth Amendment property rights. The authors in this article review the key legislative history and make recommendations to improve implementation of the ESA to counteract any movement to weaken or repeal the act. This article is still relevant today considering the recent actions of Congress to repeal the ESA.

Evans, Daniel M., Che-Castaldo, Judy P., Crouse, Deborah, Davis, Frank W., Epanchin-Niell, Rebecca, Flather, Curtis H., Frohlich, R. Kipp, Goble, Dale D., Li, Ya-Wei, Male, Timothy D., Master, Lawrence L., Moskwik, Matthew P., Neel, Maile C., Noon, Barry R., Parmesan, Camille, Schwartz, Mark W., Scott, J. Michael, and Williams, Byron K. 2016. "Species Recovery in the United States: Increasing Effectiveness of the Endangered Species Act." *Issues in Ecology* 20, Ecological Society of America. https://www.esa.org/esa/wp-content/uploads/2016/01/Issue20.pdf.
> An overview of the ESA, causes for species' endangerment, and the successes and shortcomings of recovery programs are presented in this review paper from the Ecological Society of America. The scientists present six broad strategies to increase effectiveness of the ESA.

Fabrizio, Sergio, Caro, Tim, Brown, Danielle, Clucas, Barbara, Hunter, Jennifer, Ketchum, James, McHugh, Katherine, and Hiraldo, Fernando. 2008. "Top Predators as Conservation Tools: Ecological Rationale, Assumptions, and Efficacy." *Annual Review of Ecology, Evolution and Systematics* 38: 1–19. http://www.annualreviews.org/doi/abs/10.1146/annurev.ecolsys.39.110707.173545?journalCode=ecolsys
> This is a scholarly review article about the role of predators as agents of biodiversity. The authors present both

positive and negative reports on success of top predators in establishing stability in ecosystems. Predators were successful in some systems and not in others. The scientists call for more research.

Frisvold, George. 2010. "The Economics of Endangered Species." *Resources for the Future.* http://www.rff.org/blog/2010/economics-endangered-species.

This is a political commentary on incentives to maintain habitats for endangered species in the United States and developing countries published by an independent, nonpartisan organization that conducts research and analysis to help leaders make better decisions and policies about natural resources and the environment.

Greenwald, Noah, Segee, Brian, Curry, Tierra, and Bradley, Curt. 2017, May. "A Wall in the Wild: The Disastrous Impacts of Trump's Border Wall on Wildlife." Center for Biological Diversity. https://www.biologicaldiversity.org/programs/international/borderlands_and_boundary_waters/pdfs/A_Wall_in_the_Wild.pdf. Accessed September 18, 2017.

The authors summarize the ways a border wall will affect endangered species. Included are comprehensive tables and maps. Table 1 provides a listing of the common and scientific names, status (endangered, threatened, under review, candidate), whether the species cross the border, and the state or residence of the species. Table 2 shows information about species that reside in critical habitats within 50 miles of the border. Six species are spotlighted: Jaguar, ocelot, Mexican gray wolf, Sonoran pronghorn, cactus ferruginous pigmy owl, and Quino checkerspot butterfly.

Horan, Claire M. 2017. "Defenders of Wildlife v. Jewell (D. Mont.)." *Harvard Environmental Law Review* 41: 297–320. http://harvardelr.com/wp-content/uploads/2017/05/Horan.pdf.

The article provides a good accounting of the convergence of science, politics, and the law in efforts by an environmental organization using the ESA "citizen suit" to obtain an endangered species listing from the Fish and Wildlife Service for the North American wolverine.

Julius, Susan H., West, Jordan M., Nover, Daniel, Hauser, Rachel, Schimel, David S., Janetos, Anthony C., Walsh, Margaret K., and Backlund, Peter. 2013. "Climate Change and U.S. Natural Resources: Advancing the Nation's Capability to Adapt." *Issues in Ecology* 18, Ecological Society of America. https://www.esa.org/esa/wp-content/uploads/2013/12/Issue18.pdf.
The authors make recommendation for new methods to manage ecosystems in the face of climate change.

Kaiser, David, and Wasserman, Lee. 2016, December. "The Rockefeller Family Fund vs. Exxon." *The New York Review of Books.* http://www.nybooks.com/articles/2016/12/08/the-rocke feller-family-fund-vs-exxon/.
If interested in the politics involved in climate change denial and big oil, this article will be appealing. Although John D. Rockefeller founded Standard Oil and ExxonMobil, the family is divesting its holdings in Exxon because of the company's action in leading the denial of climate change. In return, Exxon accuses the Rockefellers of a conspiracy to harm their business. The article reviews the history and politics of how and why Exxon went from a corporate leader in climate change research to a position of emphasizing the uncertainty in the science.

Lazarus, Richard J. 2013. "Environmental Law at the Crossroads: Looking Back 25, Looking Forward 25." *Michigan Journal of Environmental and Administrative Law* 2: 267–284. http://nrs.harvard.edu/urn-3:HUL.InstRepos:12956305.
Richard Lazarus, a professor of law at Harvard University, provides both a historical and future analysis of environmental law in this keynote address to the 2013 meeting

of the National Association of Environmental Law Society. He discusses three topics: Congress and the politics of environmental law, the courts and the changing relationship of constitutional law to environmental law, and the contrasting nature of the challenges that environmental lawyers and environmental law face today compared with 25 years ago.

Lee-Ashley, Matt, and Gentile, Nicole. 2015. "Confronting America's Wildlife Extinction Crisis." *Center for American Progress*. https://www.americanprogress.org/issues/green/reports/2015/10/19/123085/confronting-americas-wildlife-extinction-crisis/.

> The main theme of this article is that current policies and resources to solve the extinction crisis are inadequate. There needs to be earlier and more effective conservation of imperiled species to reduce the pressure on the ESA. An "at-risk" classification of species with declining populations that are not as yet threatened or endangered is presented and discussed as a way to accomplish this goal.

Ogden, Andrew G. 2013. "Dying for a Solution: Incidental Taking under the Migratory Bird Treaty Act." *William & Mary Environmental Law and Policy Review* 38: 1–80. http://scholarship.law.wm.edu/wmelpr/vol38/iss1/2.

> This article examines the history of the Migratory Bird Treaty Act (MBTA) and the past and present anthropogenic threats to migratory birds, including the growing hazard from wind energy development. Ogden believes that the Fish and Wildlife Service has failed to enforce the law adequately and proposes a program to permit incidental taking under the MBTA with specific guidelines starting with the wind energy industry.

Pitz, Rick. June 2013. "Proposed Ending of Gray Wolf Protection: Another Case of Setting Science Aside." *Climate Science &*

Policy Watch. http://www.climatesciencewatch.org/2013/06/09/proposed-ending-federal-gray-wolf-protection/.

When the FWS presented a plan to remove federal protection from gray wolves in the continental United States, 16 scientists signed a letter to protest the action because they did not believe the rule reflected the conclusions of their work or the best available science. In response, three of the top wolf experts who signed the letter were removed from the peer review of the plan. This article reports the events involved in this action and controversy and supplies links to the letter, news articles, and other information relating to the case.

Schiff, Damien M. 2014. "The Endangered Species Act at 40: A Tale of Radicalization, Politicization, Bureaucratization, and Senescence." *Environs: Environmental Law and Policy Journal* 37: 105–132. http://environs.law.ucdavis.edu/volumes/37/2/Articles/Schiff.pdf.

Calling the ESA a "pit bull" of environmental law, Schiff seeks to identify its shortcomings. He describes how he thinks the ESA became radicalized, politicized, and bureaucratized. The ESA is no longer successful and ill-suited to address climate change. The law protects species rather than larger biological units and has unjustified costs. Remedies for correcting and improving the ESA include paying landowners not to kill endangered species and saving species based on their utilitarian value.

Schwartz, Mark W. 2008. "The Performance of the Endangered Species Act." *Annual Review of Ecology, Evolution, and Systematics* 39: 279–299. http://www.annualreviews.org/doi/full/10.1146/annurev.ecolsys.39.110707.173538#f2.

From a review of government performance in fulfilling the ESA and the biological responsiveness of species listing, Schwartz concludes that the inability of governments to empower and implement the law is the main failure of the ESA. Listing species has not matched need, and critical habitat designations have lagged behind to result in thousands of species warranting listing to remain unlisted.

Seasholes, Brian. September 2007. "Bad for Species, Bad for People: What's Wrong with the Endangered Species Act and How to Fix It." *National Center for Policy Analysis, Policy Report* 303: 1–34. http://www.ncpa.org/pdfs/st303.pdf.
    Brian Seasholes frequently writes article arguing against provisions in the ESA. He is especially concerned about the land-use provisions that include large fines for landowners, restrictions on land use, and lack of compensation for lost value and use of the land. These provisions foster resentment by landowners toward the government, which is counterproductive because private lands harbor the majority of endangered species. He suggests new directions and the promotion of innovative wildlife conservation in the United States and foreign countries.

Smith, Mark E., and Molde, Donald A. 2014. "Wildlife Management Funding in the U.S." *Nevadans for Responsible Wildlife Management.* http://www.nrwm.org/wildlife-manage ment-funding-in-the-u-s/.
    The goal of the article is to answer the question of who really pays for wildlife in the United States. Sportsmen claim that taxes on sporting equipment and purchases of Duck Stamps and hunting licenses are the major funders of wildlife conservation and management. Not true. Ninety-four percent of the total funding for wildlife conservation comes from the nonhunting public, and only 4.9 percent of land purchases have been funded by hunters compared with 95.1 percent by the nonhunting public.

Snyder, Noel F. R., Derrickson, Scott R., Beissinger, Steven R., Wiley, James W., Smith, Thomas B., Toone, William D., and Miller, Brian. 1996. "Limitations of Captive Breeding in

Endangered Species Recovery." *Conservation Biology* 10: 338–348. https://nature.berkeley.edu/beislab/BeissingerLab/publica tions/Snyder_etal_ConsBio_1996.pdf.

> Although captive breeding of endangered species in zoos has contributed to the recovery of some species (California condor), there are still many problems associated with the activity. Snyder et al. discuss seven problems in detail and suggest ways for zoos to have more successful captive breeding programs that benefit endangered species. Captive breeding should only be used as a last resort when no other alternatives are available.

Stone, Suzanne Asha, Edge, Erin, Fascione, Nina, Miller, Craig, and Weaver, Charlotte. 2016. "Livestock and Wolves: A Guide to Nonlethal Tools and Methods to Reduce Conflict, Second Edition." *Defenders of Wildlife*. http://www.defenders.org/sites/ default/files/publications/livestock_and_wolves.pdf.

> Stone and associates provide a comprehensive summary of all the methods available for nonlethal control of wolves including use of guard dogs, erecting barrier, the value of human presence, and tools such as alarms and lighting to frighten the wolves. The authors encourage proactive measures such as switching grazing sites and scheduling calving when livestock is protected. Included is a resource directory of state agencies and other organizations that might offer financial assistance and where to report a dead wolf.

Internet Sources

Amphibian Survival Alliance (ASA) and Amphibian Specialist Group (IUCN SSG). http://www.amphibians.org/asg/.

> The ASA and SSG share a website dedicated to conservation of amphibians. ASA is a global alliance to prevent the extinction of amphibian species. The IUCN SSC is the International Union for Conservation of Nature's global

volunteer network to create a community where amphibian conservation can be achieved.

Animal Planet. "Endangered Species." http://www.animalplanet .com/wild-animals/endangered-species/.

Videos, articles, and links to conservation organizations involved in saving species are available to view. The usual megafauna is featured in addition to lesser known species such as the pangolin, sei whale, hawksbill and loggerhead sea turtles, Indus river dolphin, green turtle, bluefin tuna, and Yangtze finless porpoise.

Arkive. "Wildscreen." http://www.arkive.org.

This site is rich with information, pictures, and videos about species organized by group and conservation status (IUCN classification: extinct, extinct in the wild, endangered, threatened, and vulnerable). Species can also be viewed by habitat, country, and featured area. Free educational resources are available for ages 5–18, and fun quizzes and other interactive activities contribute to learning opportunities.

Association of Zoos & Aquariums. "Saving Animals from Extinction (SAFE)." https://www.aza.org/aza-safe.

Zoos and aquaria in the United State focus on halting the decline of 10 wild species: African penguin, Asian elephant, black rhinoceros, cheetah, gorilla, sea turtle, vaquita, western pond turtle, and the whooping crane.

Bagheera. "An Education Website about Endangered Species and the Effort to Save Them." *Endangered Species Journal.* http:// www.bagheera.com.

Bagheera is a comprehensive education resource about endangered species and efforts to save them worldwide. In addition to postings about the latest news releases and a site providing topics for further study and review, a biography of endangered species is offered to help deepen understanding of why species become endangered. There are lists of U.S. endangered species, threatened species by country, and conservation and endangered species laws by country from A to Z. Videos and a section on classroom activities are included.

Convention on Biological Diversity. https://www.cbd.int/intro/default.shtml.

The site provides the history, purpose, and description of 196 countries that have agreed to work together for sustainable development and the conservation of biodiversity within the framework of the United Nations.

Convention on International Trade in Endangered Species of Wild Fauna and Flora (CITES). https://cites.org/eng/disc/what.php.

CITES is an international agreement to protect endangered species through prohibiting international trade in live animals and plants and their products. The website offers the latest news on the wildlife trade and information on how CITES works, its structure, member countries, CITES species, and contracts and information. Information on programs for specific species such as elephants and great apes is included. There are periodic updates on export quotas.

ECOS Environmental Conservation Online system, U.S. Fish and Wildlife Service. http://ecos.fws.gov/ecp0/.

This is where to look for information about endangered and threatened species in the United States. The website contains lists and information about species by taxonomic group and region and also provides information about species with special rules, critical habitat designations, and recovery plans. Petitioned and proposed species are given as well as candidate species, their regions, and assessments.

Endangered Species International. http://www.endangeredspe ciesinternational.org.

Endangered Species International has a global focus to reverse human-induced species extinction, save endangered animals, and preserve wild places. The website includes the latest action for each month, information about the organization, projects, and overview of species. Current projects include safeguarding gorillas and rainforests, saving species from the bushmeat trade in the Congo, coral reef protection and restoration, the protection of mangrove forests, the stop of amphibian decline, stopping the illegal wildlife trade, and saving biodiversity in Colombia among others.

Environment 360. *Yale School of Forestry and Environmental Studies.* https://e360.yale.edu.

Launched in June 2008, *Environment 360* is an online daily magazine that features original opinion, analysis, and debate on a wide range of global environmental issues. It features original articles by scientists, journalists, environmentalists, academics, policy makers, and business people and is an especially good source of the latest events and issues relating to climate change.

Environmental Protection Agency (EPA). "Protecting Endangered Species from Pesticides."

EPA's responsibility is to make sure that pesticides are in compliance with the ESA and whether listed species or their habitats may be affected by the use of a product. The website describes the role of the EPA in making these determinations and its partnership with the FWS and NOAA.

EPA. "Climate Change" and "Climate Change Indicators."
https://19january2017snapshot.epa.gov/climatechange_.html,
https://www.epa.gov/climate-indicators.
>   Do not bother to look at the main EPA climate change site
>   for climate change data, because they were removed after
>   the election of Donald Trump and appointment of climate
>   change skeptics to the EPA. Links for the original, scientific-
>   based information on an archived site and the site of cli-
>   mate change indicators are provided and available at this
>   time. The information will, however, not be updated.

"Global Climate Change, Vital signs of the Planet." NASA.
http://climate.nasa.gov.
>   This site is a good place to learn more about climate change
>   from interesting and easily obtained information with
>   links to facts, articles, solutions, exploration, resources,
>   and NASA Science. The links explain evidence, causes, ef-
>   fects, scientific consensus, and vital signs of climate change
>   with descriptive graphs, illustrations, videos, and pictures.

International Fund for Animal Welfare (IFAW). http://www
.ifaw.org/united-states.
>   The IFAW works globally to save individual animals,
>   habitats, and populations. Their vision is a world where
>   animals are respected and protected. They have projects
>   in more than 40 countries and focus on saving individual
>   animals by rehabilitating them and releasing them to the
>   wild, including three critically endangered female rhinos
>   and endangered falcons in Russia.

International Union for Conservation of Nature (IUCN).
2017-2. "Red List of Threatened Species." http://www.iucnred
list.org.
>   The most comprehensive inventory of the taxonomic, con-
>   servation status, and distribution of species facing a high
>   risk of extinction.

Live Science. "Endangered Species." http://www.livescience.com/topics/endangered-species/.
> Live Science offers information about the natural and technological world and provides recent news articles on the status of endangered species.

Marine Mammal Center. "Working with Endangered Species." http://www.marinemammalcenter.org.
> The Marine Mammal Center, located in the San Francisco Bay Area, has worked extensively with endangered and threatened species of marine mammals: Hawaiian monk seals, Guadalupe fur seals, Steller sea lions, and southern sea otters. The center engages in marine mammal rescue and rehabilitation, scientific research, and education. The newly opened KeKai Ola Center in Hawaii is dedicated to saving the critically endangered Hawaiian monk seal.

The National Academy of Sciences: The Royal Society. 2014. "Climate Change: Evidence and Causes." *The National Academies Press.* http://www.nap.edu/catalog/18730/climate-change-evidence-and-causes. doi: 10.17226/18730.
> The National Academy of Science offers a detailed, but easily read and understood, summary of the causes, evidence, and uncertainties of climate change to be used as a key reference document for policy makers.

National Geographic Society. "Endangered Species." http://www.nationalgeographic.org/topics/endangered-species/.
> There are 87 links to educational content about endangered species from National Geographic Education. The content, appropriate for different ages, varies from videos and news articles to lesson plans.

National Oceanic & Atmospheric Administration (NOAA). "Endangered Species Act." http://www.nmfs.noaa.gov/pr/laws/esa/.
> NOAA has jurisdiction over 159 (65 are foreign) endangered and threatened marine species under the ESA. A table showing the year listed, status, critical habitat, and

recovery plan of these species can be accessed as well as information about how the ESA is implemented according to different sections of the law. Biennial reports to Congress provide information about species recovery, recovery grants, and partnerships.

NOAA Fisheries. "Marine Mammal Protection Act (MMPA)." http://www.nmfs.noaa.gov/pr/laws/mmpa/.
    Complete information about the MMPA enacted on October 21, 1972, is available. The site includes a description of all 217 marine mammals protected by the law worldwide. There are also sections of the law, how the law is implemented, policies and rules, and reports.

PBS Digital Studios. 2014. "The Sixth Extinction." https://www.pbslearningmedia.org/resource/the-sixth-extinction-its-okay-to-be-smart/the-sixth-extinction-its-okay-to-be-smart/#.WfjqituZNBw.
    This nine-minute video explains mass extinctions and the causes and consequences of the sixth mass extinction.

ScienceDaily. "Endangered Animals News." https://www.sciencedaily.com/news/plants_animals/endangered_animals/.
    ScienceDaily offers in-depth information based on the latest research discoveries, publications, and news from scientists. Stories are integrated with photos and illustrations. At the end of each article are references to further reading on the topic in scientific journals as well as related stories to enable the reader to accomplish further research. The articles in this publication are geared toward a non-science audience and are usually easily understood.

United for Wildlife. https://www.unitedforwildlife.org/?gclid=CIqNz__42dECFQ6bfgodesICFg#!/home.
    United for Wildlife was created by the Royal Foundation of the Duke and Duchess of Cambridge and Prince Henry to unite the world's leading wildlife organizations

under a common purpose to protect critically endangered species from being hunted to extinction. They strive for better on-site protection to reduce the demand for illegal wildlife products, improve law enforcement, reduce trafficking, and engage young people in conservation.

United Nations Environment Programme. "World Conservation Monitoring Center." https://www.unep-wcmc.org.

The UN World Conservation Monitoring Centre was established in 2000 as the world biodiversity information and assessment center for UN environmental programs. It offers a key database on statistics of biodiversity in any country.

U.S. Fish and Wildlife Service Endangered Species. https://www.fws.gov/endangered/.

The U.S. FWS is the key agency responsible for administration and enforcement of the ESA. This website provides news on endangered species, has an interactive map to learn about endangered species, and supplies links to species listed as endangered and threatened. Species proposed for listing, candidate species and their priority rank, and species proposed for status change or delisting links are also included.

Wildlife Conservation Network. https://wildnet.org/wildlife-programs.

WCN supports endangered species in 37 countries by supporting independent wildlife conservationists. There are links to the websites of individual endangered species to reveal information about the program, maps, and how to donate and be involved. Species include snow leopards, spectacled bears, African wild dogs, Grevy's zebras, lions, penguins, sharks, Ethiopian wolf, elephants, and more.

Wilson, E. O. 2014. *Life on Earth*. Biodiversity Foundation. https://eowilsonfoundation.org/e-o-wilson-s-life-on-earth/.

E. O. Wilson's *Life on Earth* is a free textbook consisting of seven units of interactive biology content. The goal is to instruct and stimulate students to appreciate and treasure biodiversity to make informed decisions about how to take care of the planet. It consists of 41 chapters and 7 units and can be accessed free from the iBook's store.

Reports

American Bird Conservancy. 2016. "American Birds 2016: Endangered Species Act: A Record of Success." *American Bird Conservancy Final Report.* https://abcbirds.org/wp-content/up loads/2016/07/ESA-Report-2016-FINAL.pdf.

The goal for the report is to assist policy makers and the conservation community in determining how the ESA is performing. The report demonstrates that twice as many bird populations are increasing as decreasing and provides recovery rates, examples of stable popula- tions, and species that are declining. A summary of the numerous species threatened and endangered in Hawaii is provided. In general, the ABC supports the ESA and provides suggestions about how it can be better funded and administrated.

"California: An Emissions Trading Case Study." 2015. *Envi- ronmental Defense Fund.* https://www.edf.org/sites/default/files/ california-case-study-may2015.pdf.

The report provides a history and analysis of the cap- and-trade program in California from 2005 to 2015. A summary of key policy features, proceeds from allow- ance auctions from November 2012 to February 15, 2015, and projected emission reductions are discussed and shown in various easily read graphs.

Center for Biological Diversity. 2017. "Politics of Extinction, Attacks on the ESA." http://www.biologicaldiversity.org/cam paigns/esa_attacks/.

The CBD presents a comprehensive report, illustrated on a large table, that shows the 303 attempts by Congress to defund, amend, and generally overturn or weaken the ESA from July 22, 1996, to December 8, 2016. The majority of "attacks" have occurred in the past five years with 135 attempts in the 114th Congress that ended in December 2016.

Defenders of Wildlife. 2011. "Endangered Species Act Summary." Harris Poll. https://www.defenders.org/publications/endangered_species_act_poll.pdf.
Results of a Harris poll revealed the extent of support for the ESA. Overall, results showed strong support of the ESA by 84 percent of the respondents. Tables of responses to questions by subject, region, and party ID are given.

Defenders of Wildlife. 2016. "Summary of Legislative Attacks on the Endangered Species Act in the 114th Congress." https://www.defenders.org/publications/Chart-of-ESA-Attacks-in-114th-Congress.pdf.
This summary of legislative action in the 114th Congress includes two lists. The first list consists of 130 bills and amendments by sponsor, title, and impact. The second list provides a history of the bill through various committees and procedures in Congress, a summary, and a scenario of the impact to endangered species if or when passed.

Department of Interior et al. 2016. "Greater Sage-Grouse Conservation & the Sagebrush Ecosystem: Collaborative Conservation at Work." https://www.doi.gov/sites/doi.gov/files/uploads/sagegrousereport_digital_10_6_2016_0.pdf.
The report highlights the accomplishments of seven federal agencies in their partnerships with 11 states, private landowners, and local communities to conserve the sagebrush ecosystem with the greater sage-grouse and more than 350 other species. Restoration projects of sagebrush habitat are underway, invasive species are being removed,

and funding has increased to manage rangeland fires and other conservation projects.

Endangered Species Coalition. 2014. "A Wild Success: American Voices on the Endangered Species Act at 40." www.endangered .org/cms/assets/uploads/2014/02/A-Wild-Success-final.pdf.
Diverse comments supporting the ESA are presented in a collection of over 100 editorials, Op-Eds, letters to the editor, and news articles to celebrate the ESA's 40th birthday. Contributions came from all parts of the United States and were written by members of Congress, governors, environmentalists, authors, journalists, sportsmen, biologists, community activists, photographers, lawyers, and concerned citizens.

Fish and Wildlife Service et al. 2016. "Northern Rocky Mountain Wolf Recovery Program 2015 Interagency Annual Report." https://www.fws.gov/mountain-prairie/es/species/mammals/ wolf/2016/FINAL_NRM%20summary%20-%202015.pdf. (See also https://www.fws.gov/mountain-prairie/es/wolf-2016 .php to see maps, tables and to access individual state reports.)
This is the latest annual report available from a cooperative effort of state and federal wildlife agencies and Indian tribes about the status, distribution, and management of Northern Rocky Mountain gray wolf population from January 1 to December 31, 2015. Follow the aforementioned links to reports from each of the five western states about the status of their gray wolf populations and how they manage livestock depredations.

The Guardian. 2012. "100 Most Endangered Species: Priceless or Worthless? in Pictures." https://www.theguardian.com/envi ronment/gallery/2012/sep/11/most-endangered-species-in- pictures.
There are pictures of 29 species taken from a list of 100 most endangered species compiled by 8,000 IUCN scientists

at the World Conservation Congress in South Korea. The entire list can be accessed at https://www.theguardian.com/ environment/gallery/2012/sep/11/most-endangered-spe cies-in-pictures.

Henson, David W., Malpas, Robert C., and D'Udine, Floris A. C. 2016. "Wildlife Law Enforcement in Sub-Saharan African Protected Areas—A Review of the Best Practices." *Occasional Paper of the IUCN Species Survival Commission* No. 58. Cambridge, UK, and Gland, Switzerland. https://portals.iucn.org/ library/sites/library/files/documents/SSC-OP-058.pdf.
Stressing the urgent need, the report identifies the most effective methods to combat poaching and wildlife crime. The report aims to take a realistic examination of which law enforcement approaches and professionals work well and which do not.

Intergovernmental Science-Policy Platform on Biodiversity and Ecosystem Services (IPBES). 2016. "Summary for Policy Makers on the Assessment Report on Pollinators, Pollination and Food Production." https://www.ipbes.net/sites/default/files/ downloads/pdf/spm_deliverable_3a_pollination_20170222.pdf
The report provides a critical assessment of the issues concerning the decline of pollinating insects, including the effects of pesticides and genetically modified foods. It concludes that pollinators are increasingly under threat from human activities, including climate change. The report also outlines a wide range of management and response options that can be used to mitigate the decline of wild pollinators, because a high diversity of them is critical to pollination even when managed bees are present in high numbers.

IPCC 2014, Climate Change 2013: "Fifth Assessment Report (AR5)." https://www.ipcc.ch/report/ar5/.
Links to reports from the Fifth Assessment Cycle of the Intergovernmental Panel on Climate Change from 2013 are

provided. IPCC Working Group I reported the physical scientific aspects of the climate system and climate change. Working Group II assessed the vulnerability of socioeconomic and natural systems to climate change, negative and positive consequences of climate change, and options for adapting to it. Working Group III assessed options for mitigating climate change through limiting or preventing greenhouse gas emissions and enhancing activities that remove them from the atmosphere. The final link is a synthesis report.

Matsumoto, Sarah, Pike, Cara, Turner, Tom, and Wan, Ray. 2003. "Citizens' Guide to the Endangered Species Act." *Earth Justice.* http://earthjustice.org/sites/default/files/library/reports/Citizens_Guide_ESA.pdf.

This is an easy to read and understand summary of the provisions of the Endangered Species Act of 1973 and its amendments and law decisions until 2002.

Millennium Ecosystem Assessment Reports. 2005. "Ecosystems and Human Well-Being: Biodiversity Synthesis." *World Resources Institute.* http://www.millenniumassessment.org/en/Reports.html.

The Millennium Assessment was established by the United Nations secretary general, Kofi Annan, in 2000 with the objective to assess the consequences of ecosystem changes for human well-being from 2001 to 2005. Over a thousand experts analyzed and assessed existing scientific information to recommend action necessary to enhance conservation and sustainable use of ecosystems and the services they provide. The resulting five technical volumes and six synthesis reports found that human actions were putting such strain on the environment that the ability of the planet's ecosystems to sustain future generations can no longer be taken for granted, but with appropriate actions it might be possible to reverse the degradation.

National Academy of Sciences: The Royal Society. 2014. "Climate Change: Evidence and Causes." *The National Academy Press*. http://nap.edu/18730.

> The report offers the current state of climate change science as a key reference document for decision makers, policy makers, educators, and other individuals. Climate scientists from the United Kingdom and United States outline established evidence, where consensus is growing, and where there is still uncertainty.

National Audubon Society. 2014. "Birds and Climate Change Report." http://climate.audubon.org/sites/default/files/Audubon-Birds-Climate-Report-v1.2.pdf.

> For birders and conservationists who wish to understand the effects of climate change on bird distributions, the Audubon Society's comprehensive analysis and distribution maps are a valuable resource that illustrate how North America's birds may respond to climate change. The maps are derived from extensive citizen science data and detailed climate data to forecast species distributions to future time based on climate estimates described by the Intergovernmental Panel on Climate Change. In-depth analysis of potential climate change impacts on 314 species can be viewed on climate change maps that predict winter and summer ranges for the years 2000, 2020, 2040, and 2080 (http://climate.audubon.org/all-species).

National Park Service. 2016. "Archeology Program." https://www.nps.gov/archeology/sites/antiquities/monumentslist.htm.

> The program includes a list of national monuments, date established, and by which president or Congress from September 1906 to September 2016. There are links to maps, monument profiles, information about the Antiquities Act, and continuing conservation and preservation.

Considering review of national monuments by the Trump administration, information in this report could be helpful.

NOAA. 2015. "Species in the Spotlight: Survive to Thrive, Recovering Threatened and Endangered Species, FY 2013–2014 Report to Congress." http://www.nmfs.noaa.gov/stories/2015/05/docs/noaa_recoveringspecies_report_web.pdf.

NOAA Fisheries reports to Congress of threatened and endangered marine species and efforts to recover and conserve their populations. Featured are eight species in most danger of extinction: Atlantic salmon, California coast coho salmon, Cook Inlet beluga whale, Hawaiian monk seal, Pacific leatherback sea turtle, Sacramento River winter-run Chinook salmon, resident kill whale, and white abalone.

Sierra Club. 2017. "The Gas Rush Locking America into Another Fossil Fuel for Decades." http://content.sierraclub.org/sites/content.sierraclub.org.naturalgas/files/1466-Gas-Rush-Report_04_web.pdf.

This report describes the rush to spend billions of dollars investing in gas, construction of new gas plants, and thousands of acres of pipelines at a time when clean energy solutions are available.

Speer, Lisa, Nelson, Regan, Casier, Robbert, Gavrilo, Maria, von Quillfeldt, Cecilie, Cleary, Jesse, Halpin, Patrick, and Hooper, Patricia. 2017. "Natural Marine World Heritage in the Arctic Ocean, Report of an Expert Workshop and Review Process." Gland, Switzerland: IUCN. https://portals.iucn.org/library/sites/library/files/documents/2017–006.pdf.

The report is a result of a scientific assessment of the unique features of ecosystems of the Arctic Ocean that are opening to human encroachment as the ice melts from global warming. It describes seven areas in the Arctic Ocean of significant biodiversity that require international efforts to preserve.

Staudt, Amanda, Inkley, Doug, Rubenstein, Aliya, Walton, Eli, and Williams, Jack. 2013. "Swimming Upstream: Freshwater Fish in a Warming World." National Wildlife Federation. http://www.atfonline.com.au/userfiles/files/NWFSwimming %20Upstream-082813-B.pdf.
    Changing climates are placing freshwater fish at risk. The report provides a summary of the economic value and the threats to freshwater fish with steps to safeguard the fish.

Union of Concerned Scientist Center for Science and Democracy. 2015. "Progress and Problems: Government Scientists Report on Scientific Integrity at Four Agencies." http://www .ucsusa.org/sites/default/files/attach/2015/09/ucs-progress-and-problems-2015.pdf.
    The Union of Concerned Scientists (UCS) reports the results of a survey of government scientists to assess the state of scientific integrity at four agencies—the Centers for Disease Control and Prevention, the Food and Drug Administration, the Fish and Wildlife Service, and the National Oceanic and Atmospheric Administration. Results indicated that problems were widespread across agencies and scientific disciplines. Federal employees at these agencies felt they were unable to communicate their scientific work openly to the public and the media, and many scientific experts feel constrained by lack of resources and respect for the scientific process. UCS offers a set of recommendations for federal agencies to improve scientific integrity.

Vincent, Carol Hardy, Hanson, Laura A., and Argueta, Carla N. 2017. "Federal Land Ownership: Overview and Data." *Congressional Research Service.* http://fas.org/sgp/crs/misc/R42346.pdf.
    This report from the Congressional Research Service was prepared for members and committees of Congress. The

report summarizes the percentage of federal land in each state and in five land agencies (Bureau of Land Management, Forest Service, Fish and Wildlife Service, National Park Service, and the Department of Defense). Discussions include current issues in land ownership, maintenance of infrastructure and lands, protection and use, and border security. Tables and graphs provide easily accessible information.

Wild Earth Guardians. 2016. "Progress for Protection: Historic Endangered Species Act Settlement Concludes 2011–2016 Report." http://www.wildearthguardians.org/site/DocServer/Progress_for_protection_October_2016.pdf?docID=17445.
Wild Earth Guardians reports the outcome of the settlement with the Fish and Wildlife Service in 2011 to address the significant backlog of imperiled species waiting ESA protection. The settlement required the service to make decisions about a total of 1,074 species, including 252 species on the candidate list that had languished there for years with no protection. So far, 193 species have received full protection and another 431 received positive findings.

Wilderness Society. 2017. "Wilderness.net." http://www.wilderness.net/NWPS/sitemap.
The Wilderness Society offers a website as a resource to learn almost everything relevant about wilderness in the United States: history, benefits, threats, stewardship, law and policy, management, research, education opportunities, maps, and community connections.

World Wildlife Fund (WWF). 2016. "Living Planet Report 2016. Risk and Reliance in a New Era." *WWF International.* Gland, Switzerland. http://awsassets.panda.org/downloads/lpr_living_planet_report_2016.pdf.
The WWF presents a comprehensive report on how human activity affects the Earth in four chapters: state of the natural planet, the human impact, the cause of losses,

and the challenge of sustainable development. They report a decline of 58 percent of species globally with the greatest loses in fresh water, primarily from habitat loss and overexploitation (81% decline). The report illustrates in easily comprehended graphics the effects as world population grows and the human impact on the planet increases exponentially with an unsustainable food system. It would take 1.6 Earths to provide the goods and services humans use each year. Seventeen goals for sustainable development are givens.

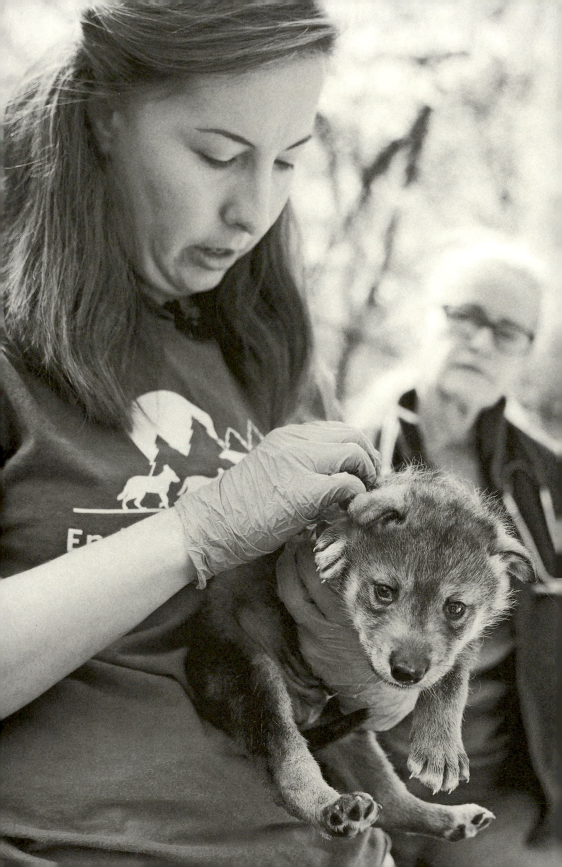

7 Chronology

Introduction

There is a rich history of the biology and events surrounding preservation of threatened and endangered species. This chapter provides dates and a brief explanation about the more important laws and actions that historically, directly, or indirectly have affected the well-being and survival of plants and animals.

384–322 BC Aristotle develops a "scale of nature" in which he organizes invertebrates and vertebrates from the lower rung of the ladder to the highest.

1735 Carl von Linnaeus begins publication of *Systema Naturae* in which he develops the binomial system of naming organisms.

1749 Comte de Buffon publishes his first 36 volumes of *Natural History* to challenge the belief that the Earth is 6,000 years old and suggests that species change over time.

1797–1876 Charles Lyell proposes that ecological formations of the Earth resulted from a slow continuous process over millions of years in *Principles of Geology*, which

A highly endangered Mexican gray wolf pup, conceived by artificial insemination, is held by the director of the Endangered Wolf Center in Missouri. There are only about 300 Mexican wolves in captivity and approximately 97 in the wild. (AP Photo/Jeff Roberson)

influenced Darwin's thinking in development of the theory of natural selection.

1809   Jean Baptista Lamarck publishes his *Philosophy of Animals* where he presents a mechanism for evolution called acquired characteristics. The theory lacks support.

1835   Charles Darwin visits the Galapagos Islands and observes finches that seem to have developed from a common ancestor on the mainland of South America.

1859   Darwin publishes *On the Origin of Species.*

1865   Gregor Mendel publishes his theory of genetics.

1872   Congress sets aside 2 million acres of public lands to create Yellowstone National Park.

1886   George Bird Grinnell proposes an organization to protect the nation's birds; the organization becomes the Audubon Society.

1891   The Forest Reserve Act ends giveaway of federal lands and grants the president authority to convert public lands into forest reserves.

1900   Congress passes the Lacey Act in response to growing concern over the decline of the passenger pigeon and other birds killed for their plumes and meat.

1901–1908   President Theodore Roosevelt creates 32 forest reserves consisting of 16 million acres and establishes the U.S. Forest Service.

1903   President Roosevelt establishes the first National Wildlife Refuge at Pelican Island, Florida, to protect wood storks, pelicans, and other water birds.

John Muir with Henry Senger, William D. Armes, Joseph Le Conte, and Warren Olney form the Sierra Club.

1906   The Antiquities Act is passed by the U.S. Congress and Signed by President Roosevelt creating 18 monuments of over a million acres.

1913   William T. Hornaday published *Our Vanishing Wildlife* in an attempt to list all species threatened with early extermination in response to the extinction of the great auk, Labrador duck, Pallas's cormorant, passenger pigeon, Carolina parakeet, and eskimo curlew.

1914   The passenger pigeon, once the most abundant bird in North America, becomes extinct.

1916   The National Park System is created.

1918   The passage of the Migratory Bird Treaty Act makes it unlawful to pursue, hunt, kill, capture, possess, buy, sell, purchase, or barter any migratory bird or bird product.

1940   The Bald and Golden Eagle Protection Act (expanded in 1962) prohibits the taking, importation, exporting, selling, and transportation of golden and bald eagles. Permits are considered only for scientific, educational, and religious purposes.

1942   The first official list of endangered wildlife by the American Committee for International Wildlife Protection is published in anticipation of international cooperation in preservation of vanishing species.

1946   The International Whaling Commission (IWC) is established for the management and protection of whales.

1948   The International Union for the Protection of Nature and Natural Resources, headquartered in Switzerland, is founded and later named the International Union for the Conservation of Nature (IUCN).

1959   Twelve nations sign a treaty to make Antarctica a demilitarized zone to be preserved for scientific research and protection of the fauna and flora and the ecosystems on which they depend.

1962   Rachel Carson publishes *Silent Spring*.

1964   The Wilderness Act is passed to create the national wilderness system that provides protected habitat for hundreds of species.

1965   The Land and Water Conservation Fund (LWCF) is created with bipartisan support to safeguard natural areas and water resources using revenues from offshore oil and gas.

1966   The Fur Seal Act is enacted to protect the northern fur seal from commercial seal trading.

Congress passes the National Wildlife Refuge System Administration Act to provide guidelines for administration and management of all areas in the National Wildlife Refuge System.

Congress passes the Endangered Species Preservation Act to provide a means to list native animal species as endangered to give them limited protection. Few species are listed.

1968   Congress passes the Wild and Scenic River Act to create a system of wild rivers to remain in their pristine, free-flowing condition.

The National Trails System Act creates a system of long-distant national trails, the Appalachian (2,160 miles) and Pacific Crest (2,665 miles) National Scenic Trails.

1969   Congress passes the National Environmental Policy Act to create the Environmental Protection Agency (EPA).

The Endangered Species Conservation Act amends the 1966 law to add international species. The secretary of interior may list foreign species and prohibit the imports of products from endangered species.

1970   The first Earth Day on April 22 increases public awareness about the environment and becomes a yearly event.

1972   The Marine Mammal Protection Act (MMPA) protects marine mammals by prohibiting take in U.S. waters and by U.S. citizens on the high seas and the importation and exportation of marine mammals and their products.

The Coastal Zone Management Act (CZMA) provides for the management of the nation's coastal resources, including the Great Lakes.

The EPA prohibits the use of DDT because of its potential to harm people and the thinning egg shells of predatory birds.

1973   President Richard Nixon signs the Endangered Species Act (ESA) that repeals the former acts and replaces them with strong provisions to provide for the conservation of threatened and endangered species of plants and animals.

1975 The Convention on International Trade in Endangered Species (CITES) of Wild Fauna and Flora is signed as an international agreement of 183 countries to ensure that animals and plants and products of imperiled species threatened with extinction are protected from commercial trade and import and export.

Congress passes the Eastern Wilderness Act to establish a wilderness system for the eastern United States.

The judge in the *TVA v. Hill* ("snail darter") case finds for Hill and halts construction of the Tennessee Valley Authority dam. Agencies and politicians realize the ESA is a strong law and a backlash against the act begins. The case eventually goes to the Supreme Court.

1976 Passage of the Federal and Policy Management Act requires wilderness review of Bureau of Land Management (BLM) lands.

1977 Surface Mining Control and Reclamation Act requires restoration of mined land to original condition.

1978 The Endangered Species Act is amended to formulize the process under Section 7 by which federal agencies consult with the FWS to ensure their actions are not likely to jeopardize the survival of listed species or adversely modify critical habitat.

The National Parks and Recreation Act makes important additions to the wild and scenic river system, national scenic trail system, and national wilderness.

The Supreme Court rules in a six to three decision that the Endangered Species Act requires halting construction of the Tellico dam. Congress responds by amending the ESA to establish the Endangered Species Committee called the "God Squad" to rule in cases when there is a controversy.

1979 The God Squad rules against finishing the Tellico dam. The decision is overruled by a rider attached to a congressional appropriations bill; the dam is finished and the last free-flowing stretch of the Tennessee River dammed.

1980   The Fish and Wildlife Conservation Act authorizes financial and technical assistance to states for the development, revision, and implementation of conservation plans and programs for nongame fish and wildlife.

The Alaska National Interest Lands Conservation Act establishes large new parks, wildlife refuges, wilderness areas, and other conservation units in Alaska.

1982   President Reagan signs the Endangered Species Act Amendment to allow, by permit, the taking of listed wildlife incidental to otherwise lawful activities provided the permit holder implements a Habitat Conservation Plan.

1985   The last surviving nine California condors are brought into captivity to begin a captive breeding program.

1987   American alligator is delisted from the endangered species list.

1989   The African Elephant Conservation Act is passed to curtail illegal trade in elephant ivory.

1990   The Fish and Wildlife Service lists the spotted owl as a threatened species, which is blamed for the decline of national forest timber sales.

1991   California condors are reintroduced into the wild.

1992   Authorization of the Endangered Species Act expires on September 30 to be implemented from then on by annual appropriations for the Departments of Commerce and Interior.

1994   The Desert Protection Act, promoted by senators from California, passes to protect areas of the California desert in the Death Valley National Park, Joshua Tree National Park, and a 1.6 million acre Mojave Preserve with five wilderness areas and two national monuments.

1995   In the "Sweet Home" [Oregon] decision, the U.S. Supreme Court affirms that alteration of a listed species' habitat is considered a "taking" of that species and can be regulated by the Fish & Wildlife Service.

Gray wolves are reintroduced into Yellowstone National Park and central Idaho wilderness.

1997   Congress passes the National Refuge System Improvement Act to direct the secretary of interior to maintain the biological integrity and diversity of national wildlife refuges.

2002   The Global Climate Change Prevention Act is a U.S. federal law to initiate studies and programs for research on climate change. The act directs the secretary of agriculture to establish a global program to coordinate issues relating to climate change.

2006   Former vice president, Al Gore, publishes *An Inconvenient Truth* to warn about the dangers of global warming.

2007   The bald eagle is delisted following recovery.

2009   The House of Representatives passes the first comprehensive global warming bill to impose limits on carbon dioxide and other greenhouse gases from power plants, factories, and refineries. The bill shifts the use of fossil fuels to renewable energy. This bill dies in the Senate.

2010   The BP oil well blows out in the Gulf of Mexico causing extensive damage and death of oil well workers.

2011   Congress removes gray wolves from the endangered species list in the northern Rocky Mountains by attachment of a rider to a budget bill.

2013   Sharks and rays gain protection under CITES.

2015   President Barack Obama announces rules designed to cut greenhouse gas emissions from power plants.

The Paris Agreement to curtail greenhouse gas emissions is negotiated by representatives of 195 countries at the 21st Conference of the Parties of the United Nations Framework Convention on Climate Change (UNFCCC) in Paris and adopted by consensus on December 12.

2016   Leaders from 171 nations meet at the United Nations on April 22 to sign the climate agreement negotiated in Paris, including the United States and China.

The Supreme Court blocks President Obama's climate change rules to curb emissions at power plants.

2017   Donald Trump becomes president. Information on climate change is removed from White House, State Department, and EPA websites. Climate change denial becomes official policy of the Trump administration and climate deniers head the EPA, State Department, Energy, and Interior.

On Earth Day, April 22, scientists and environmentalists march on Washington to protest policies of the Trump administration.

Executive order by Donald Trump mandates review of 27 national monuments spanning over 11 million acres of land and about 760 million acres of ocean designated under the Antiquities Act in the past 20 years with the intention of opening up now-protected areas to oil and gas exploration and development.

President Trump begins process to withdraw the United States from the Paris Climate Agreement signed by 195 countries. The only countries not in the agreement are the United States and Syria.

This chapter defines words and terms commonly used when talking about endangered species, the Endangered Species Act and its provisions, and the environment and related factors.

anthropocene   Current geological age in which human activity is the dominant influence on the environment.

apex predator   Predator at the top of the food chain upon which no other animals prey. Many carnivores, wolves, polar bears, lions, and tigers, are apex predators.

biodiversity   The existence of the variety and different kinds of plant and animals in an ecosystem.

biological population   Refers to a group of organisms (species) that interbreed and occupy the same place at the same time.

Candidate Conservation Agreements with Assurances   A formal agreement between the U.S. Fish and Wildlife Service and other parties to address conservation requirements of proposed or candidate species. The goal is to preclude the need for listing.

candidate list   Species of plants and animals that have sufficient biological information for listing as threatened or endangered but which are precluded by higher priority candidates for listing.

cap-and-trade system   A market-based approach to controlling pollution by providing economic incentives where participants can purchase allotments to offset their carbon emissions.

chytrid fungus   The parasitic fungus, *Batrachochytrium dendrobatidis*, thought to be responsible for a worldwide decline in amphibian populations.

citizen suits   A provision in the Endangered Species Act that a private citizen can use the legal system to enforce the law.

climate   Weather statistics (temperature, humidity, atmospheric pressure) over a long interval of decades, centuries, or millennia.

conservation banks   A contiguous or noncontiguous parcel of habitat managed for natural resource values. Similar to a financial bank, credits are established for specific sensitive species that occur on the land. When a project affects an endangered species or other natural resources credits in the conservation bank can be purchased to offset any damages.

The Conservation Reserve Program   A yearly rental payment offered to farmers by the U.S. Department of Agriculture for removal of environmentally sensitive land from agricultural production and the planting of species that will improve environmental health and quality.

critical habitats   Specific geographic area(s) that contains features essential for the conservation of a threatened or endangered species. Their designation may require special management and protection.

DDT   A pesticide widely used after World War II until Rachel Carson pointed out its negative effects on the environment in *Silent Spring* and its effectiveness was diminishing.

ecosystems   A biological community of interacting organisms and their physical environment.

ecosystem services   All the positive benefits to humans from healthy ecosystem functions.

ecotourism tourism Activities that are directed toward exotic, often threatened, natural environments to support conservation efforts and observe wildlife.

El Niño A periodic weather pattern of unusual warming of the surface waters in the east-central equatorial Pacific.

energy cycle Energy flow through an ecosystem from plants that convert solar energy to organic plant material (primary producers) to primary consumers up the food chain to the top predator to decomposition.

Federal Register Where the U.S. federal government publishes daily proposed issues and final decisions on regulation.

food chain Energy flow from producer organisms (grass or trees which use radiation from the sun to make their food) to apex predators (like wolves or grizzly bears) to decomposer species (such as bacteria and fungus).

fragmentation The process by which habitat loss results in the division of large, continuous habitats into smaller, more isolated remnants to isolate populations and stop gene flow.

Galapagos Islands Volcanic island archipelago in the Pacific Ocean off the coast of Ecuador famous for the role they played in Charles Darwin's formation of the theory of natural selection. Today, they are a prime tourist destination to view the unique animals that have evolved there.

gene flow Transfer of genes from one population to another through reproduction.

geographical range A plant or animal's spatial distribution where a species is found.

God Squad A committee created by the 1979 amendments to the ESA to mediate in situation where there is a conflict between a project and an endangered species.

Great Depression The longest and most severe economic slump worldwide in the 1930s that caused great hardship on many people, especially in industrialized countries.

gross domestic product   The total value of goods produced and services provided in a country during one year.

habitat conservation plan   Plans in the United State prepared under the ESA by nonfederal parties who want to obtain permits for the incidental taking of threatened and endangered species. The plans must describe the anticipated effects of the proposed "take" and how those impacts will be minimized or mitigated and contribute to species' recovery.

hydrological cycle   When evaporation of water from the surface of the ocean cools and water vapor condenses to form clouds to transport moisture around the globe until it returns to the surface as precipitation.

incidental take permit   Permits issued under Section 10 of the ESA to private, nonfederal entities undertaking otherwise lawful projects that might result in the death, injury, or displacement of an endangered or threatened species.

Industrial Revolution   A period of significant industrialization during the late 18 and early 19 centuries.

invasive species   Species that is not native to a specific location (an introduced species) and have spread to a degree believed to cause damage to the environment, economy, or human health.

Mercator projection   A cylindrical map used for navigation presented by the Flemish geographer and cartographer Gerardus Mercator in 1569.

mitigation   The reduction of any impact on an endangered or threatened species. This can be done through conservation banks, offsets of additional habitat or by other means approved by the FWS.

nutrient cycle   The movement and exchange of organic and inorganic matter back into the production of living matter.

old-growth forest   Forests with mature trees that have developed a long period and have not undergone any major unnatural changes such as logging.

rider on a bill   An additional provision added to a bill under consideration by a legislature. It usually has little connection with the subject matter of the bill and is used as a tactic to pass a controversial provision that would not pass as its own bill.

Rule 4(d)   A rule from Section 4(d) of the ESA which gives the FWS flexibility when issuing regulations to provide for the conservation of threatened species.

Safe Harbor   A provision under the ESA that specifies that certain conduct will not violate a given rule.

sagebrush rebellion   A revolt against federal authority during the 1970s and 1980s, originating in the western United States, that sought changes in federal control of land including a push to turn over federal lands to state regulation.

symbiotic relationships   Three types of relationships: Mutualism is where both organisms benefit; in commensalism only one benefits; and in a parasitism one organism benefits at the expense of the other.

think tanks   Experts come together to provide advice and ideas on political and economic problems. There are conservative, liberal, and nonpartisan think tanks.

weather   Day-to-day short-term changes in temperature, humidity, and atmospheric pressure.

wetlands   The link between land and water. They are some of the most productive ecosystems in the world and consist of marshes as wet grasslands and swamps as wet woodlands.

Wildlife Services   An agency under the USDA to control (kill) wildlife that come into conflict with humans.

About the Author

Jan A. Randall developed an interest in nature and biology while growing up on a family cattle ranch in southern Idaho. She has a BS in zoology, University of Idaho; MEd University of Washington, Seattle; PhD in zoology, Washington State University; NIH postdoctoral fellow at the University of Texas, Austin; visiting professor, Cornell University. She enjoyed a successful academic career with professorships in biology at Central Missouri State University and San Francisco State University. Jan is a fellow of the California Academy of Science, the Animal Behavior Society, and the American Society for the Advancement of Science. She received a career award in recognition of her seminal contribution to the study of animal behavior from the Animal Behavior Society and an Outstanding Alumni Award from the University of Idaho. She is a board member and chair of the Scientific Advisory Committee of the Endangered Species Coalition. Jan, who is a professor emerita of biology at San Francisco State University, loves to read, travel, hike, and garden. She lives in northern California with her husband Bruce.